SEMIOTIC INSIGHTS:
THE DATA DO THE TALKING

IRMENGARD RAUCH

Semiotic Insights: The Data Do The Talking

UNIVERSITY OF TORONTO PRESS

Toronto Buffalo London

© University of Toronto Press Incorporated 1999
Toronto Buffalo London
Printed in Canada

ISBN 0-8020-4705-X

Toronto Studies in Semiotics
Editors: Marcel Danesi, Umberto Eco, Paul Perron, and Thomas A. Sebeok

Printed on acid-free paper

Canadian Cataloguing in Publication Data

Rauch, Irmengard

Semiotic insights: the data do the talking

(Toronto studies in semiotics)
Includes bibliographical references and index.
ISBN 0-8020-4705-X

1. Semiotics.   2. Linguistics.   I. Title.   II. Series.

P99.R38 1999   401'.41   C99-930980-3

University of Toronto Press acknowledges the financial assistance to its publishing
program of the Canada Council and the Ontario Arts Council.

Contents

Foreword

If the ever-busy grammarians of the ancient Western world concerned themselves with nonverbal signs or perceived, by contrast with the rhetoricians of their times, any explicit functional relationships between verbal and other signs at all, they were thus engaged in a dilettante capacity only. The earliest linguists seemed to have left little or no trace of any such speculative preoccupations.

While, according to historiographers, as also observed by Jakobson, a Sumerian grammar may be the oldest known text of a linguistic character, there is every reason to believe that this too was the product of a long antecedent tradition—surely oral, and possibly recorded. Similarly, the voluminous Corpus Hippocraticum and the many treatises of (or attributed to) his distinguished successor, Galen, or even the "semiotic fragment" that survives, as noted by Eco, from the prior writings of Alcmaeon, could clearly not have constituted the initial embodiments of an evolving medical doctrine of subjective and objective signs. For these were formerly and are today variously employed in the arts of anamnestics, diagnostics, prognostics, to say nothing of the highly semioticised craft of pharmacology.

One intriguing question, still open, needs to be raised again: were our Ancient grammarians aware that they were "doing" a kind of semiotics? And did the practicing physicians of their times know that the symptoms which constituted their primary clinical data can and, in fact, must be probed by means of both verbal and nonverbal signs? In other words, rephrased more generally: how did the Greeks and the Romans and their learned successors in the Middle Ages view the relations between their versions of a general doctrine of signs and their particular theories of language? Were issues like these discussed prior to Locke—himself a medical man—who alluded to them in the concluding pages of his profound *Essay* (1690 and thereafter), threads to be extensively and vigorously embroidered upon in the next century by the Alsatian Johann Heinrich Lambert in his book, *Semiotik oder Lehre von der Bezeichnung der Gedanken und Dinge* (1764)? (I explored this and related topics, in provisional historical perspective, in an invited address to the 1986 Georgetown Round Table on Languages and Linguistics. An expanded paper based on that presentation subsequently appeared in pp. 1–18 of a volume titled *Developments in Linguistics and Semiotics, Language Teaching and Learning, Communication across Cultures,* ed. Simon P. X. Battestini (Washington, D.C.: Georgetown University Press, 1987).

The problematic, on at least an abstract level, was evidently implicit in the writings of Peirce, as, famously, in his rarefied discussion of "man as a sign," wherein he compared "man" with the vocable six as well as with this same token numeral in its diversity of scripted configurations. In a letter the mature Peirce wrote to Lady Welby on December 23rd, 1908, he listed phonetics among the subjects that had engaged him, having in his younger years paid explicit homage to "the vast and splendidly developed science of linguistics."

By the late 1930's, Charles Morris, a devoted disciple of George Herbert Mead, was advocating that semiotic be put to service as "the metalanguage for linguistics." Moreover, building further on Rudolf Carnap's claim that linguistics is "the descriptive, empirical part of semiotic (of spoken and written languages)," he proposed—alas, in vain—the schematic notion of a *lansign-system,* designed to encompass, beyond all natural spoken languages and script, such context-restricted notations as mathematics and symbolic logic, and, more vaguely, "the arts."

Peirce's ideas came to strongly and enduringly impact upon Roman Jakobson beginning with the late 1940's, and both men's writings in their turn influenced, beside a handful of other present-day linguists in the United States, Michael Shapiro; and, to name but one outstanding Peirce-saturated Continental scholar, Joëlle Réthoré of the Université de Perpignan, the publication of whose singularly exciting account of Peirce and linguistics is still eagerly awaited.

On the other hand, the programmatic schemata of Morris had seemingly little effect on professionals either here or abroad, with a few conspicuous exceptions of linguists with a decisive bent for logic, such as Joseph Greenberg in the U.S. and Roland Posner in Germany; or else occasional philosophers with a respect for linguistics, such as the late Ferruccio Rossi-Landi, in Italy. For, as the sole surviving professional linguist student of this gentle, wise, and altogether admirable man, who became my close friend after we both left the University of Chicago, I can hardly imagine that it could have been otherwise: Morris's semiotic was slipping ever deeper into the decaying orbit of behavioristic psychology in which it became at last inescapably mired when modern linguistics, espousing diverse forms of cognitive psychology, was about to move out of the sterile realms of its former habitation. (Needless to add, it was far otherwise with Peirce, who anticipated, as so much else, a sophisticated form of "cognitive psychology.")

The pivotal role of Ferdinand de Saussure in his posthumously ascribed subordination of linguistics to the "general science" of semiotics (alias semiology), and that to social and hence general psychology, is such common lore that the story need hardly be retold here once again. Yet the deeply entangled, widely ramified consequences of what in retrospect seems to have been scarcely more than a throwaway lecture-room suggestion by the Swiss master did take some fascinating turns. Were space and time to permit me such self-indulgence, it would be instructive, possibly amusing, to track these in their fullest convoluted detail from Geneva to Brussels (Buyssens); triumphantly, if but for a short while, up to Copenhagen (Hjelmslev, Uldall) and Lund (Malmberg); forking along a busy, many-tined detour throughout Central Europe (chiefly, to be sure, Brno and Prague, but also including the German Karl Bühler residing in Vienna, and many others, such as the sadly neglected Budapest linguist Laziczius); onward to Moscow (among others, the early Jakobson, who, however, eventually turned severely critical of Saussure); reverting back to Geneva (Frei, Godel, etc., amplified by the Russian Karcevkij), sliding into Paris (Greimas and his multinational epigones, with a sharp twist by Metz, with a jokey reversal by Barthes); lightly touching down in Italy (the early Eco and a host of others); and ultimately spilling over to Yale and Rice (Lamb), and even, if only biographically, Cornell (Culler).

To home in on just one, formerly conspicuous, component of this complex mosaic, it is downright mind-boggling for me to contemplate the ups and downs of Glossematics, that once inter-continentally flourishing "school" of semiotics—or, as Jakobson liked to ironically refer to it in his lectures and in private conversations, "the most overly formalized tendency in linguistics"—associated chiefly with the names of the elegantly aristocratic and erudite Louis Hjelmslev and his down-to-earth, astute would-be collaborator Hans Uldall. At the outset of the 1950's, both of the aforementioned spent, albeit of course separately, eight weeks at Indiana University upon my initiative; (it was apparent to me by then that their relationship was already beginning to fray, soon to irredeemably rupture). At work, mostly in his shady garden in the summer heat of Bloomington, Hjelmslev (assisted by Frank Whitfield) rendered the original English version of his "instant classic" *Prolegomena to a Theory of Language*—substitute Signs for the last word—and both he and Uldall taught to packed classes what passed for their quite divergent kinds of Glossematics.

When, a few years afterwards, I was cordially hosted by Hjelmslev at his home in Charlottenlund, then going on to lecture, under his auspices, in the old mid-city quarters of the Department of Linguistics of the University of Copenhagen, it was obvious that Glossematics and its "onlie begetter"—by then, since Uldall had in the meantime succumbed during an emergency operation in Africa—were supremely regnant. By this I mean not only that Glossematics had become an academic byword but also that Hjelmslev was receiving, for those days quite remarkably ample, financial support—notably (among other sources) from the Carlsberg Foundation and from his prominent publisher, Munksgaard—for his own work and that of his followers. I know of no other linguist, let alone semiotician, comparably supported at the time (but see below).

Then, some twenty years later, but not so long after the death of Hjelmslev himself, I addressed, in the course of a lecture tour in Scandinavia and Germany, mixed audiences on different semiotic and linguistic subjects at several Danish universities in Copenhagen, Odense, and Aarhus. Obedient, as is my wont, to the rule of the Ciceronian trope dubbed *captatio benevolentiae,* I more often than not began my remarks with a bow to some of the greatest ancestral ghosts populating, as it were, the local Pantheon: in this case, I mentioned Rask, Thomsen, Pedersen, Jespersen, Brøndal, and, naturally enough, Hjelmslev. To my stupefaction—I suppose I was still naive—it gradually dawned on me that, on the one hand, with the aggressive advent in Denmark of (multiple species of) generative-transformational grammar among linguists, and, on the other, of the seductions of the Parisian *carré sémiotique* among declared semioticians (the square having nowadays been all but wholly displaced by a Peircean "Semiotic Trinity," or else by a global Biosemiotic paradigm inspired by the *Umweltlehre,* or by both), the achievements of this Great Dane (again, Jakobson's epithet)—personal, authorial, as well as editorial (*vide* the excitements of essentially his "house organ," the *Acta Linguistica)*—were, though dimly remembered by older attending faculty, entirely unknown to those in their late thirties and younger. This on Hjelmslev's native heath! (In proportion that Hjelmslev's reputation fades, as it were, in the heart of Scandinavia, it continues to flourish at Europe's "periphery," this in good conformity with Bartoli's linguistic thesis, a variant of the well-known anthropological "age-and-area hypothesis" [including the so-called "Finnish method" in folklore studies]; about these, see my "Linguistics and the Age and Area Hypothesis," *American Anthropologist* 46: 382–6 [1944] [with Giuliano Bonfante]. Witness, for instance, Cosimo Caputo, *Su Hjelmslev* [Naples: Edizioni Scientifiche Italiane, 1933], as well as other recent publications, for example, emanating from the University of Bologna, that deal with aspects of Glossematics.)

As far as I can see, there are but two ways open now for linguists to productively demonstrate their vaunted expertise in a semiotic frame—to creatively situate, in Irmengard Rauch's enviably happy articulation, "the language-inlay in semiotic modalities." These alternative options are, to recycle a pair of modish clichés, "top-down" or "bottom-up."

According to the former, semiotics occupies (in Saussure's spatial imagery) a superior position which (in Roy Harris's translation) "would investigate the nature of signs and the laws governing them," an investigation which would spawn a linguistics seen as merely one branch of semiotics, to wit, a "system of signs expressing ideas, and hence comparable to writing, the deaf-and-dumb alphabet, symbolic rites, forms of politeness, military signals, and so on." One opportunity to produce a book so designed was formally proposed to The Rockefeller Foundation several decades ago by John Lotz, a scintillating American-born, Hungarian-educated, Sweden-residing linguist— professing at the time at Columbia University, later to become Director of the Center for Applied Linguistics. Lotz knew many branches of semiotics thoroughly, including metrics, script, and the signaling systems of some social insects. The last paper of his that he let me comment on was an incomparably soaring, not to say passionate, semiotic analysis of football (prevented from publication as much by his sudden, premature death as by his irresponsible literary executor who thereafter claimed to have misplaced Lotz's manuscript). My salient point is that, according to his much chewed-over proposal, which—and I am convinced that this action was unprecedented in the field on our side of the Atlantic—had been actually approved for full funding by the Foundation's Chadbourne Gilpatric, Lotz had planned to work his way "down" from general semiotic principles toward the nitty-gritty "facts" of the many natural languages—Classical and Germanic, Finno-Ugric, and some Caucasian ones to boot—that were at his easy command. That this project had to be aborted, despite Rockefeller's proffered generosity, because of Lotz's personal circumstances, I regard as a catastrophe arguably comparable in magnitude, if not in its full particulars, to Peirce's having been repeatedly rebuffed by the Carnegie Corporation a century or so before. (I included a two-part memoir about the life and works of this charismatic linguist-semiotician in my book, *The Sign & Its Masters* [Austin: University of Texas Press, 1979]).

As her readers will be able to judge for themselves, the writer of this very nearly unique book's twenty chapters, the eminent University of California Germanic linguist Irmengard Rauch, whose many scholarly and organizational contributions to general semiotics were crowned by her Presidency of the Fifth Congress of the International Association for Semiotic Studies (held on her campus in Berkeley in June 1994), still fruitfully pursues, as she has done for the past twenty years, an opposite, "bottom-up," strategy. Precisely as her subtitle specifies, "the data do the talking" throughout her meticulous work or, as one might also playfully claim, "the talking *is* the data." It is the source of her "semiotic insight"—no less, indeed, than of her consistently "semiotic outlook."

A Past President of the Semiotic Society of America, founder and steadfast guardian of the Semiotic Circle of California (some of the proceedings of which appeared in a 1989 volume she came to co-edit with Gerald Carr), and organizer of a remarkably seminal, withal multidisciplinary, semiotic conference, the results of which she and Carr published in 1980 as *The Signifying Animal: The Grammar of Language and Experience,* Rauch has launched a new journal, characteristically juxtaposing in its very title her twin academic preoccupations: "Germanic linguistics" and "semiotic analysis," both conjoined here by the adjective "interdisciplinary."

I consider it a privilege to have been associated, over the past two decades, with so formidable a scholar in an editorial capacity in the pages of *Semiotica* and other journals, and in book series produced by three major publishing houses which are supremely active in semiotics, diversely headquartered in two North American countries and in Germany. The pieces of which I speak constitute but a small portion of her prodigious output of uniformly high quality. Her reference apparatus and carefully compiled indexes will point her readers to her *opera omnia* which I recommend with admiration and enthusiasm.

Thomas A. Sebeok
Institute for Advanced Study
(Collegium Budapest), & Indiana University

Acknowledgments

Permission has been granted to reprint revised versions of articles originally published: by Gunter Narr Verlag, "The Mendacious Mode in Modern German" in *Spracherwerb und Mehrsprachigkeit,* edd. B. Narr and H. Witttje (Tübingen 1986), 343–51; by the Indiana University Press, "Between Linguistics and Semiotics: Paralanguage" in *The Signifying Animal: The Grammar of Language and Experience,* edd. I. Rauch and G. F. Carr (Bloomington 1980), 284–9, and "Evolution in a Semantic Set: Text, Discourse, Narrative" in *Language Change,* edd. I. Rauch and G. F. Carr (Bloomington 1983), 28–38; by the Institute for the Study of Man, "What Is Cause?" in *The Journal of Indo-European Studies,* vol. 9 (Washington, D.C. 1981), 319–29; by John Benjamins B.V., "Historical Analogy and the Peircean Categories" in *Proceedings of the III International Conference on Historical Linguistics,* edd. J. P. Maher et al. (Amsterdam 1982), 359–67; by Max Niemeyer Verlag, "Early New High German *e*-Plural" in *Beiträge zur Geschichte der deutschen Sprache und Literatur* vol. 113 (Tübingen 1991) 367–383; by Mouton de Gruyter, "The Language-Inlay in Semiotic Modalities" in *Semiotica,* vol. 25 (Berlin 1979), 67–76; "Semiotics in Search of Method: Narrativity" in *Semiotica,* vol. 34 (Berlin 1981), 167–76; "Semiotists on Semiotists: The Heartbeat of the Sign" in *Semiotica,* vol. 55 (Berlin 1985), 227–50; "Semiotics and Linguistics" in the *Encyclopedic Dictionary of Semiotics,* edd. T. A. Sebeok et al. (Berlin1986), 912–920; "Language and Other Sign Systems" in the *Encyclopedic Dictionary of Semiotics,* edd. T. A. Sebeok et al. (Berlin:1986), 433–8; "Peirce: 'With No Pretension to Being a Linguist'" in *Semiotica,* vol. 65 (Berlin 1987), 29–43; "Language Change in Progress: Privacy and Firstness," in *The Semiotic Bridge: Trends from California,* edd. I. Rauch and G. F. Carr

(Berlin 1989), 375–383; "Semiotics: (No) Canon, (No) Theses" in *Semiotica*, vol. 86 (Berlin 1991) 85–92; "Icon Deconstruction and Icon Construction" in *Signs of Humanity / L'homme et ses signes I*, edd. G. Deladalle et al. (Berlin 1992), 401–5; and "1994" in *Semiotica*, vol. 98 (Berlin 1994), 157–162; by Peter Lang A.G., "Basler Rezept I: Method, Medical Code, and the Polysemous Symptom" in the *Herbert Kolb Festschrift*, edd. K. Matzel and H.-G. Roloff (Bern 1989), 523–27; by the Semiotic Society of America, "'Symbols Grow': Creation, Compulsion, Change" in the *American Journal of Semiotics,* vol. 3 (Carbondale, IL 1984), 1–23 and "Deconstruction, Prototype Theory, and Semiotics" in *The American Journal of Semiotics*, vol. 9 (Carbondale, IL 1992), 129–38; by the Universitätsverlag Dr. Norbert Brockmeyer, "Medicine and Semiotics" in *Semiotics in the Individual Sciences I*, ed. W. Koch (Bochum 1990), 299–317; by the University of Michigan Department of Romance Languages and Literatures, "The Sausurrean Axes Subverted" in *Dispositio*, vol. XII, nos. 30–32 (Ann Arbor, MI 1988), 35–44; by the University of Michigan Slavic Publications, "Distinguishing Semiotics from Linguistics and the Position of Language in Both" in *The Sign: Semiotics Around the World*, edd. R. W. Bailey et al. (Ann Arbor 1978), 328–34.

Particular gratitude is extended to Professor Gerald F. Carr (California State University), Dr. Ronald Schoeffel (University of Toronto Press), Professor Thomas A. Sebeok (Indiana University), and Dr. Lihua Zhang (University of California, Berkeley) for their generous help in bringing this book to publication. *Semiotic Insights: The Data Do the Talking* is dedicated to my students and colleagues over the years in linguistics and semiotics.

Introduction: Leitmotifs at the Nexus of Semiotics and Linguistics

This book, based in part on previous research, is bifurcated into a set of eleven chapters (Part One) which lay the foundation for uncovering leitmotifs at the nexus of semiotics and linguistics, and a set of nine chapters (Part Two) which display the cooperation of semiotic method and linguistic method leading to a more adequate justification of hard linguistic data as occurring in given language growth phenomena in Indo-European, Slavic, and Germanic. The chapters in Part One address the seminal questions of what semiotics and linguistics are, indeed, the nature of their shared object, language, along with historiography of both semiotics and linguistics, as well as their interdigitation with other disciplines, especially with medicine. The chapters of Part Two demonstrate the enhanced explanation of phonological, morphological, syntactic, semantic, and pragmatic language phenomena, through the application of semiotic tools. It will be evident that the seeds of many of the discussed language phenomena are planted in Part One below.

Hard and Soft Science

Current fashion in the humane and natural sciences dictates appeal to the term "linguistic(s)" for any and all phenomena/endeavors which concern language. It has, however, not yet penetrated quotidian speech and writing to the extent that a related term such as "semantic(s)" has. The relatively young science of modern linguistics, birthed and nurtured in the flowering of nineteenth-century scientific activities (cf. Chapter 2) actually has an unofficial non-codified ancestry dating back over two thousand years. Interestingly, as the second millennium wanes, the subsequently developed modern hard science of linguistics is softening up somewhat in seeming reversion to pre-nineteenth-century rigor (cf. Chapter 1). The crucial word in the preceding sentence is "somewhat," which refers, to be sure, not only to the expansion of linguistics into a plethora of so-called hyphenated fields such as ethno-linguistics, biolinguistics and many others, but also to the admission in linguistics of less formal, less absolute approaches in analyzing linguistic data (cf. Chapter 1 and Conclusion). We ask how the latter is possible in view of the fact that linguistic data are inviolable, untouchable. Data are what they are, and no amount of manipulation can alter them (cf. Rauch 1990a). Nevertheless, linguistic data are somehow touched by the human analyst whether directly or indirectly, so that they are, in the words of Yates (1986: 358), "filtered by his [the scientist's] instruments and choices [including] his methods of subsequent analysis."

This understanding of the human touch in data analysis is ancient and hearkens back to the bifurcation of the classical Analogists and the Anomalists, whereby the notions of canon, regularity, order are pitted against the concepts of exception, irregularity, disorder, respectively (cf. Rauch 1995). Today's Analogists are the formal, purely theoretical linguists, while contemporary Anomalists represent the less formal, experiential linguists, the latter of which accordingly tend to a broader paradigm for linguistic data. Certainly tolerance for interaction with other disciplines bespeaks a broader research aura in which to analyze data. On the other hand, the admission of flesh and blood language data, not just putative or ideal language data into linguistic analysis, is the defining characteristic of this broader paradigm. In it linguistic data, in emulation of the human experience, are hardly interpreted in absolute terms, but rather in more relative terms. To be sure, this is reflective of the Analogists versus the Anomalists of Ancient times, but it is an unceasing bifurcation through history. Witness, for example, Cartesian rationalism versus Lockean empiricism, showing the current "softening up" of linguistics and science in general to be actually a rather familiar, indeed not unexpected, cyclical phenomenon.

A sample case in point is discussed in Chapter 1 which offers first-hand data on the pronunciation of the Modern German *leid* 'painful' as spoken by five bilinguals in the San Francisco Bay Area. Two methods were used to analyze the data. Method A resulted in five phonetic transcriptions of the tape-recorded pronunciation of German *leid* by the five bilinguals on the basis of the simple majority transcription of the seven or eight fieldworkers cognizing the data. Method B resulted in six, not five, phonetic transcriptions of the five bilinguals, on the basis of the validity of any transcriptions cognized by at least two fieldworkers. Obviously, in the words of hard linguistics, only five occurrences of German *leid* were spoken and tape-recorded, yet in analysis method B six occurrences were cognized— an excellent instance of so-called "softened-up" science. However, if the five taped German *leid* were subjected to machine sound spectography, (call it method C), it is possible then that still another set of five transcriptions would result. Will method B be more soft than method A and method A more soft than method C? Which cognition is the real reading, that which the machine records of the language speaker or that which the language hearer perceives? In the case of the machine reading, does it nevertheless still have a human touch?

What Is Linguistics?

What is the purpose of explaining the current status of linguistic research? It is because of the widespread non-technical use of the term "linguistic(s)" and because of the saturation of the term "linguistic(s)" in semiotic literature. To be sure, linguistics has ever been integral to semiotics. Consider, e.g., the well-know Sebeok metaphor of the semiotic tripod by which linguistics is a "fundamental semiotic tradition" along with medicine and philosophy (cf. Chapter 2). Consider also that the enormous contribution of Saussure (cf. Chapter 2) does not stand isolated in the history of modern semiotics; indeed *bona fide* linguists such as Hjelmslev, Jakobson, Sebeok (together with Saussure) outnumber as a group by fifty percent semiotists of philosophy and of medicine as designated "fathers of modern semiotics" in the words of Krampen, Oehler, and Posner (cf. Chapter 10). Surely linguistics' contribution or nexus with semiotics is not a matter of numbers. It is rather a matter of ingredients.

Semiotics and linguistics have a long history of juxtaposition. The relationships between the two fields are represented in varying literatures by scalar viewpoints with polar extremes which hold these fields as practically synonymous or as virtually unrelated (cf. Chapters 3, 4, 5, 16 and Sebeok 1994: Chapter 7). Often it is the old formal: less formal ghost that haunts the understanding of the nature of linguistics, so that a much desired definition circumscribing this discipline remains elusive. Beyond this, frequently the object of linguistics, viz. language, is used interchangeably with linguistics so that the distinction between the discipline and the object of its study tends to become obscured. This is crucial since language is the object of their disciplines as well and its definition is at least as difficult to achieve, if not more so, than that of the field of linguistics.

What Is Language?

The central position that language plays for linguistics is hardly less central for semiotics since in unison both linguists (e.g., Sapir) and semiotists (e.g., Todorov) proclaim language to be the premier sign system (cf. Chapter 3). How are we to reconcile, however, the identification of language via the Hockett/Osgood/Lyons design features of language (cf. Chapter 5) with Peirce's stunning equation of language with his own person (cf. Chapter 4)? How, moreover, do we gauge myriad other definitions of language (cf. Chapters 3 and 6), including, for example, the provocative negative definition of Mathiot by which she denies discourse as being a part of language (cf. Chapter 3).

The definition of discourse is thus made a prerequisite to the delimitation of the understanding of language. Discourse itself moves within the semantic orbit of the terms text and narrative. When the three terms, text, discourse, narrative, well-established in verbal language, particularly literature, find their extension in non-verbal modalities, discourse indeed is not *solely* a part of language but of other phenomena as well. Discourse parallels general action theory, according to van Dijk (cf. Chapter 7). A narrative component underlies all discourse; to the Greimasean narrative features of propositional macrostructures and modalities should be added the natural language category which is inferential structure (cf. Chapter 7). The third term, text, appropriately applies to all entities that house narrative and discourse. Witness now the fitting Sebeokean equation of the human being with a text (cf. Chapter 8).

Returning then to defining language, at this point we are well removed from a classical linguistic type definition such as is reflected in the simplicity of the Chomskyan axiom which associates sound with meaning (cf. Chapter 6). But even this very hard and/or formal linguistic definition of language is not at all without fallout, that is, extension, which, to be sure, points to the Cartesian rather than to the Lockean dissection of the research world (cf. "Hard and Soft Science" above). It does, however, ultimately lead also to Peirce in Chomsky's

(1972: 93) speculation that in the future it will "be possible to undertake a general study of the limits and capacities of human intelligence, to develop a Peircean logic of abduction."

To be sure, historical figures have long linked language and intellect, that is, thought, so, e.g., Humboldt. Indeed, the completion of Peirce's equation (cf. above) reads: ("language is the sum total of myself:) for the man is the thought" (cf. Rauch 1996a). If we consider the route to a definition of language via the preliminary common semiotic characteristics of both verbal and non-verbal modalities, viz. text, discourse, narrative, singling out now inferential structure of natural language (cf. above) as the ultimate feature (Peirce holds the illative relation as primary), can the functioning of the inferential feature actually be falsified and/or demonstrated? It can. Thus, not only can the innate processing or cognizing by humans of semantic primitives be shown as underlying language and paralanguage, but also as underlying non-verbal modalities such as music and architecture (cf. Chapter 6). Indeed, Peirce even extends syllogistic effects to non-humans when he speaks to the state of "mind" of his dog and to the "reasoning" of a decapitated frog. Ultimately we derive a definition of language as "signifying through an illative-type process" which is universal (cf. Chapter 6).

This understanding of language accords well with views on the origin/rationale for language. Thus Thom (1975: 309) postulated a dual need-based origin for language: "1. For a personal evolutive constraint, aiming to realize the permanence of the ego in a state of wakefulness. 2. For a social constraint, expressing the main regulating mechanisms of the social group." Thom (1975: 310) explains that the human "must 'think,' that is, seize the things lying between exterior objects and genetic forms, namely, *concepts*." To be sure, this is reminiscent of Uexküll's functional cycle whereby the outside is conceptualized/perceived/internalized by the human (cf. Chapters 9 and 10). Thom provides the catastrophe for perception, viz. the grip morphology, writing (1975: 305):

> Every perceived object is treated as virtual prey, but only objects of sufficiently promising form can initiate the capture process, while the others are weighed by perception, which in man behaves in this respect like a virtual hand. The etymology of *precipere* is "to seize the object continually in its entirety."

A practical example displaying the need-based origin/rationale for language is given by Thom with reference to so-called "wolf-children," whereby the non-association of sound with the meaning of an object (cf. Chomsky's classical definition of language, above) inhibits thought. Thom (1975: 310) writes: "The exploitation of the semantic support space of the concept is inhibited by the incoherence or absence of the sounds associated with the object; this results in the mental retardation or idiocy to which these children are condemned."

Thom, but also Lees, finds an analogue between language/thought and biology/genetics. Lees (1980: 226; cf. also Chapter 14 below) writes: "I advocate that linguistic competence (language) be viewed analogously to the genetic code as a mechanism invented by minds to serve as a scratch pad for and a repository of ideas." Similarly, Thom (1975: 313) observes: "... thought is a virtual capture of concepts with a virtual, inhibited emission of words." In describing the materialization of an SVO [subject/verb/object] syntagm, Thom writes (1975: 312): "Thought is then a veritable conception (subject/object) arising from the death of the verb, just as the egg puts flesh on the spermatozoid; thus thought is a kind of permanent orgasm."

What Is Semiotics?

The broad understanding of language as signifying through an illative-type process (cf. "What is Language?" above) displays well the affability of the semiotic paradigm. Semiotics' wide embrace not only of objects of study, but also of a plurality of approaches, has long puzzled semiotists and non-semiotists alike. Concerted efforts have been under way in rectification of a proclamation such as Eco's (1975: 17) statement that "... we may say that there does not yet exist a single unified semiotic theory." Yet the twenty years which have passed in search of an identity for semiotics show semiotics to be, in fact, diverse and plural, in the words of Yates (1985: 358–59), "synoptic" and capable of "meld[ing] the sciences." Accordingly, Eco's hope which is the second half of his 1975 (above) statement: "(we may say that there does not yet exist a single unified semiotic theory) and that we hope there never will" has proven prophetic as we near the end of the millennium (cf. Chapters 1 and 11; cf. Rauch 1996b).

This is not to deny that in the history of humankind three traditions are basic to semiotics, Sebeok's tripod (cf. "What is Linguistics?"

above): philosophy, linguistics, medicine. Genetically, semiotics was born "most likely, out of medicine" (Sebeok 1994: 105). Medicine is *the protosemiotic;* it enjoys overlap with a great many natural and humane sciences. Certainly the thought is proximate that the characteristic of medicine whereby it is neither or both a hard science and a soft science (cf. "Hard and Soft Science" above) has genetically determined the nature of semiotics (cf. Chapter 9).

No less so from the philosophical leg of the semiotic tripod do the Peircean phenomenological categories of *Firstness, Secondness, Thirdness* and their congeners read as both modern and postmodern, as soft science and as hard science (cf. above; cf. Chapter 1). Aptly, Merrell (1995: xiii) writes of "... Peirce, whose own incessant ransacking through the rubble of human thought in pursuit of the sign evinces that Faustian brand of modernity with which we are all too familiar, though his refusal to concede to determinate beginnings, endings, and centers of foci falls in line with the postmodern temper." Thus while the three categories are discrete, mutually exclusive, a semiosis requires all three as demonstrated in Peirce's (1: 339) classic definition of the sign ("A sign stands *for* something *to* the idea which it produces or modifies," cf. also Rauch 1987a) and the many triadic correlations which derive from *Firstness, Secondness, Thirdness,* such as the following:

Firstness	Secondness	Thirdness
freedom/life/freshness	*otherness/cause-effect/brute force*	*generality/continuity/habit*
possibility	*existence*	*law*
might be	*happens to be*	*would be*
past	*present*	*future*
factual similarity	*factual contiguity*	*imputed contiguity*
sign	*object*	*interpretant*
icon	*index*	*symbol*
syntax	*semantics*	*pragmatics*
abduction	*induction*	*deduction*

These concepts represent but nine of numerous trichotomies which display the machinery and/or tools of semiotics. As a set of working tools they appear different from classical binary conceptual characteristics which serve as tools for linguistics, such as *emic: etic, signifier: signified, langue: parole, paradigm: syntagm, matter: form, sound:*

meaning, diachrony: synchrony. To be sure, semiotists have borrowed tools from linguistics with varying success in explicating several semiotic modalities (cf. Chapters 3 and 5). However, a reverse trend, viz. the application of semiotic tools to linguistic data has not actually taken hold, although individual linguistic studies bear witness to selected semiotic concepts and/or notions shared by both semiotics and linguistics (cf. Chapters 1, 4, and 16). Clearly the identity problem for the two sciences of linguistics and semiotics is a red herring. The enhanced reaction of linguistic data to semiotic tools is sufficient evidence for this. Let us observe in Part Two below the objectively displayed interaction of semiotic tools and of linguistic tools on hard linguistic evidence: *the data* will *do the talking*.

Language Grows

The title of this section is in analogy to a cardinal Peircean semiotic aphorism, viz. "Symbols Grow" (2: 302). To be sure, the equation of language with symbol is obvious (cf. "What is Language?" above), but this is not the sole issue in emulating the aphorism. "Language Grows" actually speaks to identifying and treating the object of linguistics as a dynamic entity. Language can, of course, be viewed as static, a so-called snap-shot or single moment view toward data, or as dynamic, changing, whether in the *past, present, or future,* the distinction labeled *synchronic* and *diachronic*, respectively (cf. Chapter 18). This Saussurean dichotomy has widespread implications; we can trace it back to the ancient controversy of Parmenides (change is illusory) versus Heraclitus (change is continuous) or forward to the bifurcated analyses of classical American structural linguistics characterized by item-and-arrangement description versus item-and-process description. In between, Humboldt, among others, understood language as a continuous growth phenomenon and, subsequently, Chomsky propagated as one of his principal tenets the creative power of language (cf. Chapter 2).

Interestingly the growth concept of language and of other symbols was nurtured in the Darwinian milieu of the nineteenth century, in which both linguistics and semiotics take their modern roots. The medical/biological leg (cf. "What is Semiotics?" above) was clearly integral then as well as now, a century later. Regard, for example, Thom's catastrophes which display a *change* in the equilibrium of an entity, and Uexküll's functional cycle which displays the sensorimotor dynamic of *growth* (cf. "What is Semiotics?" above; cf. Chapters 2, 9, 10; cf. Rauch 1996a). The task before both linguistics and semiotics is well put by Peirce (2: 229) when he identifies it as "ascertain[ing] the laws by which ... one sign [symbol, language element] gives birth to another." The development of modern evolutionary or genetic linguistics, co-terminous with the development of modern semiotics during the Peirce/Saussure era, is indicative of an impressive set of linguistic tools in explanation of language growth/change. First and foremost this set included the highly celebrated working tool known as the Neogrammarian hypothesis of 1876, which stated that (sound) laws suffer no exceptions. For fuller justification of the data this hypothesis necessitated modern linguistic refinement and application of venerable philosophical principles of *analogy* (cf. Chapters 2, 3, 14, 15; cf. Rauch 1995, and further below). An eminent and powerful byproduct tool of linguistic analogy is the principle of *isomorphism* or *biuniqueness*, also called *invariance*, which seeks a one-to-one relationship between form and meaning. It, too, is of venerable vintage, hearkening back to Humboldt and, of course, not unknown to Peirce (cf. Chapters 3, 4, 15, 18, 19). Analogy and isomorphism are *Firstness*.

Other tools used in the analysis of language growth/change developed or refined in the fecund scientific atmosphere of the twentieth century and subsequently include the *comparative method*, i.e., systematic (re)construction of the same linguistic items across related languages, internal reconstruction, i.e., (re)construction via paradigmatic alternation within a given language, typological comparison, i.e., (re)construction of a linguistic entity by comparison across related as well as non-related languages—this last producing such linguistic notions as drift, tendencies, universals of language growth/change (cf. Chapters 2 and 14; cf. Rauch 1990). In the three sections which follow, we provide concrete examples of language growth/change data from various languages, e.g., English, German, Slavic, Czech, Latin, their hypothecated parent, Proto-Indo-European, and from various components of their grammars, i.e., phonology, (the sounds of a language), morphology (the meaningful forms, in particular the inflectional forms of a language), syntax (the combining of words into the sentences of a language, semantics (here referring to the lexical semantics or the vocabulary of a language), and pragmatics (the usage of a language). The purpose in presenting these examples of language growth/change is certainly to display the tools of linguistic analysis for the teleology of change, but, in particular, to present evidence for the additional application of the tools of semiotics (cf. "What is Semiotics?" above), effecting an enhanced *raison d' être* for how and why language grows.

Phonological Growth/Change

Primary data for reconstructing languages of the non-immediate or historical past are the written evidence of whatever kind, e.g., letters, poems or other literature, documents, records, histories. Yet writing systems display various degrees of *isomorphism* (cf. "Language Grows" above) and consistency. Ideally, each sound in a language would be written by a discrete letter or graph (isomorphism), but language is generally parsimonious in its use of letters, so, e.g., the English graph <a> is pronounced at least three different ways: *father, fate, fat*. On the other hand, the reverse occurs with the vowel in English *here* and *hear*, where the same vowel is written two different ways and accordingly is not isomorphic.

Manuscript data from very old languages, prior to the age of printing, comprise valuable empirical evidence, since such a language, being of historical vintage, lacks eyewitness corroboration. In addition, the rules of spelling for a given language of such an age were not standardized. This is the case of the oldest ancestor of present-day Low German, viz. Old Saxon, spoken a millennium ago in Northern Germany and documented in a 6000-line alliterative narrative poem entitled *Heliand* 'Healer, Savior' (cf. Rauch 1992c). Here, e.g., *heliand* is spelled *helandi, helandeo, helendi, heleand, heland, heleando, helendio*. The inclination of historical linguists is to explain such a variation via linguistic genetics, i.e., varying sources fed into these forms and often a streamlined form or phantom icon is suggested by the researchers, e.g., *heliand*. On the other hand, neither the native Old Saxon speaker of the year 1000, nor the present second language learner of Old Saxon has recourse to the genetic provenance of a word such as *heliand*, certainly not in the case of the native Old Saxon and frequently not in the case of the present learner of Old Saxon. Where does linguistic reality lie then? To be sure, it is possible that the native Old Saxon used more than one pronunciation (consider, e.g., the two pronunciations of English *either*), yet it is unlikely that there were seven or more ways of pronouncing *heliand*. Since Old Saxon had no spelling books, it is most probable that the Old Saxons had limited pronunciation variations of *heliand*. Thus, e.g., *helandeo* and *helendio* may have been spoken the same way (consider, e.g., the pronunciation of *-ible* and *-able* on words such as *legible* and *affable*). Approaching historical data from the point of view of a then native speaker rather than from the point of view of a linguistic geneticist allows for more realistic *icon* (writing habit) production in reconstructing a language of the distant past (cf. Chapter 12).

If it appears difficult to ascertain the written sounds of a language, i.e., those sounds that appear in writing, it is equally, if not more, challenging to extract that part of the written word which is not reflected in writing. These are matters of stress and pitch, known as *supraseg-mental* sounds compared with the written or *segmental* sounds. Beyond this, however, there may be any number of other unseen sounds, e.g., individual tone and/or speed of voice, varying cadence such as sing-song voice, and even characteristics such as joviality or whining. These phenomena are known as *paralanguage/paralinguistic* and, indeed, some linguists aver they belong not to linguistics but to another area, e.g., *kinesics*, and hence to semiotics. As observed in the above discussion of Old Saxon writing, the reader of the thousand-year old data from Old Saxon is confronted with a considerable amount of spelling variation for presumably one sound. Probably the most notorious case is that of Old Saxon <ō> and <ē> spellings which show up numerous ways, e.g., for <ō> we find <uo, ŏ u, V̊, ó, oo, ou>. For <ō> now, considering the most numerous variation <uo>, the question which the linguist faces is whether there is any phonetic reality to this <uo> writing, i.e., did the Old Saxons pronounce, for example, the word meaning 'good', Old Saxon *gōd/guod*, both as a monophthong and as a diphthong. Many Old Saxon researchers claim that the <uo> spelling (as well as <ie>) is just an alternate spelling which Old Saxon borrowed from its Old High German neighbors. However, there is solid evidence in the Old Saxon data to presume that a *paralanguage* feature of *drawl* actually instigated a spoken diphthong or diphthong-like vowel sound in the case of the <uo> (and <ie>) spellings (cf. Chapter 13).

The Old Saxon neighbor, Old High German, also dating from a millennium ago, is the oldest ancestor of Modern Standard German. Discerning the sounds of Old High German is thus also a task in phonological archaeology. The Old High German <ie> (noted above as possible spelling interference into Old Saxon) derives from pre-Old High German *$\bar{e}_2$. Another Old High German diphthong <eo> exists which also derives from a much earlier pre-Old High German source, viz. *eu. At about 860 A.D., these two diphthongs grow/change/merge into one and the same diphthong, which is spelled <ia> in but one dialect of Old High German called South Rhenish Franconian. This dialect is sandwiched in between Old Franconian to the North and Old Alemannic to the South, so that researchers attribute the <ia> to an amalgam of <i> from the former, and <a> from the latter dialect. Evidence that the two diphthongs actually merged soundwise is adduced from rhyme pairs of South Rhenish Franconian's chief poet, Otfried. To be sure, rhyme pairs represent *iconic analogy* (abduction), but if the rhyme pairs are assigned teleological significance, they act as cause rather than as effect; the semiotic factor of *Secondness* motivates the *iconism*, thereby offering new insight into this classical phonological change (cf. Chapter 15). Similarly, *Secondness* compels the anological regularization of the Latin paradigm for the word meaning 'voice,' *woks (as in English *vocal*) which has two roots, subject case Latin *wok- and other cases Latin *wokw-. Usually Latin chooses to change the subject case form to the majority non-subject cases form. Contrary to Latin habit, *wok- is *iconically* spread to all cases. Semiotic *Secondness* compels the direction of this growth/change, because Latin phonology does not allow a -w- between consonants anywhere in its language (cf. Chapter 16).

Secondness also plays a decisive role in linguistic data from the history of the Czech language. In the fourteenth-century Litomyšl dialect of Czech sharped labials *p*, *b*, *m* grew/changed to dentals *t*, *d*, *n*. Henning Andersen rightly attributes this Czech change in phonology to abduction (*Firstness*) on the part of the Litomyšl speakers due to ambiguity in the production and perception of the changing sounds. However, for a more adequate explanation, the dynamic (*Secondness*) which compels the change must be identified within the minor premise of the abductive inference. It is empirical reality that the sharped labials are physiologically and acoustically at least 51% dental (cf. Chapter 14).

Morphological Growth/Change

Linguistic morphology actually refers to the forms which compose the lexicon of a language (cf. "Syntactic, Semantic, Pragmatic Growth/Change" below), but also to the inflection of the lexicon, e.g., singular or plural formation of nouns and past tense formation of verbs. Thus, e.g., -*s* is a common morpheme to signal plural in English, so, e.g., *days*. German has several morphemes to signal plural, one of the more common forms being -*e* as in *Tage* 'days.' Data from the immediate ancestor stage of Modern German, called Early New High German, (circa fourteenth to the seventeenth century) bear witness to a great proliferation of noun plural morphemes, so that Early New High German plural *tag* showed up in the period also as *täg, täge, tage, tagen, ta^egen*. The -*e* forms are remarkable because of the tendency or drift toward decay of end-syllable -*e* (called apocope) which is in progress and peaks in sixteenth century Early New High German. (Compare the decay of final -*e* in English *name*, where it is not pronounced). Willi Mayerthaler correctly attributes the signaling of the plural by -*e*, in spite of the phonological trend to drop it, to an iconic principle which requires that plurality be reflected in additional morphological material. Enhanced explanatory justification for the earlier loss of -*e* and its subsequent establishment in the seventeenth century as a plural morpheme is achieved by recourse to Peircean *Secondness* and *Thirdness* principles. Thus, the earlier apocope of -*e* is coerced (*Secondness*) by the weakened stress of German on syllables containing inflectional -*e* while the later establishment of the *e*-plural is coerced (*Secondness*) by the consonant+vowel preferred syllable structure (*ta+ge*) and the suffix nature of German. Finally the established plural *e*-suffix is not a restored apocopated -*e*, since the decay of end-syllables has not reversed itself (it persists in Modern German as well as in Modern English). The seventeenth-century *e*-noun element is rather a conventionalized plural morpheme (*Thirdness*; cf. Chapter 17).

For an example of verb inflection, we look to Modern English data. Randolf Quirk claims that verbs with both -*t* and -*ed* forms signal aspectual differences, i.e., momentary versus continuous past tense, as observed in *spilt* versus *spilled*: "When I shouted, he *spilt* his coffee" versus "The water *spilled* out all day long." Of the eight verbs included in the data, Quirk's statistics show the -*ed* variants of *kneel, dream,* and *leap* to be most objectionable in expressing momentary past tense, as well as continuous past tense with the exception of *leaped*. Conversely, statistics on the eight verbs chosen show the -*t* variants of these same three verbs as the least objectionable in both the momentary and the continuous past. A crucial unnoticed observation is that *dream, leap, kneel* unlike the other five, *spoil, spill, learn, spell, burn* display an *iconic* (*Firstness*) relationship between a changing root vowel and the suffix morpheme, thus [i] + -*ed* versus [ɛ] + *t* as in *kneeled : knelt*. In addition, the exceptional behavior of *leaped* is attributable to the fact that, regardless of the spelling, *-ed* after *-p* is compelled (*Secondness*) by the rules of English phonology to be pronounced as *t*, so that the changing root vowel alone signals momentary or continuous past (cf. Chapter 16).

Secondness also distinguishes the analogies posited for the development of the perfect tense of verbs in the hypothesized ancient prehistoric parent, known as Indo-European, of the languages which have been discussed above. Kuryłowicz hypothesizes the evolution of the Indo-European perfect, which is a past tense, out of a verbal adjective by its development of personal endings in analogy (*Firstness*) to the formation of the Indo-European present tense forms. Modern English examples can depict the dynamics involved in the Indo-European development. So, e.g., English *done* in "No sooner said that *done*" is a verbal adjective. Mirroring (*Firstness*) the present active tense morphology, *done* takes on personal forms, thus "He no sooner said it, than he did (substandard *done*) it." Further, mirroring (*Firstness*) the present active tense, a passive form splits off from the original verbal adjective *done*, thus "It is *done* by him." However, the split (a *Thomian bifurcation catastrophe*) into active and passive should not be viewed simply as iconically motivated or as resulting merely from factual similarity. It is rather the necessary (*Secondness*) motivation between the active and the passive verb voice, whereby the category passive has existence only because of the existence of the active, i.e., they are in mutual dependency (cf. Chapters 2 and 15).

Syntactic, Semantic, Pragmatic Growth/Change

As observed in the section "Language Grows" (above), semantic can refer to the lexicon or vocabulary of a language. It can also refer to the semantic infrastructure throughout the various components (phonology, morphology, syntax) of a language. Similarly, pragmatic features saturate all language components. In discussing the remaining three contributions in which the data display the relevance of semiotic tools, the first, (Chapter 18), will consider primarily syntactic and semantic insights, while Chapters 19 and 20 will address primarily pragmatic relevance.

Iconism, isomorphism (cf. Chapters 3, 4, 15, 18, and 19) is central to translation theory; it is frequently held that a one-to-one translation is impossible. The rendering of a seemingly simple English phrase such as "So long" meaning something like "Farewell" or "Good-bye" demonstrates this. Heightened challenges in translation occur if the translated language is not a current language, but historical as, e.g., Old Saxon (cf. "Phonological Growth/Change" above). As mentioned earlier, the reader must break a code without the benefit of eye-witness corroboration. On the other hand, the reader does not have to appeal to the genetic history of historical data (called *diachronic* by Saussure); s/he can approach the data as though s/he were living in one and the same Old Saxon time frame (called *synchronic* by Saussure; cf. "Language Grows" above). Accordingly, attempts at rendering an Old Saxon sentence into English can be viewed as similar to rendering a modern language into English, and they may evince the strategies of an interlanguage, i.e., the imperfect grammar of a language learner. So, e.g., when the learner of Old Saxon confronts a simple sentence such as *Gaf it is uingaron forð* 'He gave it to his disciples,' s/he cognizes each word for its lexical meaning and morphological grammatical function. Through a series of cognitive decisions, the reader isolates *Gaf* as a verb in the past tense, third person singular with the lexical meaning 'gave.' Because the syntax shows the very common Old Saxon verb-first position, it is not clear to the reader whether the sentence is declarative or interrogative, both of which are licensed in Old Saxon verb-first position (the past tense excludes the possibility of imperative meaning). To disambiguate this isolated sentence, it must be compared with its immediately surrounding sentences in the text. Embedded in the larger text, the first position of *Gaf* functions to link (*Thirdness*) its sentence with the preceding sentence with which it is in iconic (*Firstness*) relationship, that is both sentences relate part of a series of actions enumerated in the text. While the immediately above data in the first portion of Chapter 18 are studied to yield a *diachronic synchrony* (cf. also Chapter 12), thus subverting Saussure's synchrony: diachrony axes, the data in the second portion of Chapter 18 are studied in demonstration of Saussure's chessboard strategies.

This lexical semantic growth/change example in Chapter 18 is of particular semiotic interest since it speaks to medical vocabulary, medicine being the proto-semiotic (cf. "What is Semiotics?" above; cf. chapter 9 below). The data come from a medical prescription written in Old High German (cf. "Phonological Growth/Change' above) around 800 A.D., the so-called Basel Recipe. The meaning of the symptom is central to medical semiosis. Following the Hippocratic axiom that our natures are the physicians of our diseases, Uexküll's belief in the reciprocal interaction of our nature with our environment is instantiated also by the semiosis of the symptom. The soft-science side of medicine is well displayed in the reading of a symptom which can refer to both evidence of the disease as well as the disease itself. Moreover, as is the case with linguistic semantics, the symptom may be liable to semantic features such as ambiguity and polysemy. While the Old High German Basel prescription is quite precise in specifying medication, e.g., some thirteen drugs (sweet cicely, juniper, red incense, pepper, white incense, wormwood, horehound, sulfur, fennel, mugwort, plantain of two sorts, homewort—each of which is to be rubbed down separately in two bottles of wine, poured together and allowed to ferment for three nights), and while the patient is given precise directions for taking the medicine (a cup in the morning and at night, in addition to fasting forty days and not eating or drinking any thing on the day it is prepared; further the patient is to be monitored around the clock), the diagnosis or the meaning of the symptom is very imprecise. The symptom, simply referred to as *it* (thus "when *it* seizes him"), is likely ambiguous if not polysemous and as in modern medicine may require variable reference in its sought-after change to *isomorphism* (*Firstness*; cf. Chapter 18).

Firstness phenomena play a dominant role in the initial stages of language growth/change. To be sure, language change/growth has a beginning and an end, with one or more possible intermediate stages, very much like all growth (cf. Rauch 1996b). The spontaneity and apparent unintentionality of speech and/or printing errors offer possible very early stage data in language change; they represent a mere maybe (a *First*), thus their presence is not necessarily guaranteed to lead to lasting change (final stage/*Thirdness*). The text chosen to display abrupt, instantaneous, unorchestrated, subliminal speech errors is the very popular Early New High German (cf. "Morphological Growth/ Change" above) "Ackermann von Böhmen: The Plowman from Bohemia," a Job-like widower's lament. Three errors in the Bamberg version of the cited chapter thirteen of the Plowman text are not entirely convincing as mere mechanical errors, i.e., slips of the hand or fingers in setting the printing type; (item 67) *wundē* 'wounds,' (item 146) *ich* 'I,' (item 163) *wol* 'certainly.' These words are embedded in the Plowman's sentences in which he addresses Death with the accusations that Death is the robber of his joys, the thief of his good days, the destroyer of his *wounds* (sic.), and of all which pledged him a happy life. He further accuses death of having snatched his faithful wife much too soon, when *I* (sic.) made him a widower and his children orphans. Miserable, alone, and of sorrow *certainly* (sic.) (the Plowman) remains uncompensated (by Death). Phonetic iconicity *(Firstness)* can account for all three errors: *ich* with the contiguous *mich*, *wundē* with the phonologically similar noun *wunnē* 'bliss,' and *wol* with *vol* 'full.' It is possible, moreover, that pragmatic/discourse iconicity *(Firstness)* may play a further role in these errors via the empathy of the printer as he identifies vicariously with the devastating experiences of the Plowman, thus the negative *wundē*, the iterating *ich* saturating the lamentation, and the *wol* lending absolute control to Death (cf. Chapter 19).

The identification by Eco and others that a basic, if not the basic, characteristic of a sign is that it can be used for prevarication informs Chapter 20, which presents data in support of a mendacious mode as an overarching mode beside the indicative and imperative modes in most quotidian language. The data derive from two telephone conversations spoken in Modern German. Grice's conversational maxims are invoked in pragmatic analysis of the data to ferret out mendacious features of varying degrees of deception by identifying the discourse catalyst, e.g., shift in topic focus leading to evading the truth in a dialogue. Grammatical structures function in prevarication, e.g., the use of the subjective to express a socially acceptable lie, and, indeed, silence in answer to a question can be a clue to mendacity. Finally, of considerable interest is whether the structures of one language are more conducive in expressing prevarication than those of another language. Initially in this section (above), it was observed that *iconism, isomorphism* is central to translation theory. Contrastive German/English evidence from a piece of holocaust literature demonstrates the added sensitivity required in rendering degrees of mendacity from one language into another (cf. Chapter 20).

Symbols grow/language changes. The nexus of semiotics and linguistics, much discussed in the literature, but little displayed empirically, is unambiguously demonstrated in this volume. Over a dozen sets of linguistic data dealing with language change/growth from the various components of language as well as from an array of languages are presented to the reader. A particular crux is pinpointed. It is shown step by step how *the data do the talking,* i.e., provide the evidence/lead the way to a resolution of the language growth/change phenomenon under scrutiny. Well-proven linguistic tools abound and are applied. Yet the application of multidimensional semiotic tools such as *Firstness, Secondness,* and *Thirdness* enhances insights into the dynamics of the language growth/change phenomenon. A felicitous by-product is the clarification of the mutual identities of the two sciences of semiotics and linguistics.

Part One

1

Semiotics: A Fire in the Belly

Why is there a lifelong fire in the belly of semiotists for semiotics? The lure of semiotics is ultimately signification or meaning. Since, as Merrell (1997: ix) writes: "Meaning is nowhere and at the same time it is everywhere; it is in the interrelatedness of the sign interaction incessantly being played out on the stage of *semiosis*", what we do in semiotics is unceasingly enticing. Moreover, this seemingly elusive task is provided with a most affable paradigm. The affability of semiotics is, nevertheless, misconceived if it is understood as a panacea for everything. It is neither a panacea nor has it everything as its object, for both concepts would lend it a closedness, the decided lack of which speaks to semiotics' affability. Rather, its affability resides in its prismatic paradigm, i.e., one which provides many and diverse foci not at all on the same plane for contemplating an object of study (cf. Introduction, "What is Semiotics?"). To be sure, the Peircean phenomenological categories of *Firstness*, *Secondness*, and *Thirdness* are universal categories, viz., valid for all times and in all places, but it is an especially welcome paradigm as the century wanes and the millennium closes, since the semiotic paradigm lets us have it both ways, so to speak; it is both modern and postmodern as aphorized in, e.g., the phrase "hard science and soft science," respectively.

As we approach the end of the millennium and perhaps more significantly the twentieth century, few humanistic methodologists will deny that this century staunchly believed in and rigorously cultivated a scientific orientation, in imitation of the nineteenth-century rigor displayed by such pure sciences as physics. Certainly the drive toward legitimization as a science is well traced in the history of the past hundred years of a discipline such as linguistics, which is informed with laws and systems that are often hypothetical in nature. So, e.g.,

Saussurean "*langue*", which encapsulates scientifically focused structuralism (cf. Chapter 2 below) not only imbued linguistics with his
paradigm, but *ceteris paribus*, semiotics, as well as seemingly anti-
structuralist paradigms such as deconstruction, germane to recent literary approaches, and prototype theory, cultivated in latter-day linguistic method. It is a remarkable realization that the scientific rigor,
the focal *sine qua non* of the past century of linguistic, literary,
semiotic research has the appearance of languishing validity. Could it
be that Eco's dogged questioning of the scientific status of semiotics
(Eco 1978: 76, "Is it enough to state that therefore a discipline [or a
science] called semiotics exists ...?) is dated or should be read tongue-
in-cheek? That is to ask, are Eco's criteria ("a precise subject, a set of
unified methodological tools, the capability of producing hypotheses,
the possibility of making predictions ..., the possibility of modifying
the actual state of the objective world") valid requirements for a science in the waning years of the millennium? Should Eco's statements
be reinterpreted for possible facetious value?

As a step in answering these questions, this chapter adduces trends
in literary and linguistic methods which seriously challenge the
"hardness" of science as adopted by humanistic enterprises in the
nineteenth and most of the twentieth century. For this purpose, grant-
ing familiarity with Saussure (cf. Chapter 2), we skim—admittedly
fragmentarily—deconstructionist thought and prototype theory concepts via recourse to a few principal actors in their respective
methodologies; we further consider whether and how these paradigms
are compatible and their relationships to the semiotic paradigm.
Lastly, we apply insights from these approaches to a sample set of
fresh empirical linguistic data to gauge their mutual interaction.

Deconstruction

Jacques Derrida, indisputably a premier theorist of deconstruction,
builds his paradigm on the deconstruction of Saussure himself by uncovering the flaw in Saussure's paradigm, i.e., that feature which subverts Saussurean thought, namely, the fact that Saussure does not develop his concept of difference far enough. Thus, for Saussure the linguistic sign derives its existence and accordingly its meaning from
differences, i.e., relationships within a system, and Saussure holds that
the meaning or signified is as inalienably united with the form of the
signifier in the sign as are, to use Saussure's well-known metaphor,

two sides of a piece of paper. This view leads to the linguistic principle of biuniqueness or *isomorphism*, whereby a linguistic entity may be unequivocally disambiguated and identified. Derrida challenges the possibility of an absolute, univocal meaning, as well as the distinction between signifier and signified, which reflects the traditional metaphysical division between matter and spirit or thought. He states (1978: 280):

> ... it was necessary to begin thinking that there was no center, that the center could not be thought in the form of a present being, that it was not a tired locus but a function, a sort of non-locus in which an infinite number of sign substitutions come into play. This was the moment when language invaded the universal problematic, the moment when, in the absence of a center or origin, everything became discourse ... that is to say, a system in which the central signified, the original or transcendental signified, is never absolutely present outside a system of differences. The absence of the transcendental signified extends the domain and play of signification infinitely.

There is no absolute meaning, no center, since in order for one to exist either the signifier or the signified must be final (Derrida says "transcendental"), i.e., incapable of referring to or differing from another signifier or signified. Each signified becomes in turn a signifier, thus muting the distinction between the two entities and extending a signification into the infinite. The maintaining of an absolute signified is called by Derrida the "metaphysics of presence," whereas infinite signification is a metaphysics of past and future as well. Presence is merely absence of what is not, i.e., difference. Thus, meaning is continually deferred, extending as he says, "the play of signification infinitely." This process frees the reader, Derrida maintains, from nostalgia for origin and a center and offers instead the joyful Nietzschean affirmation of free play and the innocence of becoming (Derrida 1978: 278–293). In the interrelatedness or system of differences, the signs, whether viewed as signifiers or signifieds, carry "traces" of one another. Derrida states (1976: 159):

> There has never been anything but writing, there have never been anything but supplements, substitutive significations which could only come forth in a chain of differential references, the

"real" supervening, and being added only while taking on meaning from a trace and front an invocation of the supplement, etc. And thus to infinity, for we have read, *in the text*, that the absolute present, nature, that which words like "real mother" name, have always already escaped, have never existed; that what opens meaning and language is writing as the disappearance of natural presence.

Beyond speaking to trace and supplement (proliferation of signifiers from an ever-deferred signified), this passage once again encapsulates fundamental concepts of Derrida and it brings to the fore his quasi-dissolution of Saussure's distinction between speech and writing, which, as with form and meaning, is derived from Western metaphysics. Plato assigned priority to speech; Derrida, however, holds this priority to be bonded with the metaphysics of presence. For him, writing exemplifies well the concept of deferral or endless commutation, the displacement of one signifier by another in an endless chain. Beyond this, writing is not fleeting; speech is fleeting and thereby tends to suppress, by its being present, the play of endless differences. Similarly, Roland Barthes speaks to the endless commutation of meaning in any text, observing (1977: 146) that "the text is not a line of words releasing a single 'theological' meaning (the message of an Author-God) but a multi-dimensional space in which a variety of writings, none of them original, blend and clash. The text is a tissue of quotations drawn from innumerable centers of culture." So too, Michel Foucault explains the intertextuality, i.e., the endless "differentially interrelated fabric" (Merrell 1984: 126), in which the text moves, as follows (1972: 23):

The frontiers of a book are never clear-cut; beyond the title, the first lines, and the last full stops, beyond its internal configuration and its autonomous form, it is caught up in a system of references to other books, other texts, other sentences; it is a node within a network ... The book is not simply the object that one holds in one's hands; and it cannot remain within the little parallelepiped that contains it: its unity is variable and relative. As soon as one questions that unity, it loses its self-evidence; it indicates itself, constructs itself, only on the basis of a complex field of discourse.

Prototype Theory

Prototype theory, at present widely applied in cognitive studies of various disciplines, owes part of its recent refinements to current linguistic methods of categorization which deal a severe blow in particular to classical distinctive feature theory. In the tradition of Western metaphysics, an entity is characterized according to Aristotelian necessary and sufficient features which are binary in nature, i.e., either absent or present, and which allow absolute and clear-cut disambiguation from another entity. In the strongly language user-oriented paradigm which prototype theory reflects, atomistic, objective, and often, abstract features are taken as unrealistic perceptions attributed to the putative user. The flesh and blood language user and not the language theorist assigns an entity to a category. The entity may not at all be perceived by the user as a distinct item; it may be categorized subjectively, i.e., relative to the user's experience, and it might be quite concretely, i.e., physically, experienced. To quote Ronald Langacker (1987: 16–17):

> Experimental work in cognitive psychology ... has demonstrated that categories are often organized around prototypical instances. These are the instances which people accept as common, run-of-the-mill, garden-variety members of the category. They generally occur the most frequently in our experience, tend to be learned the earliest, and can be identified experimentally in a variety of ways ... Nonprototypical instances are assimilated to a class or category to the extent that they can be construed as matching or approximating the prototype. Membership is therefore a matter of degree: prototypical instances are full, central members of the category, whereas other instances form a gradation from central to peripheral depending on how far and in what ways they deviate from the prototype. Moreover the members are not necessarily a uniquely defined set, since there is no specific degree of departure from the prototype beyond which a person is absolutely incapable of perceiving a similarity.

Prototype may be perceived as an entity, i.e., a particularly good example of a category, or as an abstract schema or network which represents shared features of entities or members of the category. Goodness is determined empirically by the perceiver, who infers entities as *gestalts* and judges some entities as more representative of a category than others. The inferences of the perceiver derive from quasi-encyclopedic, i.e., all his/her experiential knowledge within his/her culture rather than from isolated abstractions, so that entities are categorized by Wittgensteinean "family resemblance," described by Eleanor Rosch and Carolyn Mervis (1975: 575) as a "relationship [which] consists of a set of items of the form A B, B C, C D, D E. That is, each item has at least one, and probably several, elements in common with one or more other items, but no, or few elements are common to all items." On the one hand, family resemblance could suggest infinite relationship; on the other hand, infinite resemblance is curtailed by the necessary distinctions between category membership status and degree of representativeness within a category. To be sure, John Taylor writes (1989: 50): "Categorization makes it possible for an organism to reduce limitless variation in the world to manageable proportions."

The fact that language users speak with considerable frequency in figurative rather than in literal terms leads to category extension particularly through metaphor and metonymy. More basically, and as input to both metaphor and metonymy, however, the language user conceptualizes his/her experience through image schemas, George Lakoff's (1987: 283) "The Spatialization of Form hypothesis ... [which itself] requires a metaphorical mapping from physical space into a 'conceptual space.'" Lakoff explains (282–3):

> Recall for a moment some of the kinds of image-schemas ...: schemas for CONTAINER, SOURCE-PATH-GOAL, LINK, PART-WHOLE, CENTER-PERIPHERY, UP-DOWN, FRONT -BACK. These schemas structure our experience in space. What I will be claiming is that the same schemas structure concepts themselves. In fact, I maintain that image schemas define most of what we commonly term "structure" when we talk about abstract domains. When we understand something as having an abstract structure, we understand that structure in terms of image schemas.

Compatibility of Paradigms

Intent though we might be to espouse a discrete methodology, it is clear that a characteristic of science generally, as the century and the millennium close, is, simply put, a willingness to openness, to also look to other approaches. Richard Tarnas (1990) judges the pulse of the times well by his query: "And why is there evident now such a widespread collective impetus in the Western mind to articulate a holistic and participatory world view, visible in virtually every field!" That the nature of scientific inquiry as such has changed and is changing is voiced also by F. E. Yates, who chooses semiotics, that apparently all-encompassing, loosely fitting paradigm, as central to both natural and humane sciences. He writes (1986: 359):

> Science has been softened up by deep problems raised concerning quantum reality ... and seems to be open to new discussions of the nature of inquiry, models, theories, intentionality, explanation and meaning. Those hoary issues that in the past had to be set aside to clear the way for scientific advance now come back to haunt us once again. They are not technical issues susceptible of durable resolution in the same sense that quantum mechanics itself has been astoundingly robust under more exacting testing than has ever been applied to any other idea conceived by man. But as we build information processing machines that rival or surpass many of our own cognitive faculties, the persistent tension between linguistic [information] and dynamic views of complex systems ... generates extraordinary opportunity for semiotics to meld the sciences.

Indeed, the seeming failure of such Eco criteria (mentioned at the start) as "precise subject," "set of unified tools," may be positive characteristics which help accord semiotics its "melding" prowess. It is likely, then, that the two questions posed in Chapter 11 below ("A Canon and Theses for Semiotics") may attract a negative and an affirmative answer, respectively: "Should we, at long last, rid ourselves of this nagging on us of concern for semiotics without canon, without theses (and institutionalize both for the record)? Or is this burden's existence, after all, the semiotist's *raison d'être*—i.e., is the best canon indeed no (conventionalized/delimited) canon; are the best theses indeed no (conventionalized/delimited) theses?"

With semiotics thus necessarily joining in the interdigitation of deconstructionist thought and prototype theory, let us extract, by recalling particularly salient insights from the citations given above, some surprisingly clear analogies, indeed similarities, to which deconstruction, prototype theory and semiotics are mutually open. The destruction of a monolithic signification which permeates the given citations is voiced, e.g., in Derrida's "extends the domain and play of signification infinitely" (cf. "Deconstruction," above) beside, e.g., Langacker's "there is no specific degree from the prototype beyond which a person is absolutely incapable of perceiving a similarity" (cf. "Prototype Theory," above), beside Peirce's (2§302) simple aphoristic encapsulation "symbols grow." That signification is grounded in experience is reflected, e.g., in Derrida's "not a fixed locus but a function ... the absence of a transcendental signified" (cf. "Deconstruction," above), beside Langacker's "prototypical instances occur the most frequently in our experience" (cf. "Prototype Theory," above) and Lakoff's (1987: 154) negative reply to the question: "Are concepts and reason 'transcendental,' that is, independent of the nature and bodies of the reasoning beings?" beside Uexküll's autoambience theory which holds that (Uexküll 1940: 61, translation mine): "The body likened to a house is, on the one hand, the creator of meaningful signs, which inhabit its garden, and, on the other hand, it is the creation of these signs which intervene as motifs in the construction of the house." Notice the interplay with prototype theory, which also espouses various kinds of both biological and linguistic relativity (cf. now Lakoff 1987.335: "I am convinced by Whorf's arguments that the way we use concepts affects the way we understand experience"). The concretization of features within endless signification is a common motif, thus e.g., Barthes' "the text is not a line of words releasing a single 'theological' meaning (the message of an Author-God) but a multi-dimensional space" and Foucault's "it is a node within a network" (cf. "Deconstruction," above), beside Lakoff's "image-schemas" (cf. "Prototype Theory," above) and Langacker's (1987) "trajector/landmark" schema, beside René Thom's (1975) "archetypal morphologies" or "elementary catastrophes." (Cf. further Chapter 10, especially "Semiotic Architectonic," below.)

Needless to say, these few commonalities alone whet the appetite. In completing Chapter 1, let us test the mutual interaction of the three paradigms on a fresh, albeit small, sample set of linguistic data taken from the very physical linguistic component, phonology. The evidence is part of Phase Four of the San Francisco Bay Area German Linguistic Fieldwork Project (Rauch et al. 1985). In eliciting the pronunciation of the German word *leid* 'painful' from five children of German descent living in the San Francisco Bay area, each fieldworker transcribed phonetically the word as s/he heard it on the tape of the recorded informant. The informant spoke each word twice by reading it from a card; accordingly, the phonetic transcription should yield two entities, each of word length. However, the fieldworkers, averaging seven to eight per transcription session, did not perceive the taped evidence uniformly. All perceptions recorded by two or more fieldworkers were considered viable. Two different methods led to the extraction of the phonetic bits. Method A yielded five phonetic transcriptions for the five informants by opting for the simple majority perception of the fieldworkers, thus: [la^{l}d̥ , l$^>$a^{l}d, li·t, li^{l}t, li·ʔ] in the case of the informants' first reading. Method B applied to the recorded data yielded six transcriptions perceived by at least two or more fieldworkers: [la^{l}d̥ (14%), la^{l}t (6%), li·ʔ(22%), li^{l}t (14%), li·t (25%), l' a^{l}d (14%)]. The fact that six instead of five transcriptions for five informants demonstrates beautifully how perception may influence reality. The prototype schema on the data differ accordingly, although both may well differ from a possible third set, if the taped data were subjected to sound spectrography. The question is, what are the phonetic realia? Might an informant have in fact actually pronounced [la^{l}t] or still other phonetic configurations? We are inclined to rely on machines rather than the human ear, yet the newer wave, as argued above, also recognizes human perception as a factor in science. Compare Kelly and Local (1989: 8) who "do" phonology by ear: "Instrumental findings, though crucial to our understanding, in quantitative terms, of phonetic exponency, do not in themselves contribute to the elaboration of phonological entities.

The deconstructionist enterprise not only comes to the fore in the variable interpretation of the *leid* data by the fieldworkers, but also by three speakers' displacement of a hypothesized prototypical pronunciation of the vocalic nucleus of the word. The two [i·] and one [i:] pronunciations are certainly not central to the prescribed standard [a^l] actually spoken by at least one of the first generation speakers in the word *leid*. The deconstruction takes place by the graphic confusion of <ei> with <ie> (possibly through interference from English) as found in the German word *Lied* 'song.' Needless to say, the Peircean categories underlie all of the above observations; thus, e.g., while a prototype as an instantiation of goodness fit is *Secondness*, the <ei> <ie> analogy is, by way of abduction, *Firstness*, and the majority perception of the fieldworkers results in *Thirdness* or convention.

Phonological data, such as those recorded on tape and/or the sound spectrograph, are about as hard linguistic data as may be found. If we consider but one piece of hard evidence, e.g., [liːt], both a mispronunciation of the elicited *leid* and a correct pronunciation of the non-elicited *Lied*, the semiotic paradigm can reflect the mere hard data [liːt] as *Secondness*. With a slight turn of the multidimensional prism, [liːt] can appear as an abduced possibility, while the major premise in the analogy underlying the falsely abduced [liːt] evinces *Thirdness*, to be sure, another plane of the [liːt] prism and, at that, harder than that of the abduction, which is the minor premise (cf. Chapter 6). There are many further configurations in the prism which display semiotics' affability, and accordingly its relative power, compared with both hard and soft sciences. On the other hand, the softening of linguistics is a very recent and not universal (i.e., in all methods) reoccurrence, as will be perceived in Chapter 2.

2

Saussure: Roots of Today's Linguistics

Today's linguistics was nurtured in the flowering of nineteenth-century scientific activity which, in its drive for legitimization, cultivated the roots of science, in particular affinities with physics and biology. Saussure's action and his reaction to these roots account for a great deal of his thought. The interlacing effects of biology and physics are, accordingly, evident in semiotics as well (cf. also Chapter 9 below).

Language/Life

Arnold Toynbee writes in his book *Change and Habit* (1966: 89):

> The study of human affairs has to adjust itself to their nature. Human affairs are a part of life, and life has two salient characteristics; it is perpetually on the move through time and space, and it is plural, not singular. The approach to the study of human affairs in the time dimension is necessarily genetic ...

This certainty, that it is the nature of human affairs to be "perpetually on the move," is not an unchallenged truth throughout the ages. Recall, e.g., the Greek Eleatic school of philosophy, foremost Parmenides of Elea, who asserted that reality is one unchanging whole, and that the changes we observe through our senses are but illusion. Parmenides' contemporary, Heraclitus of Ephesus, held an opposing view: "Upon those who step in the same river, different and ever different waters flow down," meaning that we cannot step into the same river twice, since neither we, nor the river, are the same the second time. Needless to say, both Parmenides and Heraclitus are correct in part, in view of the newer concept of homeostasis which considers all living systems to be in dynamic equilibrium—a self-regulating process whereby systems persist or remain stable, while constantly undergoing change or adjusting to conditions. The quasi-equilibrium is the outcome of evolution, which creates systems, and the understanding of which, again in the newer viewpoint, can be approached through dynamic game and problem solving theory. (So, e.g., Werner Leinfellner, "Ontology of Evolution: Ontology of Becoming or Becoming of an Ontology" at the 6th International Wittgenstein Symposium, Vienna 1981).

In semiotics the homeostatic nature of a sign as a system has most innovatingly been proposed by Sebeok, who, in fact, equates life with sign creation; he writes: "... people, animals, plants, bacteria, and viruses—are only a sign's way of making another sign" (1979: xiii). This chapter considers *life*, that is *creation*, (Peirce's "Symbols grow", 2: §302), in the semiotic modality of linguistics. Thus it speaks to language. But, one might object that language is not the province of linguistics alone. It belongs to all disciplines. That is correct; as Martin Heidegger (1971: 189) puts it simply:

Man speaks. We speak when we are awake and we speak in our dreams. We are always speaking even when we do not utter a single word aloud, but merely listen or read, and even when we are not particularly listening or speaking but are attending to some work or taking a rest ... It is as one who speaks that man is—man ... Language belongs to the closest neighborhood of man's being.

Still, language is all that linguists have. It is the sole object of their discipline. And, as one of the all-time leaders in the field, Emile Benveniste (1968: 85), observed: "The evolution of a language taken as a sign system consists in the mutation undergone by its categories ... those form classes which are distinctively characterized and capable of grammatical function." In turn, the changes in language, "the eternally self-generating stuff" according to Wilhelm von Humboldt, are to be viewed in terms of "laws of creation" (quoted in Chomsky 1964: 56, translation mine)—a statement fascinatingly close to the Peircean assignment to semiotics of the "task ... to ascertain the laws by which ... one sign gives birth to another" (2: §229). And within the laws of mutation or change, the rules which speak to causation are in Hume's judgment those on which "All reasoning concerning matters of fact seem to be founded ... By means of them (the laws of causation) alone we go beyond the evidence of our memory and senses" (quoted in Thompson 1917: 4 fn. cf. Chapter 14 below).

Linguistics/Semiotics as Science

What is this paradigm called linguistics? If it is that framework usually associated by semiotists with Saussure, is there then, we might ask further, life after Saussure? or without Saussure, and, let us say, without those linguists who in most semiotic literature impress as neo-Saussureans such as Hjelmslev, Jakobson, or Chomsky? (cf. also Chapter 10 below).

The majority of semioticians accept the science of linguistics as one of the "three fundamental semiotic traditions" along with the medical and the philosophical traditions to form "the semiotic tripod" in the words of Sebeok (1976: 181). There is, then, hardly a semiotist who would do their semiotics without some knowledge of linguistics, philosophy, and medicine. We know through the extensive historiographical chronicles of Sebeok, e.g., his "Semiotics: A Survey of the State of the Art" (1974), that linguists from Saussure onward have laid claim to their input into semiotics. Thus, Adrien Naville, a colleague of Saussure and Dean of the School of the Literary and Social Sciences at the University of Geneva, writes in 1901 in his *New Classifications of the Sciences* (104, translation mine) of Saussure's

> ... very general science which he [Saussure] calls semiology, whose object would be the laws of creation and transformation of signs and their meaning ... Since the most important sign system is the conventional human language, semiological science in its most advanced form is linguistics, or the science of the laws of life of language. Linguistics is, or at least tends to become, more and more a science of laws.

What we are looking for in this citation is not so much the oft-quoted foresight of Saussure in conceiving "a very general science which he calls semiology," but rather we are looking for Saussure's usually neglected impression among semiotists of what linguistics is. We do not pursue here the question of whether "semiological science in its most advanced form is *linguistics*," the linguistics-semiotics hierarchy controversy, or the Barthes heresy, so to speak (cf. however, Chapter 3 below). We are interested in two insights which the Naville quote yields that are by far more productive, namely, first: in conjunction with the title of our presentation, that the "object" of Saussure's semiology "would be the laws of creation and transformation of signs and their meaning" and, secondly: in conjunction with the immediate discussion, that the Saussurean definition of linguistics is, in Naville's words, "the science of the laws of the life of language. Linguistics is, or at least tends to become, more and more a science of laws."

What are semioticians dealing with when they admit linguistics into their tradition and background? In the opening of the present century, Naville referred to linguistics as a "science" treating "laws." In the final quarter of this century, the philosopher Jacques Bouveresse, when queried by Herman Parret in his dialogues with linguists (1974: 310) on "What activates the linguist's mind?" answered: "I think that, as in any other empirical science, the observable regularities set the linguist's mind in action ..." Accordingly, despite the fecundity and the ongoing linguistic breakthroughs of the twentieth century, rivaled perhaps only by the linguistic activity of the immediately preceding century, we read no fundamental difference in these two accounts, namely, *science* and *rule* or *law* in the Saussurean conception of linguistics and in the conception of, let us say, Chomsky.

What in particular we have been dealing with as semioticians, or, at least, are reputed to be dealing with in regard to linguistics is, of course, structuralism. Robert Young, in his 1981 collection *Untying the Text: A Post-Structuralist Reader*, says outright (3): "Semiology [or, in the USA, after C. S. Peirce, semiotics] is not easy to distinguish from structuralism." Of structuralism he writes (1): "'Structuralism' as a proper name includes a number of diverse practices across different disciplines in the human sciences. What they will have in common is a use of Saussurean linguistics." There is nothing here about structuralism that surprises us as semiotists, yet Young's words do give us a sense of the seemingly unbridled reign of so-called structuralism throughout today's humane sciences—in fact, structuralism is now often construed as a shapeless mass, a trend word, an undefined panacea for humanistic endeavors. It is not our intention to touch this, so to speak, "can of worms," namely, the many faces of structuralism. It is, however, our intention to go back to the irrefutable basic notion of *structure* that Saussure borrowed from Wilhelm von Humboldt (†1835), which holds that a language has an outer and an inner form. The outerness, let us call it that, translates into Saussure's *parole*, that is, the empirical data, the actual substances, stuff of language (sounds, sentences; in kinesics, facial gestures, for example). The innerness translates into a hypothetical, non-real, that is, it can't be seen, heard, or touched, construct, Saussure's *langue*, the underlying form of a relational network or system of rules that accounts for a language being what it is. This is the "bottom line" on linguistic structuralism which we witness as dominant over a hundred years after Humboldt in the galvanizing Chomskyan paradigm.

But why is it that we, as we look to the twenty-first century in our semiotic and linguistic methods, are so grounded in the nineteenth century, whether via Peirce, Humboldt, or Saussure? As semioticians we are keenly aware of the identity discussions surrounding semiotic method. Aside from the several equations into which semiotics is brought, such as that of Young, which we spoke of above, there is continual questioning of the scientific status of semiotics. Consider the nagging concern of Eco, e.g., just during this last decade, in which he writes: in 1975 (17) "... here does not yet exist a single unified theory;" in 1978 (83) "... semiotics, more than a science, is an interdisciplinary approach;" and finally in 1981 (177, translation mine): "Today semiotics exists as a discipline (be it as a unified science or as a unified viewpoint which relates to one object shared by various sciences)" (cf. Chapter 1 above, Chapter 11 below). Interestingly, the linguistic leg of the semiotic tripod has wrestled with the same identity problem since its modern rebirth, also somewhat over a hundred years ago. It should not come as a shock, then, that as recently as 1981 John Lyons, in his *Language and Linguistics*, still entitled a section (2.2) "Is linguistics a science?" and reminiscent of Eco above, Lyons says (5): "Linguistics ... has natural links with a wide range of academic disciplines." But the *idée fixe* of the scientific status of these disciplines hearkens back to the intellectual climate of the nineteenth century. Peirce in his "Classification of the Sciences" (1: §§183, 186, 189, 191, 200)—note this is the same title as that of Naville's *(New) Classification of the Sciences*—readily accommodates semiotics as deriving from logic, a normative science branching from philosophy, and he assigns linguistics to classificatory psychics or ethology branching from the psychical sciences, which, in turn, branch from idioscopy. Philosophy and idioscopy are the "sciences of discovery"—all "theoretical sciences." There is no doubt about their scientific status in Peirce.

Nineteenth-Century Science

Modern linguistics was birthed in a golden age of the expansion of science into new fields. First and foremost, two paradigms influenced all scientific activity, that of physics and that of biology. Physics primarily lends to linguistics the parameter of rigor which seeks regularities, in the case of linguistics, regularities in language structure, and views these regularities as laws just as laws are formulated in the description of the regularities and patterns of physical phenomena, so, e.g., in Carnot's laws of thermodynamics. This is the characteristic of linguistics which Saussure's colleague (Naville) referred to in 1901, saying: "Linguistics is, or at least tends to become, more and more a science of laws." It explains as well Bouveresse's 1974 answer that "the observable regularities set the linguist's mind in action" (both quoted above). The nineteenth-century biological paradigm of evolution which culminated in Darwin's *Origin of Species* (1859) is accountable for Naville's wording of "linguistics [as] the science of the laws of the *life* of language" (above; emphasis mine). The biological paradigm lends to linguistics the notion that a language, like plant and animal life, is an organism or quasi-organism with *life*, which implies that language experiences birth and death as well as continual change, including growth. Recall our opening sentence from Toynbee: "[life] is perpetually on the move through time and space." Contemporaneous with Darwin's *Origin of Species*, the linguist August Schleicher, in an attempt to harness the ever more accumulated data on the world's languages, proposed in his *Compendium of the Comparative Grammar of the Indo-Germanic Languages* (1861) the family-tree (Stammbaum) theory of the interrelationship of various species of language. In 1863 followed then Schleicher's treatise entitled *Darwin's Theory and Linguistics*. As might be expected, there is some controversy in the literature as to who said what first, so, e.g., the Stanford linguist Joseph Greenberg in his article "Linguistics as a Pilot Science" (1973: 50) claims: "The acceptance of evolutionary explanations [in linguistics] preceded that in biology by about half a century." To be sure, a quarter of a century before Darwin's *Origin*, the linguist Franz Bopp in 1836 spoke of the fact that "Languages ... must be regarded as *organic bodies*, formed in accordance with *definite laws*" (1, translation and emphases mine). Yet, in periods of monumental scientific breakthroughs, preliminary glimmers or indications of a particular discovery commonly permeate the universal intellectual climate or atmosphere, so that it is often impossible to pinpoint the actual moment of innovation. Again, as with the linguistics-semiotics priority discussion, linguistics-biology precedence arguments impress largely as futile. It is more relevant to notice the title of Schleicher's *Compendium of the Comparative Grammar of the Indo-Germanic Languages* or of Bopp's twenty-year (1833–52) study entitled *Comparative Grammar of Sanskrit, Zend, Greek, Latin, Lithuanian, Old Slavic, Gothic and German*. Indeed, and again in consonance with the methods of the other sciences, comparative investigations were in vogue, as we can observe, e.g., even in the pre-nineteenth-century Humboldt, who in 1795 wrote a *Plan for a Comparative Anthropology*.

To recapitulate, we turned to Naville as a lead to understanding the interdigitation of semiotics and linguistics, especially the intellectual setting which accounts for the emergence of linguistics as one of the three traditions of modern semiotics. We have amplified his description of linguistics as "the *science* of the *laws* of the *life* of language" (emphases mine). Before leaving Naville let us turn briefly to another part of the same quotation, namely, that the "object [of Saussure's] semiology would be the laws of creation and transformation of signs and their meaning." At this moment, we do not concern ourselves with the major part of this statement, which is, of course, "the laws of creation and transformation of signs and their meaning," but let us take a fleeting glance at the "would be." Saussure, himself, through his editors Bally and Sechehaye (1959: 16), records this futuristic approach in the well-known Saussure citation which reads:

> A *science that studies the life of signs within society* is conceivable; it would be a part of social psychology and consequently of general psychology: I shall call it *semiology* ... Semiology would show what constitutes signs, what laws govern them. Since the science does not yet exist, no one can say what it would be; but it has a right to existence, a place staked out in advance.

Is this part of the Saussurean legacy to semiotics perhaps the origin of the identity crisis which continues to haunt semioticians and feeds such statements as that of Tullio de Mauro (1975: 41) that "Semiotics ... is a science still *in statu nascendi*" and causes Eco (cf. section above) to agonize over whether there does or "there does not yet exist a single unified semiotic theory"? Is it the same force that prompted the Danish theoretical linguist, Louis Hjelmslev, to stand back from his excruciatingly intricate Glossematic paradigm—construed by Trabant (1981: 146; cf. "Trabant on Hjelmslev," Chapter 10 below) not as a "language science" but as a "sign science"—and muse that "For the scholar nothing is more beautiful than the sight of a science that is still to be created"(cited in Fischer-Jørgensen 1965: xxii). We refer now to this seemingly minor thought—Naville's and Saussure's "would be," de Mauro's "*statu nascendi,*" Eco's "not yet exist(ence)," Hjelmslev's "science still to be created" —only to show that if our answers to the last several questions are in the affirmative, then these respected semiotists were and are not only scientists, but at heart they were Romantics as well. This is meant seriously, for it is but one more small piece of evidence again pointing to the ambience of that explosive nineteenth century, wherein it was fashion to begin so much and to ever strive for a completion that was, however, admittedly out of reach. Witness Peirce himself, the "... pioneer, or rather ... back-woodsman, in the work of clearing and opening up ... *semiotic,*" sighing: "I find the field too vast, the labour too great, for a first-comer" (5: §488).

Saussure and Diachrony

We are aware that there are innumerable other catalytic characteristics and factors of that century which contribute to an explanation of what linguistics is and, therefore, what role linguistics plays in semiotics. However, when we return to our earlier question as to whether there is life, that is, research life, without or after Saussure or so-called neo-Saussureans, such as Hjelmslev, Jakobson, or Chomsky, we encounter a most peculiar phenomenon. It amounts to the fact that Saussure only told us half the story, so to speak. In a sense, then, there is research life without Saussureans. Still, this is qualified as only in a sense, be-cause Saussure knew it all and, indeed, he functioned, i.e., researched, with complete knowledge—knowledge which he failed to acknowl-edge in the linguistic paradigm that he bequeathed to semiotics. In fact, he purposely excluded it—an incredible influence which still produces many a closet-linguist in current linguistic circles. This con-cealed half of the linguistic model is, shockingly so to an emerging era of Sebeokian biosemiotics, that portion of linguistic method derived principally from the biological paradigm of the nineteenth century.

Saussure short-circuited the crowning achievement of nineteenth-century linguistics, the so-called comparative method. He rejected the idea of the organic nature of language, saying (1959: 231) "We now realize that Schleicher was wrong in looking upon language as an organic thing with its own law of evolution ..." He became disenchanted with the notion of law itself for linguistic phenomena, saying that (91) "... speaking of linguistic law in general is like trying to pin down a ghost." In his celebrated bifurcation of the empirical realm of linguistics into *synchrony* and *diachrony*, the first considering language states, which was understood as current states, and the second considering language over time and most frequently associated with evolutionary linguistics, Saussure claimed that data from neither realm meet the criteria of law-likeness, viz., that they be, according to him, both *imperative* and *general* (91, 95). He attacked evolutionary linguistics, holding that (82):

> Ever since modern linguistics came into existence, it has been completely absorbed in diachrony. Comparative Indo-European philology uses the materials at hand to reconstruct hypothetically an older type of language; comparison is but a means of reconstructing the past. The method is the same in the narrower study of subgroups (Romance languages, Germanic languages, etc.), states intervene only irregularly and piecemeal. Such is the tendency introduced by Bopp. His conception of language is therefore hybrid and hesitating ... Classical grammar has been criticized as unscientific; still, its basis is less open to criticism and its data are better defined than is true of the linguistics started by Bopp.

In spite of Saussure, the dominance of evolutionary linguistics was still evident in the first third of the present century. The Danish linguist-semiotist whom we quoted above, Louis Hjelmslev, had to write two dissertations. His 1928 *Principles of General Grammar* was considered too theoretical and unhistorical to be acceptable for a dissertation, so that he produced his 1932 *Baltic Studies*, which, in the words of his eulogist, Eli Fischer-Jørgensen (1965: vii), was "good old traditional historical phonology, as it was required to be." During the second third of this century, however, particularly in the United States, Saussure's dictum that (1959: 90) "... diachrony and synchrony ... are not of equal importance ... the synchronic viewpoint predominates" took firm hold, largely by dint of necessity. Synchrony was the only realm available in capturing the hundreds of previously undescribed indigenous American Indian languages. There was concern to record these languages, many spoken only by a small band of native speakers, before they might become extinct, since their written documents, if any, were minimal. The required prodigious fieldwork, recording especially the native languages of North America, was undertaken by Franz Boas under the aegis of the Smithsonian Institution, resulting in his 1911 *Handbook of American Indian Languages*. Boas represents the initiation of American synchronic linguistics, which includes the familiar names of Sapir and Bloomfield and those so-called descriptivists who, again by dint of necessity, applied the methods of synchrony to break the Japanese code during World War II. We refer to the American School to show that Saussure's synchrony dream did indeed achieve fairly early realization in the United States. In itself this is entirely positive, but it was done at the expense of diachrony. The complete story of the emergence of synchronic linguistics in the first two-thirds of this century is labyrinthine and fascinating (cf. Chapter 18 below).

Nineteenth-Century Linguistics

Diachrony was thus put into the closet. The Saussure-induced reaction against evolutionary linguistics reached such a high pitch that the Swedish linguist Bertil Malmberg in his 1963 *Structural Linguistics and Human Communications* lamented (4):

> The orientation towards change, evolution, and history which put its mark on 19th century science as a whole and for a long period to come determined the methods and aims of a whole series of humanistic branches such as literary and aesthetic analysis, social anthropology, and philosophy, saddled linguistics with an approach to language study which is, in fact, inconsistent with the basic functions of the object itself and overemphasizes one of its aspects—and a secondary one—to the detriment of the others. For the establishment of linguistics as an autonomous science, it was no doubt unhappy that its early development should coincide with a period of romanticism and its final shape should be determined by evolutionary influences and biological analogues.

At the very time of this citation, Noam Chomsky expressed thoughts which, so to speak, compelled Saussure's words (cf. section above) to come back to haunt him. In his 1964 "Current Issues in Linguistic Theory," based on his 1962 "The Logical Basis of Linguistics Theory," Chomsky observed (60):

> Modern linguistics is much under the influence of Saussure's conception of *langue* as an inventory of elements ... and his preoccupation with systems of elements rather the systems of rules which were the focus of attention of traditional grammar and of the general linguistics of Humboldt. In general, modern descriptive statements pay little attention to the "creative" aspect of language ...

We have come full circle with the theme *creation/growth*. Before demonstrating a concrete case of growth in a language, let us turn now to view, to requote Saussure (section above), "the linguistics started by Bopp" upon which Saussure turned his back, and which, accordingly, semiotists did not inherit from him via structuralism. It is one of the most remarkable ironies of this account, which we have been tracing, that the comparative method, which we designated as the crowning achievement of nineteenth-century linguistics, and which Saussure characterized as "but a means of reconstructing the past" (section above) was *the* very paradigm which provided Saussure with the approach necessary for his brilliant hypothesis of the existence of laryngeal sounds (sounds emanating from the larynx and pharynx) for Proto-Indo-European. In 1879 Saussure published his *Memoir on the Primitive System of Vowels in the Indo-European Languages*, introducing the world of learning to his masterful conjecture that there must have existed at some time an Indo-European language which possessed laryngeal sounds that were not present in any of the then known Indo-European languages, but whose effects can only be found in these known languages. Saussure died in 1913, too early for the discovery of the Hittite finds which, to be sure, occurred in 1906 by Hugo Winkler at Boğazkoy, Turkey (94 miles east of Ankara), but whose cuneiform clay tablets were not deciphered until 1915 by the Czech Bedřich Hrozny. What an ironic triumph it would have been for Saussure to have witnessed the confirmation of his elegant comparative inference in the identification in 1927 of the actual laryngeal sounds in the Hittite material by the Polish Indo-Europeanist Jerzy

Kuryłowicz. Perhaps it would have softened Saussure's attitude toward diachrony and comparative method, which, in turn, could have changed the course of current linguistics and, consequently as a leg of the semiotic tripod, could have introduced from mainstream linguistics a strong biological orientation into modern semiotics as early as the opening of this century. This could have been achieved without necessarily detracting from synchrony.

Contrary to Malmberg (above), we should then reword the Malmberg citation to read "... it was no doubt (*felicitous*) that its (linguistics') early development should coincide with a period of romanticism and its final shape should be determined by evolutionary influences and biological analogues." Thanks to the interests of romanticism, researchers considered curiosity about the past of their own culture, folklore, and language as a legitimate area of study. The preceding eighteenth century had already been marked by expansive study of languages around the world, which, in turn, has been prompted by an ever shrinking world. Eighteenth-century linguistics had been characterized by massive data collection which, by dint of necessity, that is, fueled by needs identical to those of American synchrony, required systematization. The missing link for uniting the several languages of eighteenth/nineteenth-century Europe was Sanskrit, with which contact had been made through British colonialism in India and the romantic curiosity of Friedrich von Schlegel, leading to his book entitled *Concerning the Language and the Wisdom of the Indians* (1808), in which for the first time the words *comparative grammar* are used. Suddenly European linguists had a classical language other than Latin and Greek to compare to their continental languages. Surely, language similarities with Sanskrit could not be attributed to geographical and, accordingly, cultural contiguity within Europe. It incited Sir William Jones to conclude in 1786 that the relationship of Sanskrit to Latin and Greek (cited in Pedersen 1931: 18):

> ... bears a stronger affinity, both in the roots of verbs and in the forms of grammar, than could possibly have been produced by accident; so strong, indeed, that no philosopher could examine them all three without believing them to have sprung from some common source, which, perhaps, no longer exists ...

By 1813 T. Young termed this suspected common source "Indo- European," and in 1816 Bopp came forward with his volume *Concerning the Conjugational System of the Sanskrit Language in Comparison with that of the Greek, Persian and Germanic Language.* Although Bopp spoke of "definite laws" of languages (cf. "Nineteenth-Century Science" section above), and although he was actually the first to use the phrase "sound law" (in 1824), his nascent linguistic comparative paradigm could not move beyond the elementary stage of pointing out agreements in the inflections, that is, the noun and verb endings of these languages, as a criterion in establishing the interrelatedness of the languages. In fact, Bopp made serious errors; for example, he identified the Malayo-Polynesian language group as Indo-European solely on the basis of vocabulary comparison. To claim identical origin by vocabulary comparison alone is like claiming genetic relationship between two persons on the basis of their wearing the same suits. It took the Danish linguist, Rasmus Rask, to require of himself the discipline for a strict comparison of languages on the basis of their innermost core, that is, their sounds, which allowed the certain reconstruction of the genealogical relationship of the languages compared. This *is* what we mean by the comparative method (cf. "Analogy in Linguistics," Chapter 15 below) in linguistics. In 1818 Rask completed his prize-winning work on the comparison of the sounds of the major European languages, and in 1819 Jakob Grimm showed that the regularities of Rask's sound agreements between languages are the result of systematic sound change; hence Rask's discovery is known as Grimm's Law rather than as Rask's Law. The startling fact of this comparative method is that it can demonstrate, to give an extreme example, that the English word for the numeral *two*, for instance, is sound for sound genetically identical to the Armenian word for "two," viz., *erku*. In short, these two words had but one organic parent, the same single source, origin. Such certainty, of course, required exhaustive knowledge of sound changes that occurred in each individual language, since the language had left the parental nest, so to speak. In spite of the ever more comprehensive knowledge of the private sound laws peculiar to each language of the world, there remained unexplained residue. By the end of the nineteenth century, then, the final linchpin for a fail-safe scientific linguistic comparative method was proposed by August Leskien in 1876 through the brusque remark "sound laws know no exceptions." We will not detail the furor and infighting this proclamation caused at the time among linguists. Suffice it to say that the dictum of Leskien and his supporters, known as the Neo- or Young Grammarians, revolutionized the linguistic scene in a manner reminiscent of Chomsky's transformational-generative linguistics in our time. What is remarkable is that there is not one linguist today, whether working with synchrony or diachrony, who would forfeit the Neogrammarian hypothesis of the exceptionlessness of linguistic laws as a working hypothesis in his own investigations.

Linguistic Analogy and Semiotic Abduction

There was, however, one exception allowed by the Neogrammarians; it was the celebrated corollary to their hypothesis, namely, the accounting for the residue to uniform linguistic change by means of analogy. The vicissitude encountered by *analogy* in linguistic explanation is again a story in itself, and we will have to cut it very short here. As can well be imagined, from the moment of its recognition by Leskien, declared in the same breath with his exceptionlessness principle, analogy became the automatic cure-all for all language changes hitherto defying causal explanation. Within seven years the Indo-Europeanist August Fick viscerally attacked what he called "The fashionable child's disease of analogizing" (1833: 583, translation mine). Fick was not far from the mark, however, since drawing analogies is something that children and, for that matter, adults do extremely well—it is *abduction*—a fact which philosophers and perhaps psychologists of Fick's time understood, but which eluded linguists, who saw analogy simply as an unscientific excuse (cf. Chapter 6, 15 below). Almost a full decade earlier Peirce had outlined his three modes of reasoning ("On a New List of Categories," 1867). Needless to say, some linguists took on the challenge posed by analogy, first and foremost the Polish scholar of laryngeal theory, mentioned earlier, Kuryłowicz. Kuryłowicz (1945–49) and his countryman Witold Mańczak (1958) have formulated a set of linguistic principles governing analogy which constrain somewhat the Aristotelian proportional formula *a: b: : c: d* used in linguistics. Edgar Sturtevant, who happens to be another laryngealist and a prominent American linguist, offers an imaginative example of linguistic proportional analogy in the word **nosigate* abduced by his own son in analogy to the word *irrigate*, which the son had related to the word *ear*. The study of linguistic analogy received another hard blow at the hands of generative grammar, which simply swept it under the rug. This blow resulted, of course, in a counter-blow which ultimately led to the written admission one hundred years after Leskien by Raimo Anttila (1972: 180), who understands analogy as abduction, that "The different mechanisms of [linguistic] change share a common analogical core" (cf. Chapter 15 below). Similarly, Henning Andersen in 1973 in an article "Abductive and Deductive Change" wrote (778): "We have seen that the conception of language acquisition assumed for our model of phonological change involves processes that are basic to all activities of the human mind" (cf. Chapter 14 below). Andersen means by these processes abduction; the attraction for linguists is, of course, that abduction results in creation. However, while it is obvious that processes which are fundamental to all activities of the human mind are a necessary ingredient in linguistic cause, it must also be obvious that such processes cannot be decisive in identifying cause in a given linguistic innovation. Unfortunately Andersen, Anttila, and Kuryłowicz before them, constructed the teleology of linguistic change through, in a certain sense, an indiscriminate view of linguistic analogy. In brief, in their discussions all analogy is alike (cf. Chapter 14, 15, 19 below).

The linguistic paradigm of language innovation stands to gain everything if, at this point, it resorts to Peirce. Let us demonstrate the enormous contribution that can be made on the part of semiotics to linguistic causation by considering, for a moment, a concrete case of *change* discussed by Kuryłowicz. In an intricate formulation (1964) Kuryłowicz hypothesizes the creation of the perfect tense in the languages that we use, Indo-European. For the purposes of our presentation, this is the semantic distinction, although not the form distinction, between, e.g., English *is* and *was*, *see: saw, sell: sold*. In prehistoric times, it is hypothesized, man managed with a present tense only. The perfect tense, it is claimed, originated in *analogy* to the present. The proto- or parent form of the perfect tense (let us refer to it in our discussion semantically, as "past" tense) is conceived simply as an adjective with no indication of time, e.g., *said* and *done* in the sentence *No sooner said, than done*. In order to make *said* and *done* real tenses they have to combine with persons in a manner in which the present tense operates, thus *He no sooner said it, than he did it*. The past tense paradigm mirrors the present; semioticians, but not linguists, could readily distinguish this analogy as iconic, that is, the past is now factually similar to the present tense. Semantically, the past tense is derived by Kuryłowicz out of a medial voice, again in unspecified analogy to the present active tense. We admit of three voices in language: active voice, e.g., *He sees*, in which the subject acts upon something, an object; passive voice, e.g., *He is being seen*, in which the subject is acted upon; and medial voice, e.g., *He appears*, in which the subject acts upon itself. Consider the sentences with the medial verbs: *Newports smoke better* or *smoother* (from a cigarette ad of some years ago), or *That house sells well*. In the case of *smoke* and *sells*, the subjects *Newports*, *house*, respectively, are neither acting upon an object (active voice), nor are they acted upon (passive voice). But they can readily be converted into actives and passives by saying: *He smokes Newports, Newports are being smoked by him*. Let us take our primordial tenseless adjective *done* of *No sooner said, than done*. If we no longer wish to have it as an adjective, but instead have it join the ranks of verb tenses, then according to Kuryłowicz's thinking, it should imitate the present active tense. *He does* should then yield *He did*, better yet for our purpose substandard: *He done it*. The Kuryłowicz explanation of the past tense, that is, perfect, from a tenseless adjective in analogy with present tense semantics, namely, with the active, is again one of *iconic analogy*. However, semiotics can explain to linguistics that the word *done*—indicating a resultant state from a previous action upon it (e.g., *That meat is well done*, meaning someone had cooked it; *The portrait is well done*, meaning it had been artistically painted by someone)—the word *done* splits into an active (*He done it*) and, accordingly, into a passive (*He is being done*, that is, painted by an artist), because underlying the iconic analogy to the present tense is an *indexical analogy* whereby an active has its existence solely because of the passive, and the reverse. It is *Secondness*, or the factual contiguity between the active and passive, whereby one is meaningless without the other, that activates or compels the past tense into being. We see that abduction as explanation for linguistic cause, in this case analogy, is of little interest unless we require that the dynamic of direct *compulsion* (Secondness) within the abduction be sought and identified (cf. Chapter 15 below). In linguistic literature we call this creation of the perfect tense a semantic split; needless to say, it is representative of Thom's bifurcation catastrophe (cf. section below).

Physics' Law and Biology's Growth

Although analogy looms large in causation theories of language change, a vast array of widely ranging catalysts of change has been proposed and systematized over the years since Leskien (cf. Chapter 14 below and Rauch 1990a). However, to render a more complete picture of those linguistic insights which Saussure chose not to pass on to semiotics, let us return briefly just once more to our discussion of nineteenth-century linguistic achievements. While the law-likeness of linguistic change had come from the physics paradigm, the organic progression in the change came from the biological paradigm. The two views, often considered tantamount to cause, were not in conflict; in fact, they mutually reinforced one another. The biological view that replacement of one species by another is not a random change (although individual mutations may be), but rather a change from lower to higher by survival of the fittest, led directly into the typology of languages. In 1818 August Schlegel (the brother of the Sanskritist Friedrich) proposed that all languages can be classified according to three types of structure: first, an analytic type in which words have no inflections or endings, e.g., Chinese; secondly, an agglutinating type in which words have ending-like suffixes, but they stand as separate units, e.g., Turkish; and thirdly, a synthetic type in which words and endings are melded together in one unit, e.g., Latin. Schleicher, whom we had mentioned above, proposed his language family tree on the model of the evolution of biological species. He suggested that the synthetic type, in this case Latin represented the most advanced stage in the evolution of language. It is quite clear that value judgments on the typology of languages are, to say the least, prejudicial; from the scientific viewpoint they are simply erroneous. It is very similar to saying, e.g., that English *I am, you are, he is* is a more advanced mode of expression than English *I see, you see, he sees* because the forms are more complicated in the former group. To say the reverse and to claim that the simpler forms are more advanced is equally prejudicial. The argument, naturally, does not hold in the area of lexicon in language as reflective of thought; it does not refer, for instance, to the advanced thought status of the vocabulary of nuclear science versus the vocabulary of gourmet cooking, if you will.

The great advantage, however, of this typological classification, intiated by Schlegel, is that it leads to the study of which characteristics (so-called tendencies) are common in many languages and which features are even universal to all languages. This again renders to linguistics a parameter of predictability. Jakobson explains (1958: 20):

Typology discloses laws of implication which underlie the... structure of languages: the presence of *A* implies the presence (or on the contrary the absence) of *B*. In this way we detect in the languages of the world uniformities or near-uniformities ...

A great many typological schemata have been proposed by linguists as cause for change; for example, André Martinet (1955) would likely hold in our above example of linguistic change that the perfect tense developed in Indo-European from the pressure of a lacuna within the system, which is so identified from typological comparison with the other languages of the world. This line of thinking actually claims to derive from Saussure's analogue of language to a chessboard in which the play moves from one state of *equilibrium* into the next. Saussure, as we know, did not view language organically; nevertheless, some of his closet successors did. So, e.g., van Ginneken, in considering the moves from one language state to another, wrote in 1930 (575) that every language system "is an organic whole which grows and flowers and develops, but also drops overripe fruit and casts off dry branches." In order to restore equilibrium to a language system, van Ginneken speaks of Jakobson's proposed universal or panchronic typological laws in terms of "therapeutic, healing processes," of "sworn comrades, that is favorable tendencies" within a language, and alternately of "incompatible or hostile tendencies [which] inevitably fight to the death." To be sure, we recognize in this effort on the part of linguistic typology not only a common link with evolutionary theories (e.g., survival of the fittest), but a common link with Thom's (1975: 323) morphologies—all of which are attributable to "conflict, a struggle between two or more attractors." Recall that the evolution of the Indo-European perfect tense, detailed above, was conceptualized in linguistics as a semantic split which is represented in Thom's bifurcation catastrophe. Although I am speaking like a fighting linguist, that is, implying that genetic linguists have proposed typological configurations for language change quite some time prior to Thom, we realize that Thom's theory is universal and that the so-called moot questions of language change, e.g., whether change is abrupt or gradual, could gain insight by the application of Thom's paradigm (cf. Chapter 10 below).

Even a neo-Saussurean like Sapir (1921), who was certainly no closet linguist, speaks of the typological growth tendency of a given language in terms of "drift," interpreted by Yakov Malkiel (1981: 566) as "an evolutionary strain or streak." Such a strain or streak, according to Vennemann (1975: 274) "remains alive over long periods of time;" by it Sapir "feels safe to predict certain further, similar changes for the future." Once more the methods of linguistics display its predictive capacities and, accordingly, its continually sought-after scientific status. It appears with the outgoing twentieth century that even mainstream linguists, and surely Chomsky still first and foremost among them, are beginning to dare to speak of "the language capacity virtually as ... a physical organ of the body" (1980: 185).

Peirce was able to unite the two paradigms from physics and biology. Of the "observable regularities" which (to requote Bouveresse, cf. "Linguistics/Semiotics as Science" section above) "set the linguist's mind in action," Peirce would have to say (6: §13) "... the only possible way of accounting for the laws of nature and for uniformity in general is to suppose them as results of evolution." And, of course, there is no doubt of the organic nature of language in Peirce after his celebrated equation (6: §314), "my language is the sum total of myself."

But Sebeok, a trend-setter among linguists, has prepared the way for a return of evolutionary linguistics to the linguistic paradigm, put into the closet by Saussure or, more precisely, by his interpreters. In particular, Sebeokian biosemiotics offers via Thom's catastrophes, which display a change in the equilibrium of an entity, and via Uexküll's functional cycle, which displays the sensorimotor dynamic of growth (Sebeokian biosemiotics) the ultimate paradigm to date for the understanding of *how* "symbols grow."

Slightly over one hundred years ago the English jurist and professor of law, Sir Henry Maine, successfully applied comparative method modeled on linguistic comparative method (1871 *Village Communities in the East and West*). At present a few tremors are already detectable for the revival of the evolutionary linguistic model. In anthropology, ever cognizant of method dealing with language, we hear from Lévi-Strauss (1980) that synchrony customarily governed investigations because it was easier to get at, but that diachrony should be introduced whenever possible. In the 1983 volume 5 of *Zeitschrift für Semiotik*, we read of Werner Enninger's diachronic hypotheses with regard to codes of clothing. In 1969 Brent Berlin and Paul Kay, in their book *Basic Color Terms*, undertook a comparative study of color terms in ninety-eight languages, which, they claim, is an evolutionary study. Although they found that all color vocabularies evolve from eleven basic color categories, they are still not able to explain why for instance, if we use Hjelmslev's classic example of form and substance, the four English color substances *green, blue, gray, brown* designate the same form area which is subsumed by three substances only in Welsh *gwyrdd, glas, llwyd.*

Considering the linguistic leg of the semiotic tripod, the time is ripe—a century and a third after *Origin of Species* and about a century after Peirce—to exploit linguistic diachrony, evolutionary or genetic linguistics, its comparative method, the law-likeness of its rules of change, in direct relationship with Peirce's *Firstness, Secondness,* and *Thirdness,* to pursue the answers as to *why* "symbols grow." Part Two of this volume does exactly that. However, first the nature of linguistics and of semiotics and their interdigitation require further understanding.

3

Linguistics and Semiotics Juxtaposed — 1

The intimacy of the relationship between semiotics and linguistics is accountable on the one hand to the role assigned to *language within semiotics*, and on the other hand to the role assigned to *linguistics within language*. Specifically, the arrangement of the arguments of these "within" relations prefigures the controversial hierarchical entanglements between and among semiotics, language, and linguistics. Just as today's linguistics finds its recent roots in the nineteenth century (cf. Chapter 2 above), so too does semiotics, in North America primarily in the person of Peirce, and on the continent in the person of Saussure.

Linguistics

Recent linguistic history on semiotics has its roots in the semiology of Ferdinand de Saussure, whose widely read *Course in General Linguistics* (1959) dominates linguistic semiotics in the twentieth century. While Saussure's semiology would elevate linguistics to the position of "the master-pattern for all branches of semiology" (68), it is obvious in the final decade of the century that the Saussurean observation "Linguistics is only a part of the general science of semiology" (16) is proving to be more prophetic.

In Peirce's taxonomy of the sciences (1: §183, 186, 189, 191, 200), linguistics is assigned to classificatory psychics, or ethology branching from the psychical sciences, which in turn, branch from idioscopy. In contrast, Peirce derives semiotics from logic, a normative science branching from philosophy. Nonetheless, Peirce foreshadows the glory days of linguistics in his appraisal of "the vast and splendidly developed science of linguistics [among the] studies of mental performances and products" (1: §271). This value judgment on linguistics is echoed throughout the century by linguist and non-linguist alike. Leonard Bloomfield (1939: 25) states confidently that "Linguistics is the chief contributor to semiotic," and with equal conviction Jean Piaget (1968: 25) writes "La linguistique est sans doute la plus avancée des sciences sociales." The movement toward recognition that the "problem of interrelations between the sciences of man appears centered upon linguistics" (Jakobson 1970: 26) culminates in Roland Barthes' (1968: 11) inversion of Saussure's declaration (Saussure 1959: 16 "Linguistics is only a part of the general science of semiology"): "linguistics is not a part of the general science of signs, even a privileged part; it is semiology which is a part of linguistics."

In the early seventies Thomas A. Sebeok's Volume Twelve of the *Current Trends in Linguistics* series addresses Linguistics and Adjacent Arts and Sciences. In that volume semiotics is a self-contained topic somewhat on the same level with such disciplines as philosophy; the verbal arts, subsuming poetics, folkloristics, rhetoric, stylistics, literary genres, and metrics; artificial languages; translation; psychology; anthropology/sociology; economics; education; bio-medicine and computer science. This assemblage of linguistics-related arts and sciences rests upon a widespread conviction that linguistics functions for them as a "pilot science" (Marcus 1974: 2871), "the primary science which serves as the unifying focus of the language sciences as a whole" (Garvin 1974: 2890).

With the maturation of the discipline of semiotics, however, the singular glory of linguistics begins to assume the characteristics of a burden, since the linguistic model, which is understood as a structuralist model (cf. below), is expected to account for "any study concerned with the production and perception of 'meaning'" (Pettit 1975: Preface). By the late seventies then, that is, within half a decade, the linguistic model, the "'archetype'...for semiological inquiry" (Pettit: 109) experiences a stark shift in its hierarchical position among related sciences. Sebeok's sobering characterization of linguistics as being "alias semiotics" (1979: 66) signals the turning point. Nevertheless, linguistics is singled out as the essential paradigm for semiological research because it claims language as its primary research object. Accordingly, the literature is rife with the indiscriminate synonymizing of linguistics with language. There is no doubt that with or without linguistics, language is a most powerful organ. At the same time, it remains a fact that linguistics is an extremely successful structural model.

The Sign System Par Excellence

Tzvetan Todorov (1975: 97), echoing others such as Edward Sapir and Uriel Weinreich, declares language to be "the sign-system par excellence." Certainly the amenability of language, specifically the linguistic sign, to the scrutiny of structural principles supports the esteem for language as a sign system. In fact, it leads to an array of studies treating non-linguistic signs via language-analogical tools (cf. "Linguistic Semiotics" section below). But language, for the moment now without reference to any one discipline, traditionally holds a superior position in writings on the sciences of man. Witness, for example, George Steiner's view (1978: 208): "The creative well-being of an organic system depends on intricate balance between stimulus and response, between use and recuperation. This balance, in turn, derives from adjustments between inner and outer environment. Language constitutes both in the most immediate and dynamic sense. It is the pulse and skin of conscious being." In this context, Bloomfield's view (1939: 55) that "In the cosmos, language produces human society, a structure more complex than the individual, related to him somewhat as the many-celled organism is related to the single cell, appears rather as an anomaly, since Bloomfield is customarily interpreted as antimentalistic. Finally, we see in Edmund Leach's statement (1976: 88): "From some points of view spoken language is not only a part of culture, but prototypical of *all* culture," the rapid acceleration toward deification of a particular phenomenon, this time not the linguistic model, but language itself. Once more Sebeok intervenes in a seeming reversal of the trend with his comment "Genetic copying is the semiotic process par excellence" (1979: 120). The reversal, however, is a mirage.

Sebeok's biologically based semiotics is not entirely novel (cf. Baer 1979: 354), nor, of course, does he claim it to be. The Bloomfield quote (immediately above) can be said to prefigure it serendipitously. The Steiner quote (also above) accords well with concepts embodied in von Uexküll's "Funktionskreise" (1940: 9) which, thanks to Sebeok's efforts, represent the most current stream of semiotic research. The main current in this stream is the catastrophe theory of René Thom. Most importantly for the present discussion, Thom's explanation of the rationale for the existence of language

(1975: 309–11): "1. For a personal evolutive constraint, aiming to realize the permanence of the ego in a state of wakefulness; 2. For a social constraint, expressing the main regulating mechanisms of the social group," shows Sebeok's epitomical genetic copying on one plane to underlie another "paramount" (Sebeok 1979: 63) phenomenon, which is language, on another plane (cf. also "Baer on Sebeok," Chapter 10 below).

The Language Inlay

The reputed role of language within semiotics is understandably richer than that of linguistics within language (cf. above). This is eminently reasonable since "One can raise an enormous variety of questions about language. Language is used for a great diversity of purposes, it affects many different aspects of personal and interpersonal activities, it has its physical qualities in terms of sound patterns, it evokes reactions from people, etc. It is senseless to expect that there should be one unitary science [linguistics] that would answer all these questions" (Moravcsik 1975: 11). Beginning with Saussure (as a point in recent history) we read that (1959: 17) "the characteristic that distinguishes semiological systems from all other institutions shows up clearly only in language." Emile Benveniste (quoted in Todorov 1973: 125) formulates a simple axiom, stating "The configuration of language determines all semiotic systems," while Jakobson avidly exploits this axiom in his work; he is convinced that "any human communication of non-verbal messages presupposes a circuit of verbal messages without a reverse implication" (1970: 32). Again we witness a steam-roller effect when Claude Levi-Strauss (1963: 83) postulates that "language comes into play" in the exchange of messages, of goods, and of mates—the linchpins of his interpretation of society within the science of communication. One of the most current and explicit reiterations of the Benveniste axiom is found in the thinking of Sebastian Shaumyan, who attributes the ability of natural language to translate a message from any sign system into itself to the "cognitive flexibility of natural language" (1976: 60). And finally, we may note that it does not appear accidental that on occasion Francis Whitfield, in translating Hjelmslev's *Prolegomena to a Theory of Language*, employs English 'semiotic' as a gloss for Danish *sprog*. Hjelmslev, after all, forms another link in that chain of thought which holds that "a language is a semiotic into which all other semiotics may

be translated—both all other languages and all other conceivable
semiotic structures (1963: 109; cf. "Trabant on Hjelmslev," Chapter
10 below).

It seems crucial that, in the maze of literature dealing with language
as underlying semiotics, at the very least a clear distinction ought to
be drawn between metalanguage, sometimes called metasemiotic (cf.
Chapter 5 below), and language infrastructure or inlay. Sebeok, quite
rightly, bursts yet another inflated concept when he questions the
"asymmetrical convertibility of codes" (1979: 256), that is, the
translatability of any semiotic message into language but not
necessarily the reverse. Certainly language as a representative or
surrogate for another semiotic system (metalanguage) cannot modify
the nature of that system (cf. Chapter 5). Accordingly, the translatability problem is trivial. The case is otherwise, however, if features or
characteristics of language are integral to another semiotic system
(language inlay). Here, we are dealing with the Soviet semiotists'
concept of secondary modeling systems, that is, systems based on the
so-called primary system, which is language. In fact the Soviet School
(Lotman et al. 1975: 76) defines culture as a system of secondary
modeling systems, and Lotman considers it to be more complex than
natural language, or, for that matter, biological systems (Rewar 1979:
282, 276). As always in discussions of crossdisciplinary systems, a
healthy skepticism for the value of, indeed the justification for, positing degrees of complexity among the systems is in order. There is,
however, no disputing the fact that the problem of the language inlay
in semiotic modalities resides ultimately in the nature of language (cf.
Chapter 6).

Defining Language —1

"If we are to discover the true nature of language we must learn what
it has in common with all other semiological systems." This dictum of
Saussure (1959: 17) represents the Sisyphean task confronting linguist
as well as semiotist. Among the most common parameters characteriz-
ing language are the features verbal versus nonverbal and human versus nonhuman. Adam Schaff defines verbal as follows (1970: 114):
"By verbal signs I mean the proper parts of the sound language used
by men for the purpose of communication (written language being
treated merely as a peculiar transformation of sound language)."
While Schaff's definition is incisive, it is debatable since "language

also contains non-verbal components, such as the prosodic features of intonation and stress, which serve to distinguish meaning and should thus be counted as 'verbal signals'" (Schmitter 1979: 146). Prosodic features are frequently relegated to paralanguage, the delimitation of which is obviously as uncertain as that of language itself (cf. Chapter 13 below). The expanding bounds of language are implied in Erving Goffman's observation (1979: 6) that "the terms 'speaker' and 'hearer' imply that sound alone is at issue, when, in fact, it is obvious that sight is organizationally very significant too, sometimes even touch." These bounds become virtually unlimited in the provocative statement of Madeleine Mathiot (1979) that "Discourse is not a part of language."

Schaff's definition indicates that language is a human property. Although there is an increasing tendency to expand the application of the term language, the tendency is not necessarily accompanied by an expansion of the traditional concept of language reiterated by Ronald Wardhaugh (1977: 3): "Linguists are in broad agreement about some of the important characteristics of human language, and one definition of language widely associated with linguistics may illustrate areas of agreement. This particular definition states that *language is a system of arbitrary vocal symbols used for human communication.*" Thus Noam Chomsky (1979: 32), for example, is willing to extend the application of the term language beyond the human species, "If by *language* we mean *symbolic system*, or *system of communication.*" Nevertheless, Chomsky holds firmly that "human language ... is outside of the capacities of other species, in its most rudimentary properties. The differences appear to be qualitative; not a matter of 'more or less'" (43). Contrariwise, William Orr Dingwall writes (1980: 78) "the determination whether one communicates in a human manner cannot be made in absolute terms; rather some gradient measure must be employed." Clearly, Dingwall's statement reads as postmodern compared with Chomsky's (cf. Chapter 1 above; cf. also Chapter 5 below).

Even though it is obvious that linguists are, in fact, actively divided on a definition of language, the question of what in the nature of language is semiotic, namely, Saussure's dictum above, is rarely pursued directly. Jakobson's insight that (1971c: 703): "The cardinal functions of language—referential, emotive, conative, phatic, poetic, metalingual—and their different hierarchy in the diverse types of messages have been outlined and repeatedly discussed. This pragmatic approach to language must lead *mutatis mutandis* to an analogous study of the other semiotic systems" serves as a lonely beacon and at that a weak one, since the *mutatis mutandis* remains unspecified. More fruitful is his conviction that (1971c: 708): "only natural or formalized languages are able to generate ... judgments, general and especially equational propositions," for it can be challenged as being human-language specific. Frequently intention is entailed in the production of a proposition. John Lyons (1977: 32–3), who considers language as but one instrument of communication, requires of all communication that it be intentional. Even this requirement can be circumvented for non-human communication since, according to Jonathan Bennett (1976: 205) "intention is significantly like biological function." Indeed, Peirce determined a syllogistic effect in the pinching of the hind legs of a decapitated frog, namely "the way a decapitated frog reasons when you pinch his hind legs" (Fann 1970: 28). Accordingly, "the illative relation is the primary and paramount semiotic relation" (Peirce 1932: 2.§441n.1). If language is posited as an inlay in all modalities of communication, whether human or nonhuman, verbal or nonverbal, it is due to acceptance of the exceptionally broad definition that "Language is signifying through an illative-type process" (cf. Chapter 6 below).

Linguistic Semiotics

Structuralism, whether in linguistics, biology, genetics, physics, chemistry geology, or sociology, holds that being resides in relationship, that a structure or system consists of elements having certain mutual relations rather than of a mere accumulation of independent items to apply structural strategies comparatively easily, in particular feature analysis. In the second third of the century, the emulation of the successful application of structural principles to nonphonological data was, however, not as facile, since semantic data, which become primary, are not automatically amenable to the analytical tools of phonology. Linguistics' concentration on semantics has led into another member of the semiotic triad, pragmatics. Pragmalinguistics, as well as attempts to extend the linguistic paradigm to nonverbal data, encourage the refinement of the structural model through action theories in the final third of the twentieth century.

Saussure (1959: 120) considers a linguistic system to be "a series of differences of sound combined with a series of differences of ideas." The differences are perceived by Saussure and the Prague

Phonologists as dyadic oppositions. In fact, Saussure's linguistic model rests largely on binary conceptual characteristics such as signifier : signified, langue : parole, paradigm : syntagm, matter : form, sound : meaning, diachrony : synchrony. This pervasive habit of the linguist of bifurcating his cosmos continues to permeate semiotic method. Consider, for example, Sebeok's (1977a) characterization of the zoosemiotic features of human communication in terms of binary components, or Lotman's (1977) discussion of a dynamic model of a semiotic system by means of the antinomic features systematic : extrasystematic, monosemic : ambivalent, nucleus : periphery, description : nondescription, necessary : superfluous.

It is quite another challenge, however, to define and isolate features which are minimal and distinctive internal to a semiotic system. The linguistic method employed in ferreting out features is commutation (Hjelmslev 1963: 73), whereby the substitution of one feature by another in a given context may effect a difference in meaning. In analogy to phonemic structure, semiotic method seeks to identify the mytheme, filmeme, danseme, vesteme (Greimas 1971), proxeme (Hall 1972), kineme (Birdwhistell 1970), among other -emes (cf. "Object Semiotic, Chapter 5 and "Complementary Tools," Chapter 16 below), but such data from semiotic modalities other than language tend to defy their definitive reduction to discrete elements consisting of distinctive features (cf. Jakobson 1971a: 105–6; Lange-Seidl 1977: 15–1 9).

As dyadic as feature analysis in the linguistic framework may seem to be when used in an act of signification or semiosis, a feature necessarily participates in a triadic act. The language act itself consists of an organism (a human being) producing an expression (a sound, orthographic sequence, gesture) in order to refer by it to something (an object) (Carnap 1961: 8–9). Thus, the language act, comprising a speaker, an expression, and a designatum correlates directly to Charles Morris (1955: 217–19) tripartite division of semiotics, namely, pragmatics, syntactics, and semantics, respectively. In turn, the members of these two sets correlate further to the interpretant, sign, and object integral to Peirce's definition of a sign (1: 339): "A sign stands *for* something to the idea which it produces or modifies."

Of the three divisions of semiotics, semantics "occupies a central place" (Shaumyan 1970: 244). That signifying essentially entails meaning is confirmed by Rulon Wells' observation that "Semiotic has two groups of affinities ... communication, and ... meaning" (1971:

95), and it is again reflected in Paul Ricoeur's statement that "meaning is the noematic correlate (the 'what') of all that which deserves to be called experience" (1979: 171–2). However, as Jerzy Pelc (1973: 109) explains: "relativization *only* with regard to *meaning*, which may sometimes be adequate in *pure semantics* and also in descriptive semiotics of *artificial* language, gives a *static* image when we confine ourselves to it in the analysis of *natural* language: it discloses the expressions of that language as *isolated lexical items* and fails to disclose the actual *functioning* of words, phrases and sentences in language *context* and *extralinguistic situation*." Linguistic method, which in the first half of the twentieth century is strongly influenced by the Prague school and the subsequent Bloomfield phoneme construct, turns in rapid succession by the second half of the century to the development of syntactic theory (1957, Noam Chomky's *Syntactic Structures*), then to semantic theory (1963, Jerrold J. Katz and Jerry A. Fodor's "The Structure of a Semantic Theory"), and finally to pragmatic theory (1969, John Searle's *Speech Acts*). The way is thus open for a linguistic return to the text.

Language is "prototypical of *all* culture" (cf. "The Sign System Par Excellence" section above, Leach 1976: 88) and "culture consists of a plethora of texts" (Silverman 1979: 258). *Text* in the broad sense, accordingly, equates with culture, with language, with man himself (Peirce 5: §314 wrote "the word or sign which man uses *is* the man himself"). In a more narrow sense text refers to the "abstract theoretical construct underlying what is usually called *discourse* (van Dijk 1977: 3). Nevertheless, Teun van Dijk's delimitation is tenuous in view of the fact that "discourse is systematically related to communicative action" (loc. cit.), and accordingly recycles into cultural behavior (cf. "Defining Language—1" section above, Mathiot 1979: "Discourse is not a part of language").

The transdisciplinary status then that text enjoys calls for a transdisciplinary model, which is currently action theory. Linguistic pragmatics is exploiting an action theory of its own with a basis in speech act theory. Special focus is placed on the category narrative because of its general nature. Thus A. J. Greimas writes (1977: 23): "narrative structures can be identified outside of the manifestations of meaning that occur in the natural languages: in the languages of cinema and of dream, in figurative painting, etc." In fact, Greimas' narrative appears to parallel van Dijk's discourse which contains such universal features as propositional macrostructures, modalities, and inferential structure (cf. Chapter 7, 8 below). Not surprisingly then, "conventional organizations of discourse ... [parallel those] of the corresponding global speech acts, and of action in general (van Dijk 1977: 245–6).

Semiotic Linguistics

Given the trend in development of linguistic method in the twentieth century, it can hardly be unexpected that the awakening of a semiotic linguistics has been delayed until the final quarter of this century. Traditions of influences such as the Prague School, which contribute so much to the refinement of feature analysis, at the same time have stunted the Saussurean discernment that all language is a semiotic, the existence of which depends on the interrelationships of sound with meaning. In other words, a linguistic form of any sort without a meaning correlation is paramount to non-existence.

The fuller acceptance of Saussure's semiology is accompanied by the incorporation into linguistic method of the Peircean division of signs and his phenomenological categories. Peirce's theory of abduction is found to account for language acquisition strategies and language change, that is, the creative aspect of language.

Linguistic iconicity, whether in speech, writing, or sign-language, gives a deceptively simple impression when viewed in isolated data, for example onomatopoeic images as English *click, clack, cluck* (Wescott 1971). However, diagrammatic schemata involving entire systems of a language are extremely intricate and sophisticated, for example, the analysis of the morphology of the Russian verb in terms of the fit between the phonological representation and the meaning of the morphemes (Shapiro 1969, 1980, 1991). The main principle at work in determining the fit is that of *markedness*, whereby feature values of an opposition in one component of the grammar correlate with feature values of an opposition in another component of the grammar.

Whereas the morphology and the syntax of a grammar are strongly diagrammatic, the lexicon is predominantly symbolic (cf. Jakobson 1965, Valesio 1969). Other than iconic elements in the vocabulary, indexical relations compose deictic words such as pronouns and morphemes of time and place; the remaining symbolic component then comprises the largest mass of dictionary items in a language (cf. Chapter 4 below). A language can thus be called arbitrary only in certain parts of its lexicon. Saussure's oft quoted statement (1959: 67) that "*the linguistic sign is arbitrary*" has been misinterpreted and applied without restriction to the whole of language structure. As Saussure himself cautions (133): "Everything that relates to language as a system must, I am convinced, be approached from this viewpoint, which has scarcely received the attention of linguists: the limiting of arbitrariness."

One of language's most powerful strategies, if not its single most effective universal maneuver, is *analogy*. In its multifaceted functionings analogy displays a strongly iconic character, but also an indexical one. A basic mechanism of analogy is well expressed in the "iconic principle whose ideal is 'one meaning, one form'" (Anttila 1972: 100; cf. "Language Grows" section of Introduction above), which clearly checks arbitrariness. The indiscriminate use of analogy in linguistic explanation, however, is curtailed by requiring the identification of discrete relational strategies operative within the analogical processes. Thus, for example, if *Secondness* is determined as the main function in a given linguistic analogy, contrary to an analogy based on *Firstness*, the highly valued predictability factor in linguistics as a science is strengthened (cf. Chapter 2 above and Chapter 14, 15, 16 below). This is not to say that analogy is necessarily less widespread than formerly thought; it does say that analogic explanations, in order to be valid, must be held more accountable. Indeed, analogy's universality stems from the fact that the analogical process is an abduction, and hence it results from those laws of inference which are responsible for language creation or growth.

Growth, comprising language change and acquisition, proceeds by a model "which recognizes, on the one hand, that the verbal output of any speaker is determined by the grammar he has internalized, and on the other, that any speaker's internalized grammar is determined by the verbal output from which it has been inferred" abductively, but also inductively, and deductively (Andersen 1973: 767; cf. also Savan 1980). Ultimately, it is the teleology of language change, of language acquisition, of why "symbols grow" (2: §332), which semiotic method imparts to linguistics as a haunting legacy and challenge for the twenty-first century. Part Two of this volume displays the interaction of semiotic tools with linguistic tools in ferreting out cause of change in hard linguistic data.

4

Peirce and Linguistics

Notwithstanding the fairly facile, non-teleological application of Peirce's icon, index, symbol to language data, e.g., the iconic positioning of the protasis before the apodosis in a conditional sentence, or the indexical relationship of a pronoun to its referent, or the symbolic structure of that part of the lexicon which is arbitrary (cf. Chapter 3 above, "Semiotic Linguistics"), Peircean categories are generally neglected and/or underutilized in restructuring or grammaticalization discussions on language data. Thus, Dressler and Mayerthaler (1987: 17) note: "The important role of diagrams [iconicity] has become clearer since Jakobson ... and is a dominant theme in Natural Morphology."

Linguists and Firstness

The type of iconicity involved in teleological linguistic research is not imaginal; rather, it is the extremely intricate diagrammatic iconism, namely, that similarities are postulated between form and meaning based on the relations of their parts. The cornerstone of diagrammatic iconism is the time-honored principle of *isomorphism*, biuniqueness, stated in the formula "one form: one meaning." This isomorphism, invariance, biuniqueness of verbal signs is called the "law of semiotic relevance" by Shaumyan (1984: 235).

Shapiro (1980) gives several excellent examples of linguistic diagrammatic iconism. One of these is his "explication," not mere "description" or "rule formulation" (1980: 67), of the verb desinences of the Russian non-preterite indicative. The first person singular *-ú* ending incorporates the highest degree of deflection for the marked person category with unmarked number, while the third person plural

ending incorporates the maximally marked number category with unmarked person. The greatest semantic differentiation between person
and number value is in the first person singular, followed by the third
person plural. This distinction in content is then mirrored (iconically
reflected) conversely in the forms, where, for example, the -ú of the
first person singular desinence is highly underdifferentiated; it is
marked for neither the flat nor the diffuse distinctive feature (Shapiro
1980: 80). It would be folly to hold that the iconic principle is an explanation for all linguistic relations, or (as Shapiro claims) for "why
the data cohere as signs" (1980: 91). The principle is a working hypothesis, not a proof.

It is precisely the purpose of John Haiman to underscore on the one
hand the power of isomorphism, while on the other hand to show that
it is but "nearly universal" (1980: 515). Haiman aims to account for
homonymy, which is as impossible as synonymy under the principle
of biuniqueness. He is unable to explain the anticipatory subject morpheme on the medial verb in Hua, a Papuan language of Eastern New
Guinea, through isomorphism. because the morpheme in question has
one invariant form with three different meanings. Accordingly,
Haiman seeks an answer outside of isomorphism, and he finds it in the
universal principles of coreference, subject-verb agreement, and the
nominal character of medial verbs. Haiman writes that such
"principles ... are universal, and override bi-unique correspondence or
isomorphism wherever they conflict with it" (1980: 519). In fact, he
claims that "the value of the iconic assumption lies in the impetus it
provides toward the discovery of such (otherwise unnoted) principles." This view differs considerably from that of Shapiro, for whom
the value of iconicity in coherence between sign and meaning lies in
its hermeneutic force.

Robertson (1983: 529) hypothesizes a correlation between the
iconic or symbolic character of a grammar and Huntington's Law,
which holds that "the number of elements in every logical field must
be 2^m where $m = 1, 2, 3 ...$," 2 represents plus or minus a semantic
value, and the variable m equals the number of semantic values.
Robertson maintains that strongly iconic language structures favor
many logical possibilities, and conversely, that a symbolic system
tends to be syncretic. Examples from English are the "hierarchically
defined grammatical system" (HDGS) of the verb which admits of
logical possibilities such as the future, past, progressive, present perfect and others (1983: 530). On the other hand, in the HDGS of the

third person plural pronoun *they*, few logical possibilities are realized—the logical meanings *he*, *she*, and *it*, that is, singular of all three genders, are syncretized in the symbol *they*. Robertson displays the Mayan evidence showing Common Mayan to have been syncretic and symbolic in its HDGS for pronouns, but to have developed into an iconic, less syncretic HDGS. Needless to say, it is difficult to agree that Robertson's appeal to the Peircean categories explains how linguistic data realize Huntington's theorem; they simply corroborate what has already been observed linguistically. Moreover, Robertson has totally overlooked *Secondness*, which should be his point of departure in utilizing the categories dynamically—making them work in the system, rather than appending them as superficial similes (cf. Chapters 14, 15 below).

Haiman (1983) has in the meantime addressed linguistic iconicity again, where he establishes an economic/iconic correlation between a linguistic form and its conceptual category. For example, appealing to Greenberg's universal which reads: "In no language will the linguistic distance between x and y be greater in signaling inalienable possession, in expressions like 'x's y,' than it is in signaling alienable possession," Haiman (1983: 793) demonstrates that in many Austronesian languages distance between the conceptually alienable *my* and *house* is iconically mirrored morphologically by the fact that *my* is a separate word. Thus in Nakanai one says *luma taka* 'house my,' while the conceptually lesser distance or the intimacy between *my* and *hand* is narrowed by the fact that *my* is an affix to its possession, thus one says *lima-gu* 'hand my.' A familiar case in point in demonstrating the economic/iconic correlation between linguistic expression and conceptual distance is seen in the set of what Haiman (1983: 803) calls introverted verbs (e.g., English *wash*) as contrasted to his set of so-called extroverted verbs (e.g., English *kick*). In the phrase *Max washed*, the reflexive object is incorporated into the verb, mirroring closeness, while in the phrase *Max kicked himself*, the reflexive object is less close, that is, not incorporated into the verb, and accordingly requires overt expression (cf. Rauch 1987b). The second semiotic principle that dominates the recent applications of semiotic theory to linguistics is *abduction*, which represents *Firstness* and hence iconicity as well. Andersen (1973) speaks to the abductive replacement of the sharped labials /pbm/ by the dentals /tdn/ in the Litomyšl dialect of Czech during the fourteenth century, with their subsequent reversion to plain labials in the nineteenth century (for discussion cf. Chapter 14 below, cf. also Newmeyer *Language* 1992).

Peirce *qua* Linguist

We have just discussed several linguistic viewpoints which explore Peircean thought. Let us now turn to several viewpoints of Peirce *qua* linguist. Robin (1967) lists some ten pages with 126 entries of linguistic topics addressed in Peirce's writings. Robin's subtitles read "Classification and Synonyms" (1967: 133–134), "Dictionaries" (1967: 134–137), and "Spelling") (1967: 137–140), with four pages (140–143) entitled "Miscellaneous." This last subtitle subsumes the 126 items listed in cue words, e.g., item 1210 (1967: 140), "Notes on Chemical Suffixes and Prefixes," or item 1248 (1967: 142), "The Cardinal Digits in Several Languages." Although Robin's listing provides an index of sorts, it goes without saying that it is no substitute at all for combing Peirce directly for his insights into linguistics (cf. also "Oehler on Peirce," Chapter 10 below).

In his classification of the sciences, Peirce (1: 183, 186, 189, 191, 200) suborders linguistics under the order classificatory psychics or ethnology, which derives from the subclass psychical sciences, which falls under the class idioscopy, belonging to the subbranch science of discovery, part of the branch theoretical science. He classifies language as the seventh genus of the classificatory sciences of intellectual performance (7: 385), deriving from classificatory psychology (as does linguistics). Peirce (1902: 242) wrote:

> This seventh Genus is stupendous, embracing not only Speech, but all modes of communication such as sign language; and under speech studying all dialects, not merely in their grammar and vocabulary, but also in their styles of composition. It will also embrace studies of Diplomatics, of Alphabets, etc.

Without dwelling at this point on Peirce's own stupendous definition of language, namely the famed (5: 314) equation which reads "my language is the sum total of myself," we should observe Peirce's dialogic commentary on language. He explains "dialogic" thus (5: 497): "I write in the form of a dialogue, because it is in that form that my thoughts come to me ..." Pragmatist (5: 533) states: "The brutes are certainly capable of more than one grade of control; but it seems to me that our superiority to them is more due to our greater number of grades of self-control than it is to our versatility." Doctor Y (5: 534) asks: "Is it not due to our faculty of language?" Pragmatist replies:

> To my thinking that faculty is itself a phenomenon of self-control ... All thinking is by signs; and the brutes are signs. But they perhaps rarely think of them as signs. To do so is manifestly a second step in the use of language. Brutes use language, and seem to exercise some little control over it. But they certainly do not carry this control to anything like the same grade that we do. They do not criticize their thought logically.

In one breath Peirce, "though with no pretension to being a linguist" (2: 328), foreshadows both of Lyons' premier characteristics of human language: "reflexiveness" (1977) and "versatility" (1981), indeed using the identical term for the latter (cf. "Object Language," Chapter 5 below). Note, too, that Peirce does not circumvent outright the question of language in animals. He (7: 379) speaks to the

> Instincts of Communication; for some kind of language there is among nearly all animals. Not only do animals of the same species convey their assertions, but different classes of animals do so, as when a snake hypnotizes a bird. Two particularly important varieties of this Species of study will relate to Cries and Songs (among mammals and birds chiefly) and to facial expressions among mammals ...

He adds that "I can tell by the expression of face the state of mind of my horse just as unmistakably as I can that of my dog or my wife."

Peirce addresses the linguistic principle of biuniqueness, also known as invariance (cf. Haiman 1980, 1983; Robertson 1983), *isomorphism*, or Shaumyan's "law of semiotic relevance." He writes (2: 222): "As an ideal to be aimed at ... each word should have a single exact meaning ..." (cf. "Language Grows," Introduction, and "Semiotic Linguistics," Chapter 3 above; and cf. 'Medicine and Linguistics, Chapter 9, "Causation in Linguistics," Chapter 14, "New Growth," Chapter 17, "Toward Isomorphism," Chapter 18 above). Peirce also speaks to linguistic change, specifically semantic change, saying: "For every symbol is a living thing, in a very strict sense that is no mere figure of speech. The body of the symbol changes slowly, but its meaning inevitably grows, incorporates new elements and throws off old ones."

The experience of reading that "In most languages that have nouns and adjectives, the participial adjective follows the noun" (4: 56) is that familiar linguistic one of reading about a universal of linear syntax. Equally, if not more, sought after by linguists is a definition of a sentence, such as can be found in Peirce (3: 461): "The proposition, or sentence, signifies that an eternal truth, a permanent conditional force, or law, attaches certain haecceities to certain parts of an idea." Peirce's definition, however, strikes the linguistic ear as less familiar, since it typifies the classic Peircean definition of a sign.

Peirce's interest in linguistic pragmatics goes without saying. Obviously this statement is somewhat misguided, since it is only in the last quarter of the century that many a linguist began to understand the position of pragmatic considerations in linguistic structure and description. Peirce (3: 419) demonstrates the pragmatics of verbal interaction or discourse grammar:

Two men meet on a country road. One says to the other, that house is on fire. "What house?" "Why the house about a mile to my right." Let this speech be taken down and shown to anybody in the neighboring village, and it will appear that the language by itself does not fix the house. But the person addressed sees where the speaker is standing, recognizes his right hand side ... estimates a mile ... and looking there sees a house. It is not the language alone, with its mere associations of similarity, but the language taken in connection with the author's own experiential associations of contiguity which determines for him what house is meant. It is requisite then, in order to show what we are talking or writing about, to put the hearer's or reader's mind into real, active connection with the concatenation of experience or of fiction with which we are dealing, and, further, to draw his attention to, and identify, a certain number of particular points in such concatenation.

The more conservative linguist may relate to Peirce's discussion of sentence function for including pragmatics in his (the linguist's) own work. Thus Peirce (4: 57) maintains:

The distinction between an assertion and an interrogating sentence is of secondary importance. An assertion has its *modality*, or measure of assurance, and a question generally involves as part of it an assertion of emphatically low modality. In addition to that, it is intended to stimulate the hearer to make an answer. This is a rhetorical function which needs no special grammatical form. If in wandering about the country, I wish to inquire the way to town, I can perfectly do so by assertion, without drawing upon the interrogative form of syntax. Thus I may say, "this road leads, perhaps, to the city. I wish to know what you think about it." The most suitable way of expressing a question would, from a logical point of view, seem to be by an interjection: "this road leads, perhaps, to the city, eh?"

As a logician Peirce naturally deals with various parts of speech; he is intent on explaining, for example, subjecthood, verbness, the nature of the preposition and the noun. Thus, concerning subjecthood, Peirce (2: 338) writes:

I term those occasions or objects which are denoted by the indices the *subjects* of the assertion. But these will not coincide with the objects denoted by the grammatical subjects ... That which is called the *subject* is the noun which is in the nominative, although, even in our relatively small family of Indo-European languages, there are several in which that noun which in Latin, Greek, and the modern European languages is put in the nominative, is put in an oblique case. Witness the Irish and Gaelic.

He (4: 438) writes further:

Each part of a proposition which might be replaced by a proper name, and still leave the proposition a proposition is a *subject* of the proposition. This, it will be remarked, makes what modern grammars call the direct and indirect objects, as well as much else, to be *subjects,* and some persons will consider this to be a bad abuse of the word *subject.*

Feistily, Peirce continues, "Come, let us have this out," and he proceeds to explain the origin of the logical definition of subjecthood according to Boethius and Cicero, predating by more than a millennium that grammatical notion of subjecthood which insists on a surface nominative. Subjecthood in linguistic deep structure grammars, for example case grammars, coincides nicely with Peirce's local concept of subject.

Peirce (3: 458) considers the preposition "an essential part of speech ... in that no language can exist without prepositions, either as separate words placed before or after their objects, as case-declensions, as syntactical arrangements of words, or some equivalent forms." He has little use for the common noun (as we will point out further below). Comparing the preposition to the noun, he (2: 341) writes: "It is absurd, indeed, to erect this unnecessary part of speech (the noun) into a logical form and leave the indispensable prepositions unrepresented, merely because in Indo-European languages they often appear in the form of terminations." From the more recent linguistic viewpoint, Peirce expresses the sentence-like or propositional character of the exocentric prepositional phrase (cf. Rauch 1979c).

Peirce's lengthy and frequent discussions of the dispensability of the noun generally go hand in hand with his understanding of the primacy of the verb. He (2: 328) observes: "It happens to be true that in the overwhelming majority of languages there are no general class names and adjectives that are not conceived as parts of some verbs ... almost every family of man thinks of general words as parts of verbs." Further (2: 341): "common nouns ... are mere accidental grammatical forms which happen to be very prominent in the languages most familiar to us, but which hardly exist, or at least are far from prominent, in the vast majority of tongues, and are really not needed, at all, and ought to be unknown to the *Grammatica Speculativa*." And further still Peirce (3: 440) writes: "The common noun happens to have a very distinctive character in the Indo- European languages. In most other tongues it is not sharply discriminated from a verb or participle. 'Man,' if it can be said to mean anything by itself, means 'what I am thinking of is a man.'" This notion is repeated nineteen sections later (3: 459):

Our European languages are peculiar in their marked differentiation of common nouns from verbs ... it is probably true that in the great majority of the tongues of men, distinctive common nouns either do not exist or are exceptional formations. In their meaning as they stand in sentences. and in my comparatively widely-studied languages, common nouns are akin to participles, as being mere inflections of verbs.

Two additional statements of Peirce on the position of the common noun will serve as a prelude to the final topic we will consider in the interdigitation of linguistics and semiotics. Peirce (4: 56, italics mine) writes:

> There are more than a dozen *different families of languages, differing radically in their manner of thinking*; and I believe it is fair to say that among these the Indo- European is the only one in which words which are distinctively common nouns are numerous. And since a noun or combination of nouns by itself says nothing, I do not know why the logician should be required to take account of it at all. Even in Indo-European speech the linguists tell us that the roots are all verbs. It seems that, speaking broadly, ordinary words in the bulk of languages are assertory. They assert as soon as they are in any way attached to any object. If you write GLASS upon a case, you will be understood to mean that the case contains glass.

Finally Peirce (7: 385, italics mine) says:

> The Indo-European languages are singular in having the common noun distinctly and fully developed as a separate part of speech, and by more or less development even of abstract nouns. I do not mean to say that the common noun is not fully developed in any other language, but only that such a phenomenon is exceptional in every other great family of speech. *This requires and evidences considerable power of thought on the part of those who use these languages.* With the exercise of a little ingenuity it is possible to express anything in these languages, provided no higher relations than dyadic ones enter. Only very simple propositions can be expressed involving higher relations; and *those whose mental education is limited by the powers of these languages* are unable to grasp the meaning of a complex triple relation ...

Peirce before Sapir—Whorf

It is important in cogitating these two statements to shift attention from the common noun to Peirce's implication that the structure of a language and the thinking of its speakers are intimately related, perhaps in a cause and effect relationship. In the final section of this chapter, viewing Peirce "with no pretension to being a linguist," we will consider something known to linguists as the Sapir-Whorf hypothesis. Alternately we may wish to consider our concluding discussion under the rubric Peirce: "those whose mental education is limited by the power of these languages."

First to the linguists. Although the premises contained in the Sapir-Whorf hypothesis are manifold, the basic or central proposition holds, in the words of Whorf's editor, John B. Carroll (1956: 23), that "the structure of a human being's language influences the manner in which he understands reality and behaves with respect to it." The hypothesis so entitled by Carroll after two linguist-anthropologists of the first half of the twentieth century, Edward Sapir (1884–1939) and Benjamin Whorf (1897–1941), is otherwise known as the theory of "linguistic relativity" or "linguistic relativism." Relativism itself actually holds that human languages are relative in their structure, since it claims there is no absolute universal structure; reality, it claims further, attests to endless diversity among languages. Sapir-Whorfian relativity incorporates also the concept of "linguistic determinism," which holds that language determines thought. This combination theory commonly admits of two degrees, a stronger version and a weaker version—the former maintaining that language determines cognition and action, the latter maintaining that language merely influences cognition and action. Statements of Sapir (1931: 578) asserting, for example, that "Such categories as number, gender, case, tense ... are not so much discovered in experience as imposed upon it because of the tyrannical hold that linguistic form has upon our orientation in the world," and of Whorf (1964: 136) proclaiming that "linguistics is fundamental to the theory of thinking" are most frequently construed as representative of the stronger version of linguistic relativity.

The juxtaposition of thinking and language is, of course, a venerable topic. Twentieth-century linguistic relativity derives from theories of the interrelatedness of thought and language which enjoy an uninterrupted succession from Ferdinand de Saussure through Wilhelm von Humboldt, Johann Gottfried Herder, and Johann Georg

Hamann—all of whom considered our world view to be directly influenced by language. Penn (1972) traces the hypothesis of the influence of language on thought as far back as Plato, and Brown (1967: 13) implies a broad network of Humboldt-influenced linguists, philosophers, psychologists, and anthropologists since Sapir and Whorf, many of whom are still active today (Cassirer, Weisgerber, Trier, Bally, Levi-Strauss, Piaget, Sommerfelt, and Wittgenstein).

In fact, evidence of the linguistic relativity concept is ubiquitous. The linguist-semiotist Rulon Wells, speaking of evolution, writes (1964: 306, second emphasis mine): "It is customary to speak of *the* Darwinian hypothesis, as though it were a singular, individual, and determinate object. This is a way *in which our language misleads us* into steps and paths which it is all-important to avoid." Another case in point is found in the appendix to Orwell's *1984*. Orwell describes the official language, Newspeak, of his imagined Oceania: "It was intended that when Newspeak had been adopted once and for all and Oldspeak forgotten, a heretical thought—that is, a thought diverging from the principles of Ingsoc—should literally be unthinkable, at least so far as *thought is dependent on words*" (emphasis mine).

Let us turn now to Peirce on linguistic relativity. Peirce (2: 67–70) speaks directly to linguistic relativity as one "of a swarm of different methods of establishing the truths of logic." He (2: 69, emphasis mine) writes,

> I must acknowledge ... there are a number of eminent linguists who maintain this method in its extremest possible form ... When Sayce [a linguist] says that "had Aristotle been a Mexican, his system of logic would have assumed a wholly different form", I am willing to admit that there is a good deal of truth in that. It is lucky that Aristotle's only language was one that led him into as few errors as did the Greek. But so far am I from finding in this remark any encouragement to trust to the indications of language as evidence of logical necessity, that it seems to me to go quite the other way.

Let us consider a few more citations from Peirce where he addresses linguistic relativity indirectly. Peirce (3: 430) observes that speculative grammar "must analyse an assertion into its essential elements, independently of the structure of the language in which it may happen to be expressed." He notes (3: 481): "It is a curious example of the degree to which the thoughts of logicians have been tied down to the accidents of the particular language they happened to write (mostly Latin) ..." Describing a scenario for the origin of language, Peirce (7: 384, emphasis mine) writes: *"Language gave man distinct conceptions, and awakened in him the idea of understanding things."* On the other hand, Peirce (1902) writes: "It seems to me that the broadest classes of speech are determined by the general character of the thought which they represent." On balance, Peirce appears, if not in word then in deed, to hold the weaker version of the linguistic relativity hypothesis. This is not surprising in view of Bertalanffy's (1968) identification of linguistic relativity as a part of general scientific relativism. Another facet of scientific relativism is known to semiotists as Uexküll's theory of autoambience (cf. "Uexküll on Uexküll," Chapter 10 below).

To be sure, Peirce predated Sapir-Whorf (twentieth-century formulations of linguistic relativity), but he profited from a virtually uninterrupted line of predecessors with regard to linguistic relativity and many other fundamental linguistic principles (cf. Rauch 1996a), not the least of which is language as the mediator between one's inner world and one's outer world. While language as mediator later accords extremely well with Uexküll's theory of autoambience, whereby a human being and their ambience mutually generate one another, and Thom's (1975) grip catastrophe or loop catastrophe, which both depict the internalization of external stimuli, it reveals coherence with previous thinkers, so, e.g., once again the linguist-philosopher Wilhelm von Humboldt. Compare, e.g., Humboldt's (1836 [1988]: 214) statement: "... it is a general law of man's existence in the world, that he can project nothing from himself that does not at once become a thing that reacts upon him and conditions his further creation," with that of Peirce (5: 313):

Man makes the word, and the word means nothing which the man has not made it mean, and that only to some man. But since man can think only by means of words or other external symbols, these (the words) might turn round and say; "You mean nothing which we have not taught you, and then only insofar as you address one word as the interpretant of your thought." In fact, therefore, men and words reciprocally educate each other; each increase of a man's information involves, and is involved by, a corresponding increase of a word's information.

5

Semiotics as Metalanguage

Metalanguage and Object Language

Semiology is defined by Hjelmslev (1963: 120; cf. "Trabant on Hjelmslev," Chapter 10 below) as a metasemiotic, and the science of language is called *semiotic* by Carnap (1942: 9), who considers it to be composed of pragmatics, semantics, and syntax. Reichenbach (1947: 15) holds that metalanguage is divided into syntax, semantics, and pragmatics, "corresponding to the three arguments of the sign relation." One could infer, accordingly, that semiotics is metalanguage, and the reverse, relegating the term *metasemiotic* to redundancy. (For the separate issue of the varying distinctions accorded syntax, semantics, and pragmatics, cf. Lyons 1977: 4.4.)

The object language is L_1 in Carnap's (1942: 3–4) definition: "If we investigate, analyze, and describe a language L_1, we need a language L_2 for formulating the results of our investigation of L_1, or the rules for the use of L_1. In this case we call L_1 the object language, L_2 the metalanguage." Metalanguage of object language is, for example, definition, what Bentham (1969: 44) calls "paraphrasis" (cf. also Weinreich 1963: 130; Leech 1980: chap. 2). The object, however, need not be a language, in which case Morris (1955: 179) speaks of object signs and, in fact, metasigns, "where these are language signs." It would seem that as long as the metamedium is language, metalanguage is the appropriate designation. Nevertheless, Morris (1955: 180–1) restricts semiotic to metalanguage of scientific and logico-mathematical discourse. He thus excludes from semiotic metalanguage poems about poems. Contrariwise, Lotman (1977: 197–98) speaks, for example, of works of art describing works of art in the age of Classicism, or of the changing of the guard as a metasystem of

Russia's military, bureaucratic utopia during the time of Paul I. In the case of music, we might want to consider such compositions as Brahms's "Variations on a Theme of Haydn" or Chopin's "Variations on '*Lei darem la mano*' of Mozart's 'Don Giovanni'" as metamusical.

Whether the object is identical with the metasemiotic or not, an important characteristic of the dichotomy is its potential for an infinite hierarchy. Thus, Tarski (1949: 60) observes: "If ... we become interested in the notion of truth applying to sentences, not of our original object-language, but of its meta-language, the latter becomes automatically the object-language of our discussion; and in order to define truth for this language, we have to go to a new meta-language—so to speak, to a meta-language of a higher level." Another requirement of Tarski's, that the metalanguage contain the object language or, as he (1949: 61) writes, that "the object-language can be translated into the meta-language," may hold for human object language, but certainly cannot be a general requirement for all objects of metasemiotics. Sebeok (1979: 257) strongly rejects the translation theory, stating that "there is no compelling evidence for the view that every non-verbal sign must invariably address somebody verbally." He removes metatheory from language in semiosis by referring to metacommunicative signing, which may or may not include language in its operation.

Related to Sebeok's (1979: 256) conviction that some object semiotics, including animal sounds, "are incapable of being paraphrased" is the observation that even if paraphrase is possible between an object and its metalanguage, the fit should not be such as to obscure the distinction between object and metalanguage. Borerz (1969: 11) cites as an example the "heuristic metaphor ('gravity', say) to explain some musical phenomenon suggestively, followed by the invocation of all the deductive and inductive consequences of the metalinguistic term as it is used in the metalanguage as though it were consequentially explanatory, or analogously significative, in the object-linguistic domain, without further justification." Clearly, the only object that is fully capable of translatability into metalanguage is language, due to its *reflexivity,* which, Lyons (1977: 5) writes, is "One of the most characteristic features of natural languages (and one which may well distinguish them, not only from the signalling-systems used by other species, but also from what is commonly referred to as non-verbal communication in human beings ...)." On the other hand, it is possible that metalanguage has no object at all. Gopnik, in her discussion of

"Scientific theories as meta-semiotic systems" (1977), marks the possibility of the mere hypothetical existence of an object as the characteristic distinguishing the human sciences from the natural sciences.

Object Semiotic

It is the case that an object semiotic (in distinction to object language) is commonly studied through metalanguage. Because of the success in treating object language through the metalanguage of linguistic structuralism, an array of language analogical tools has been applied to nonlanguage sign systems. The varying degrees of lack of success in their application show that there are no one-to-one correlations between object and language and object semiotic, and in fact their failure elucidates the differences between the two objects. One of the most frequently employed concepts is that of isolable features minimal and distinctive internal to an object semiotic. Stokoe (1974: 367), working with sign language, suggests as the minimal gesture the "chereme," specifically the place, operator, action (or tabula, designator, signation features, respectively), whereas Birdwhistell (1952) refers to the minimal motion distinguishing meaning as a "kineme," which may be combined to form "kinemorphs." But it is difficult to claim minimal distinctiveness for all these language analogues. Thus, Edward Hall (1972: 269) prefers to characterize his study of spatial behavior as "more concerned with proxetics than proxemics," and in the case of film semiotics, Lange-Seidl (Lange-Seidl 1977: 18) considers Worth's (1969) *videme* (image shot), *cademe* (camera shot), and *edeme* (editing shot) as "in reality abbreviations for technical procedures, not minimal units isolated theoretically in the sense of structuralism." The *behavioreme* of Pike certainly was a concept ahead of its time, reading more familiar today than in 1954. Yet, as recently as 1973, Greenberg (1973: 55) observed of Pike's behavioreme, such as a church service or a football game, that "while [it is] in a very broad sense meaningful, [it] does not send messages, as it were, with such precision that we can say when the message is the same or different." Cultural object semiotic- "emes" on the whole tend to defy reduction to meaningless features in contrast to the acoustic distinctive features of object language phonology.

The phonological, morphological, syntactic, semantic, and lexical levels of language are transferred as levels to object semiotics. A well-known study is Uspenskij's *Semiotics of the Russian Icon* (1976), in which he demonstrates a primary level, devoid of meaning, but which provides the conventions (compare alphabet) for transmitting three- or four-dimensional space on a two-dimensional surface. The language-analogous levels of semantics and syntax for the icon intersect in, for example, the position of one object relative to another. Thus, in the fresco "Adoration of the Magi," in the monastery of St. Therapont, the Magi face the viewer, but their bodies are turned away from the viewer toward the Virgin and Child, conveying the meaning of adoration. Further, conventions such as clothing, idiosyncratic to a particular saint in an icon are held to function analogously to idioms in the lexicon. The similarities between object language system and object semiotic system remain mere analogies.

Another case in point is the often proposed analogue of music to linguistics—a much exploited model at the Rome 1972 International Symposium on the Problematic of Today's Musical Notation. Nattiez's paper (1972) establishes "notemes," which represent ideal sound relations that may have manifold renderings. Stefani (1972) identifies duration, intensity, pitch, and timbre as "morphological aspects of a discourse," which although they are "acoustic properties of sound ... are in reality cultural categories filtered through the perception and organized according to convention;" examples might be duration peculiar to Ars Nova, timbre to Baroque. For syntax in music, Ruwet (1967: 83–84) considers the possibility of the recursive mechanisms of conjunction and embedding. Although he cannot attribute recursion to all kinds of music, Ruwet observes that "there is, at least in the tonal system, a specific harmonic (tonic—sub-dominant/dominant—tonic) which may, by itself, provide the basis of a musical work and may, by means of transposition, be self-embedded indefinitely." Eco, in his *Theory of Semiotics* (1976: 11), expresses the familiar view that music is a semiotic without a semantic level, yet he writes: "there are musical 'signs' (or syntagms) with an explicit denotative value (trumpet signals in the army) and there are syntagms or entire 'texts' possessing pre-culturalized connotative value ('pastoral' or 'thrilling' music, etc.)."

Whereas musicologists such as Ruwet, Stefani, and Nattiez attempt to exploit similarities between object language and object music, the linguist Jackendoff, who, pursuant to a Massachusetts Institute of Technology seminar on music, linguistics, and aesthetics, wrote (with Lerdahl) a monograph *Toward a Formal Theory of Tonal Music*, restricts the similarities between language and music to metatheoretical considerations, Thus they (1980: 2) write: "we demand strong motivation, formal rigor, and predictive power for every part of the theory." However, they (1980: 5–6) make amply clear that

> Whatever music may "mean," it is in no sense comparable to the semantic component in language; there are no substantive parallels to sense and reference in language, or to such semantic judgments as synonymy, analyticity, and entailment. It is in the domain of syntax that the linguistic approach has relevance to music theory. Yet even here there are no substantive parallels between musical structure and such grammatical categories in language as noun, verb, adjective, noun phrase, verb phrase, and so forth. The concepts of musical structure must be developed in terms of music itself.

Object Language

Study of the differences between language (herein taken as human language) and other sign systems has frequently been based on the sixteen design features of verbal language postulated by Hockett (1963: 6–14): (1) vocal-auditory channel for communicating; (2) broadcast transmission and directional reception of the sign; (3) rapid fading of the sign; (4) interchangeability in being the transmitter or the receiver; (5) complete feedback of the sign; (6) specialization of the signal for communication; (7) semanticity; (8) arbitrariness; (9) discreteness; (10) displacement in that the sign may refer to things remote in time or space; (11) openness in that a sign may be created; (12) tradition of passing on signs by teaching and learning; (13) duality consisting in a phonology and morphology for signs; (14) prevarication may be accomplished through signs; (15) reflexiveness in that a sign can be a sign of itself; and (16) learnability of more than one sign system.

Sign systems such as written language, African drum signals, and bee dancing, as well as all nonvocal systems, differ from language by criterion (1). Nonauditory sign systems such as silent films, or for that matter any semiotic systems involving touch, smell, taste, or sight but not hearing, differ from language by criteria (2) and (3). Nonanimate sign systems as well as certain animal communication systems, such as the restriction of the transmission of the chirp to the male cricket but its reception by both male and female crickets, are differentiated

from language by criterion (4). Nonanimate sign systems as well as
the visual-kinetic communications of certain animals (Hockett's example is "the courtship dance of sticklebacks," 1963: 7) resist criterion
(5). The stock example for showing the high degree of specialization
(criterion [6]) that language has is exhibited in the difference between
the kinetic-visual system used by a person setting a dinner table in the
sight of hungry family members and the verbal communication
"Dinner is almost ready" in prompting the kinetic-visual approach to
the table by the family.

Lyons writes of criterion (7), semanticity, that "It would seem to be
little short of tautological to say of any semiotic system that it has semanticity" (1977: 79). He introduces two sets of useful distinctions to
differentiate language from other sign systems on the basis of this
criterion: (1) Communicative signs involve intention on the part of the
sender, while informative signs do not. The latter are simply meaningful to the receiver and are the only signs of nonhuman systems; (2)
Verbal communication refers to human language communication,
while nonverbal communication refers to the signing behavior of both
humans and nonhumans. Verbal communication tends to convey descriptive meaning, and nonverbal communication tends to convey so-
cial-expressive meaning. It is debatable whether nonhuman semiotic
systems convey descriptive meaning. Lyons concludes (1977: 80):
"There are certain kinds of meaning that appear to be unique to language (and more especially to its verbal component) and there are
others which language shares with nonhuman semiotic systems."

Criterion (8) is equated by Hockett with noniconicity; it is accordingly too strong for human language, since, in fact, iconic features do
exist in human language. However, compared with object semiotics,
object language strongly exploits arbitrary signs. Object language is
characterized also by employing discrete (criterion [9]) signs rather
than gradient signs, at least in its phonological, morphological, and
syntactic components. Non-human communication systems as well as
object language admit of criterion (10), displacement, in signing objects that are removed in time and place from the sign (e.g., the bee
dance or a dog approaching door signaling his need to go out). Criterion (11), openness, otherwise called productivity, is frequently relegated to object language only, but with lingering doubts (Hockett
1963: 9; Lyons 1977: 76–77) as to the possible productive nature of
the bee dance. Both object language and animal communication are
transmitted by learning (criterion [12]), although the communicative

ability of animals and the language ability of man are in part genetically determined (e.g., organs of sound). Despite the object semiotic analogues to linguistic phonology and morphology, object language alone is credited with criterion (13). Criterion (14), prevarication (recall Eco [1975: 12] "the fundamental characteristic of the sign is that I can use it to lie") is certainly shared by object semiotic as witnessed, e.g., in the expression "playing possum." There is general agreement that criterion (15), reflexiveness, is strictly bound to object language. Experiments carried out on birds (Thorpe 1972) attest to their ability to learn more than one sign system (criterion [16]), as do humans.

While Lyons (1977: 79) singles out arbitrariness, duality, discreteness, and productivity as questionable for object semiotics, Osgood (1980: 14) considers a type of productivity, viz., the ability to combine signs indefinitely and in novel combinations, as characteristic of an object semiotic such as the bee dance. On the other hand, Osgood extends the defining characteristics of object language to a requirement that states: "The distribution of message forms over time on a linear 'left-to-right' basis requires temporary storage and integration of information" (1980: 21). He offers several additional nondefining characteristics, "some of them absolute but many of them only statistical universals" (1980: 26) of object language: propositionalizing, translatability, selection and combination rules, a progressive differentiation principle, a least effort principle, affective polarity, and a Pollyanna principle wherein affectively positive structures are more easily processed cognitively than affectively negative structures.

Osgood's presentation is written from the viewpoint that object language is unmarked, while Sebeok (1977a: 1060) reverses the focus in "Zoosemiotic Components of Human Communication," stating: "Anthroposemiotic systems are always marked, in contradistinction to the zoosemiotic systems that comprehend them." Similarly, Dingwall (1980: 70) studies the differences between object language and object semiotic, specifically animal communication, on the basis of a biological model. This model results in features which, "in contrast to those presented by Hockett, can be used to measure the complexity of primate communication systems, and, at the same time, are phylogenetically relevant." Interestingly, Chomsky (1980: 185), who writes that "we may regard the language capacity virtually as we would a physical organ of the body," combines parameters from the Hockett and Dingwall approach in his consideration of human language along "six

dimensions of inquiry ... (a) structural principles; (b) physical mechanisms; (c) manner of use; (d) ontogenetic development; (e) phyloge-
netic development; (f) integration into a system of cognitive structures" (Chomsky 1979: 33). The initial state in human language competence, Chomsky (1979: 31)claims, is species-specific and distinguishes "a human from a rock or a bird or a chimpanzee." What might
be most stimulating in this last observation is the bold reference to
"rock," since a great deal of comparison between object semiotic and
object language centers in animal communication for the former.
However, "rock" can indeed play a role in communication, e.g., as a
"ready-made object(s) ... ostension" (Jakobson 1971c: 702) in a rock
garden display, as an instrument in a street fight, as a guide along a
path. Study of mute, inanimate object semiotic is ultimately not trivial
in ferreting out the differences between language and other sign systems.

6

Language as Inlay in Semiosis

So pervasive and ubiquitous is the concept of the role of language in semiotics (cf. Chapter 3 below) that in this chapter we seek to confront head-on how language, as an infrastructure or inlay in semiosis or the semiotic act, can be conceived to function.

Defining Language — 2

In spite of Kristeva's (1975: 47) unwavering conviction that "What semiotics has discovered in studying 'ideologies' ... as sign-systems is that the *law* governing, or, if one prefers, the *major constraint* affecting any social practice lies in the fact that it signifies; that is, that it is articulated *like* a language," and Jakobson's attractive observation (1971: 703) that "The cardinal functions of language—referential, emotive, conative, phatic, poetic, metalingual—and their different hierarchy in the diverse types of messages have been outlined and repeatedly discussed. This pragmatic approach to language must lead *mutatis mutandis* to an analogous study of the other semiotic systems ...," statements such as these remain obscure as to their implementation or application.

Among the many definitions of language (cf. "Defining Language—1," Chapter 3 and "Object Language," Chapter 5 below), Bruce Liles (1975: 36) reverts to Sapir's classical definition of language, namely: "Language is a purely human and noninstinctive method of communicating ideas, emotions, and desires by means of a system of voluntarily produced symbols." Appealing to Lenneberg (1967), Liles has reservations about Sapir's term "noninstinctive"; further, disputing Sapir's "purely human" classification, he notes that recent research in animal communication obviates its summary exclusion from human communication. One wonders then why Sapir's definition is worth salvaging or revitalizing? Liles' intention is to emphasize to the linguistic world that the purpose of language is "Communicat[ion] of ideas, emotions, and desires," since in the first quarter of his book he stresses nonverbal as well as verbal communication, language-like structures as well as language structures. Interestingly, Liles attempts to discuss semiotic areas such as systems of signals, eye movements, mime, interpretive dancing, kinesics, and paralinguistics, without so much as a reference to the word *semiotics*. In point of fact, his statement (16): "There is currently no scholarly framework within which nonverbal signals can be discussed" reflects at best either lack of information or subtle rejection of the discipline of semiotics. Obviously, the treatment of the subject matter of semiotics in Liles' standard introduction for linguists bears testimony to the coming of age of semiotics in the minds of those whose primary business is the defining of language.

Liles notwithstanding, we are left without a definition which might attest to progress (since Sapir) in the understanding of language, a definition which is necessary in order to account for the language-inlay in semiotic modalities. It is in order, then, to exploit the two parts of the definition which Liles at least nominally qualified, viz. "noninstinctive" and "purely human" (cf. below). Concerning 'noninstinctive,' there is no denying that the transformation revolution, against the backdrop of the discoveries in this century of the genetic code, has established as a working hypothesis in linguistics the concept of the innateness of language ability. Significantly, this transformational innateness of language ability was associated with Peircean innate powers of the mind by Wells in 1971 (102 ff.). However, concrete examples which might relate the two fields of thought remain limited, and certainly no attempt at establishing a relationship has been made with examples involving nonverbal data.

Universal Semantic Primitives: Length [L]

It would seem that the comparison among diverse semiotic modalities of massive or large-scale relationships, as represented perhaps in the cardinal functions of language as outlined by Jakobson (cf. above), is somewhat premature. On the linguistic side, we may have more success in relying on what is recognized as a principal time-proven tool of all modern linguistic methodolgies, viz., the ability to isolate and identify discrete elements. Of the several theories of semantic development, the universal primitives hypothesis proposed especially by Postal (1966: fn.10) and extended by Bierwisch (1967: 1–4, 34–6, and 1970: 181–2) in particular appears to connect with semiotic theory. In effect, these linguists hold that the real world, or input into the human organism, is interpreted in the form of universal semantic components or primitives in a species specific manner.

Such universal semantic components or primitives may be represented, for instance, by the four sensory attributes of Miller and Johnson-Laird (1976: 15), "quality, intensity, extension, and duration." In this chapter no distinction is made between extension and duration; they are subsumed under one attribute, i.e., length. (In fact, length and intensity are quantitative, thus somewhat interchangeable; insofar as certain types of quality may be represented in extremes, it too may become quantitative.) In an effort to uncover the language-inlay in nonverbal as well as verbal modalities, this chapter isolates the primitives of quality, intensity, and length in four semiotic modalities, viz., language, paralanguage, music, and architecture.

The primitives of quality [Q], intensity [I],and length [L] are more transparent in certain structures than in others. These primitives appear less identifiable in the nonphonological components of language, even though language resides in all semiotic modalities. To be sure, those components of language become increasingly abstract, while the sensory attributes (primitives) seem more physical; on the other hand, this observation may be indicative of our traditional concept of language. To an extent, imposing on language features which are generally perceived as basically physical is a provocative reverse analogue to imposing language components on nonlinguistic semiotic systems. That is, in seeking the language-inlay in semiotic modalities, efforts are frequently made, for example, to identify a syntax in music, or a semantics in architecture. It must be remembered that an adequate definition of language is still lacking, and that the components of semantics, syntax, morphology, and phonology are by no means considered commensurate with such an adequate definition. Similarly, apparent lack of more than one linguistic component in music and in architecture here does not imply denial of their existence. Rather, our aim is to identify at least one example of each primitive in each modality. Language component analogues to music and architecture are obviously the object of a separate study.

[L] in Language

In the semantic component, e.g., in the English sentence *A mile is longer than a kilometer,* the perception of the primitive [L] is more direct than on the syntactic level, which may be exemplified by gapping in, e.g., *John reads Dickens, Joe Hemingway, and Jill Kant* as opposed to *John reads Dickens, Joe reads Hemingway, and Jill reads Kant.* The primitive [Q] is obtained semantically, e.g., in such oppositions as the positive and the negative, the active and the passive, or even content and functor words. In syntax, a [Q] distinction obtains between parataxis and hypotaxis, for instance. The primitive [I] for semantics is found in redundancy data, e.g., reduplications as in the Spanish *pocititito* 'very, very little' or in the German tautology *Tigertier* 'tiger(animal)'; for syntax [I] is evident in multiple hypotaxis, for example.

For morphology the distinction of the [L] primitive often cited in semiotic literature for its iconicity is the comparative versus the superlative suffix in Indo-European adjective comparison, where the suffixes mirror a stratified phoneme increment, e.g., in English *older* versus *oldest.* In turn, a morphological [Q] distinction can be adduced for suppletive adjective comparison between, e.g., Eng. *good* and *better.* The [I] feature for morphology may well be identified in terms of syllabicity where, e.g., the morpheme English *be* has a higher degree of syllabicity than the morpheme English *beat.*

On the phonological level, the primitive [L] is, of course, perceptible where it alone distinguishes one word from another, thus in Kamba, a Bantu language, three degrees of vowel length are contrastive, e.g., *kwelela* 'measuring,' *kwele·la* 'moving backwards and forwards,' and *kwele: la* 'aiming at.' One of the most widespread [Q] phonological features is represented in the Indo-European *e/o* ablaut; the [I] feature is represented in phonological stress or loudness.

[L] in Paralanguage

Phonology leads us technically into what have been considered borderline linguistic levels, specifically what Trager in 1958 first called "paralanguage" (cf. "Delineating Paralanguage," Chapter 13 below). His so-called voice qualifier of extent, which would oppose drawl to clipping, for example, represents the feature [L] on the paralinguistic level. The feature [Q] in paralinguistics is certainly reflected in voice pitch but also in timbre as, e.g., a raspy or jerky voice. The [I] feature in paralanguage opposes an overloud voice to an oversoft voice.

[L] in Music

Let us now move to the semiotic system of music. It is striking that we actually retrace the phonological component of both language and paralanguage, since the three primitives [L], [Q], [I] are reflected on both the phonological level, where beat, pitch, and loudness are incorporated, and on the paraphonological level where the features slower-faster, smooth-staccato, and softer tone-louder tone are incorporated. Consider as a specific example the choral sequence of the first twelve notes of equal [L] in the "Ode to Joy" of Beethoven's Ninth Symphony. Excepting performance modifications, the playing of any one of the twelve notes shorter or longer relative to its adjacent notes would be perceived as incorrect. Not surprisingly, Gerald Warfield, who (1976: xi) explicating the highly structured principles underlying tonal music, stresses that "… music can be (and is, most of the time) understood intuitively …"

[L] in Architecture

If music, including so-called concrete music, is considered an abstract art form, then sculpture and architecture, including so-called abstract sculpture, can be considered the polar opposite, viz., concrete art forms. The identification of the three primitives in a concrete art form is less concerned with the auditory sense than with the visual sense, so that here [L] is represented in extension; [Q] is reflected in tactile features, e.g., hardness and softness or visual features, e.g., color, hue, or texture; while [I] records lightness or brightness, for instance. In architecture, man's most common form of construction is the basic box, be it a house, a skyscraper, or whatever. In conceptualizing an object in space, e.g., a box, Miller and Johnson-Laird (1976) distinguish between two systems: (1) a deictic system which is relative to the speaker's ego location and the coordinate axes of an object, and (2) an intrinsic system which is relative to the coordinate axes of the object itself. In the case of the box, if the horizontal dimension, labeled A, is its maximal dimension, it is intrinsically the [L] or longer than the secondary horizontal dimension, labeled B, which is its width or shorter than A. Interestingly, Miller and Johnson-Laird write (1976:

404): "Recognizing the intrinsic nature of the parts of some objects seems something that users of English manage to do without self-consciously conceptualizing it."

Abductive Processing of Features

Let us recall our working hypothesis that language, undefined though it be, underlies all semiosis. Accordingly, we seek the common denominator among the reflexes of these semantic primitives in language, paralanguage, music, and architecture. It is precisely the processing of these shared features which can be broadly referred to as an Innateness theory that links linguistic thought with Peircean thought. Postal (1966: fn. 10) argued that "... that relation between the semantic primitives and their combinations which are part of the combinatorial structure of language and the world is not learned but innate." Bierwisch (1970: 181) hypothesized that "... all semantic structures might finally be reduced to basic dispositions of the cognitive and perceptual structure of the human organism." Apropos of the nonlinguistic modalities, viz., music and architecture, let us bear in mind the observations of Warfield and Miller/Johnson-Laird (cf. above).

This innate ability (to process semantic primitives) expounded by Postal and Bierwisch may find an explanation in the theory of inference of Peirce (2: 444.n.l), who holds that ... the illative relation is the primary and paramount semiotic relation." According to Peirce we experience external objects as percepts and interpret them through a cognitive operation. All cognition involves inference and the type of inference which Peirce holds to be the most common kind of reasoning is *abduction*, whereby the minor premise is derived from the major premise and the conclusion (cf. "Abduction = Essential Preliminary Trigger," Chapter 19 below). Our first premises are perceptual judgments, viz., the formation of a mental proposition concerned with our sense experience when making a judgment. Peirce (5: 54) defines this innate manner of interpreting an experience or a perceived object as "... a judgment asserting in propositional form what a character of a percept, directly present to the mind, is." Meaning thus originates in the perceptual judgment, which may itself be regarded as an extreme case of abductive inference. The term "educated guess" closely approximates the abductive process, which Peirce claims is instinctive. Thus the interpretation of the primitive [L], e.g., as displayed in the various semiotic modalities, derives from one and the same innate ability of judgment and hypothesis formation, an ability which characterizes the semiotic modality of language. Compare Jakobson (1971: 708): "... only natural or formalized languages are able to generate, ... judgments, general and especially equational propositions." Once more we accept this statement contingent upon an adequate definition of language.

The [L] cognition then of the nonlinguistic modalities discussed here projects a language-inlay for those modalities.

Music
Major premise: Each of the twelve notes equals one beat.
Conclusion: E equals one beat.
Minor premise: Therefore, E is one of the twelve notes.

Architecture
Major premise: Maximal dimension equals the length.
Conclusion :   A equals the length.
Minor premise: Therefore, A is the maximal dimension.

Language
Major premise: *-er* adjectives equal 'more.'
Conclusion: (*long*)*er* equals 'more.'
Minor premise: Therefore, *longer* is an *-er* adjective.

Illation and the Signifying Animal

Let us return now to the definition of language. Liles' second reservation concerned the "purely human" qualification in the Sapir definition. To be sure, it is not difficult to find reflexes of the three semantic primitives in nonhuman communication. Consider the primitive [L] again. Sebeok (1972: 46–7) describes what we may discern as distinctions of [L] in the bee dance among six races of bees. The distance between the hive and the food source is calculated at six different [L]s in revolutions per fifteen seconds: Italian 7.95, Austrian 8.4, German 9.0, Punic 9.05, Caucasian 9.8, Egyptian 9.25. Sebeok observes that an encounter between, e.g., an Austrian bee and an Italian bee would therefore precipitate confusion of signals. The mystery question is, of course, why this confusion, or what strategy underlies this confusion, i.e., do the bees react to the primitive [L] or lack of it by any process emulating abductive inference, possibly what Chambers (1961: 49) terms "a rudimentary syllogistic movement"?

Current linguistic and psycholinguistic method remains adamant in divorcing animal from human communication; thus, e.g., O'Grady, Dobrovolsky, Aronoff (1993: 9) state: "There is every reason to believe ... that humans have a special capacity for language that is not shared by other creatures," and Kess (1976: 1) in his introductory psycholinguistics book reiterates : "The essence of human language, which distinguishes it from the communication systems of other animals, is the quality of abstraction." Perhaps, however, Chomsky's (1974: 54) insistence, for example, that "... a general theory of the human mind ... postulate a *language faculty* with special properties that are in part unique to it ...," could be pursued without necessarily placing it into opposition to his (1967: 73) admission that "... both [animal communication and human language] systems are propositional, syntactic, and purposive ..."

Significantly, this is achieved, at least by quasi-synthesis, in the work of some philosophers. Thus, e.g., Jonathan Bennett (1976: 11, 202–3), following Grice, holds that meaning is a type of intention, and he therefore reserves meaning for intending beings only, which excludes nonhumans. This is clearly in striking agreement with the Chomskyan definition of language which reads (1972: 115): "At the crudest level of description, we may say that a language associates sound and meaning in a particular way; to have command of a language is to be able, in principle, to understand what is said and to produce a signal with an intended semantic interpretation." How, then, does Bennett achieve a synthesis between "intention-dependent evidence" (human communication) and "display-dependent evidence" (nonhuman communication)? For Bennett the function of both human and nonhuman language behavior is to communicate; the control which intention effects in the former, natural selection effects in the latter, since according to Bennett (1976: 206, 205) "... individual intention is significantly like biological function."

In turn, Bennett's simile coincides with Peirce's own comparison of abduction to the instincts of animals for feeding and breeding; he declared with confidence (2: 754): "... all human knowledge, up to the highest flights of science, is but the development of our inborn animal instincts." In fact, Peirce even determined a syllogistic effect in the pinching of the hind legs of a decapitated frog, i.e., "... the way a decapitated frog reasons when you pinch his hind legs" (writes Fann

1970: 28). The internerve nerve habits are analogous to the major premise, the pinching is analogous to the minor premise, and the act of jumping is analogous to the conclusion.

Doubtless, for Peirce, man was first and foremost a "signifying animal." Sebeok heightens this realization even more when he writes (1977a: 1060): "Anthroposemiotic systems are always *marked*, in contradistinction to the zoosemiotic systems that comprehend them." Possibly, then, a viable working definition of language might be: Language is signifying through an illative-type process. While this definition transcends such moot questions as language ability, i.e., the possession of humans or of humans and nonhumans, and language behavior, i.e., a function of communication or of thought, it nevertheless invites exploitation of Blanshard's (1940: 91, 63) seminal idea that "... there is at work in the perceiving mind (of man, infant, ignorant man, and animals) an implicit universal."

7

The Narrative Inlay in Semiosis

While language is thus construed as signification via illation (cf. Chapter 6 above), illation or inference is instantiated in the concept of narrative, which finds refinement and applicability to both verbal and nonverbal semiosis in action theory.

Nonverbal Sign Theory

In the "anything goes" era of Paul Feyerabend (*Against Method*, 1978), it would seem that semiotists might content themselves to bask in the sun of the necessarily multimethodological input which channels into the theory of signs from innumerable disciplines (cf. Chapter 1 above). Once it is understood and accepted that semiotic method by nature can only be heterogeneous, the mirage of sought-after methodological uniformity will disappear. Such was the spirit of the special session on Theory and methodology in semiotics held at the Third Annual Meeting of the SSA (Providence 1978), with T. Sebeok, J. Umiker-Sebeok, J. Ransdell, N. Baron, and N. Bhattacharya participating. Similarly, Bouissac (1976: 381) attacks "The 'Golden Legend' of Semiotics," which seeks to anchor semiotic method in "... the diachronic listing of a hypothetical and highly selective genealogy." Eco, too (1978: 83), while affirming that semiotics meets the three requirements of a science, maintains that "... semiotics, more than a science, is an interdisciplinary approach—even though I could have also surreptitiously put forth the idea that it may be a sort of unified metatheoretical point of view governing a new encyclopedia of unified science."

It would seem, then, that the search for some sort of preconceived, uniform method is at an end. Interestingly, however, efforts to establish a nonhomogeneous semiotic method have taken the curious turn of singling out a scapegoat which is viewed alternately as a culprit and a casualty. Thus A. Lange-Seidl (1977: 25) writes: "We must ask ourselves ... if a sign theory determined by the model of linguistics could solve all the problems connected with signs, or could even begin to treat them." While not abandoning language theory outright ("The theorization of nonverbal signs on the one hand depends on language theory, on the other hand has to develop its own methods," 1977: 42). Lange-Seidl (9) holds that "... semiotists hesitate at recent developments in linguistics." Lange-Seidl (42) perceives the "develop[ment] of its own methods" in the "interdisciplinary connexions" of nonverbal sign theory and particularly in its "being absorbed into philosophical action theories." Accordingly, Lange-Seidl should welcome linguistic action theories, which are, in fact, relatively recent developments. On the one hand, she (24) writes of Searle's speech act theory that "... there is the risk that sign science attached to action would irreversibly reduce its descriptive phase for the benefit of action theories and that, thereby, sign science would lose distinctness and precision." On the other hand, Lange-Seidl (45, n.27) advocates the writing of an essay, "How to do things with signs," parallel to Austin's classic work.

Clearly, then, we are left floundering in the wake of Lange-Seidl's purported theoretical vacuum for nonverbal semiosis. Her parting thoughts to us stress once again intention, pragmatics, and action systems; however, a program for the implementation of these elements is not outlined in her 1977 volume. Let us consider the question: Is this purported vacuum a reality? Interestingly, current linguistic theory does indeed feed into a program for the implementation of intention, pragmatics, and action systems. The program is that of discourse analysis avidly pursued by A. J. Greimas and T. A. van Dijk, among others. Surprisingly, Lange-Seidl does not take a turn in their direction. In the following sections we propose to exploit linguistic discourse theory, in particular that of *narrative* relative to nonliterary narrative, in an effort ultimately to approach nonverbal signs via narrative theory.

Attitudes toward Narrativity

If in the course of applying, let us say, for a research grant, among the several directives such as providing information as to the type of aid requested, materials required, and the like, one is asked for a "narrative" or "narrative account" of the project, precisely what would be perceived under this requirement? That is, would one without hesitation proceed with a description of the research problem? Would it include background? Would it include working hypotheses and projected possible solutions? Or would the term narrative cause the researcher to pause and consider the felicity of the term "narrative" or "narrative account" vis-à-vis perhaps "lyric" or "lyric account" of the research project? If "lyric account" obviously strikes one as incongruous, why then is it possible to characterize nonliterary discourse as narrative? We propose to answer this question in order to proceed beyond nonliterary narrative and consider whether it is possible even to entertain a nonverbal narrative.

In seeking an answer to the application of narrative in a nonliterary context, we must peruse the existing options open to us in "narratology" (Genette 1972: 68). Time and again these emerge in the form of binary schools of thought, certainly a characteristic of linguistic method, but apparently also of the Western mode of thinking in general. Certainly Saussure's and Jakobson's linguistic concept of the basic signifying role of binary opposition underlies narratology; however, the latter-day linguistic return to narratology is prompted by an entirely separate catalyst, namely the linguistic recognition of the third component in the semiotic triad, pragmatics, that ingredient which transforms sentential grammar into discourse grammar.

The term *discourse* itself requires clarification; it, too, is variously defined (cf. below). Such a lack of terminological hygiene actually obviates a distinctive feature chart consisting of plus/minus features to characterize narratological schools. Thus, for example, Scholes' (1974: 157–58) distinction between "high structuralist" and "low structuralist" contrasts starkly with Doležel's (1976: 6) bifurcation of "functionalists" and "compositionalists." For Scholes, "high structuralist" somewhat vaguely embraces the capability of timeless, even dazzling philosophical/literary texts and includes such persons as Lévi-Strauss. "Low structuralist," on the other hand, serves as a reference (again somewhat vaguely) to those producing immediately useful but ultimately supersedable works and includes such persons as Propp. Doležel considers as "functionalists" those who posit a finite number of elements with a finite combinability for the plot of a text, and as "compositionalists" those who seek the Aristotelian concept of organization in the narrative action through such categories as exposition, complication, peripety, and catastrophe. Note well that in Doležel's scheme, Lévi-Strauss and Propp find themselves as bedfellows under the functionalist rubric.

On the other hand, Proppean functionalism is somewhat distinct from other divisions based on *function*. Language function, strictly speaking, refers to linguistic types such as statement, question, and command, which indeed come into play in narratology. At the same time, language function in semiotics as well as in narratology bespeaks rather the Jakobsonian (1971b: 703 and "Defining Language 2," (Chapter 6 above) functional dimensions: "'referential, emotive, conative, phatic, poetic, metalingual.'" Accordingly, van Dijk (1972a: 310) maintains: "The distinctions among types of texts are also derivable from their *functions* in a linguistic process of interaction. Thus, articles in a newspaper have 'informative' function, while literary texts are traditionally said to have 'esthetic' function." And Labov and Waletzky (1967) study "'referential'" and "evaluative" functions in oral narratives of personal experiences.

Finally Propp's function, linguistic function, Jakobson's, van Dijk's, or Labov and Waletzky's function differ in turn from Corti's use of function, which in essence restricts narrative to literary language. Corti writes (1978: 52):

> ... the mere application of linguistic grids in the examination of literary language misses its specific properties and sign-functions; in fact, if it is true that alliteration, rhythmic solutions, tropes, parallelism, etc., appear also in everyday language at the spoken level, what is lacking in these cases is the constructive, interrelated function that is typical of literary language.

The immediate observation here is Corti's distinction between literary and nonliterary language. Her coherence claim is taken up below.

In search of a definition of the narrative, we have thus far witnessed the repeated construction of binary options, viz. high structuralist versus low structuralist, compositionalist versus functionalist, plot function versus language function, and literary versus nonliterary. Let us mention one final bifurcation in schools of thought since it is so proximate to the literary versus nonliterary division, namely that of written versus oral data. Banfield (1978: 416–17) states: "It is writing which releases language from the communicative function and allows other functions of language to be apprehended in their pure form." We notice again the emphasis on function and its division into communicative versus the rest. Banfield continues: "If writing has its own laws, as many have recently claimed, then they are the principles of narration. These principles are not counterposed to those of language itself, but to those of the communicative function." Finally, she boldly states (448): "I define narration accordingly: an expression which may or may not contain a speaker, but which has no addressee/hearer" —a definition which cannot be reconciled with action theories. Before closing this survey of possible attitudes toward narrative, suffice it to say, we have hardly scratched the tip of the iceberg. So, for example, the very important use by Todorov-Barthes (*Communications* 8, 1966) of function as a subset of story could not even be skimmed here.

Narrative versus Nonnarrative

How then is the problem initially presented affected by the parameters of these several schools? That is, can they explain the use of narrative in the context of a research proposal? Most concrete is of course the opposition *oral* versus *written,* and unless this research proposal requires an oral defense the opposition is hardly directly interesting. *High structuralism* versus *low structuralism* appears somewhat ethereal and is, in a sense, immediately uninteresting. *Literary* versus *nonliterary* can be rather unambiguously decided with regard to standard research proposals if literature refers to the *belles lettres.* Jakobsonian language function sheds light on the narrative of the research proposal in that it is obviously cognitive or referential, delineating that function of language which transmits information—a very broad function which, to be sure, does not single out narrative, whatever it might be.

A more incisive parameter is provided by the pair *functional* versus *componential,* not, however, for the divergences of the two but rather for the shared implications proceeding from both their methods; in particular we refer to their common concern with the dichotomy of *narrative* versus *quotidian* language. Greimas, whom Doležel (cf above) would align with the functional school, insists (1971: 793): "Narrative structures are distinct from linguistic structures because they can be revealed by languages other than the natural languages (in cinema, dreams, etc.)." On the other hand, van Dijk, a so-called compositionalist, wrote in his *Some Aspects of Text Grammars* (1972b: 200): "All approaches to a definition of literature that try to reduce it to a specific 'use' of standard language or to a specific 'function' of language ... thus overlook the important fact that it is a *specific language-system, within a language L but different from L_N, describable by an autonomous but not independent grammar*." Van Dijk's 1972 formula thus reads $G_L - G_N = C$, where the Literary Grammar less the Nonliterary Grammar leaves the rules distinctive to literary. (Contrast van Dijk's support of function, cf. above and below). Finally, Crodian, in a talk entitled "Narratology" given at the Purdue Film Conference (March 1979), postulates as a point of departure for text typology the distinction *narrative* versus *nonnarrative,* which universal distinction "... is not yet sufficiently clear to allow the proposing of very rigorous hypotheses ..." but nevertheless is perceptible through "... our competence for a natural language," as are other "... universal constraints on narrative structure." In effect, this echoes van Dijk's claim (1972a: 298) that the "fundamental ability ... [of the native speaker] ... to differentiate the universe of texts and to recognize different types of texts ... is part of linguistic competence."

We propose now to challenge a *narrative : nonnarrative* distinction proceeding from natural language competence. The issue is not immediately one of competence versus performance or pragmatics, which Lyons (1977: 573) attempts to finesse by proposing a "communicative competence" to include contextualized sentences, of which linguistics is a part. Rather, the immediate issue is what makes narrative—narrative in this instance in the context of nonliterary discourse, e.g., a research proposal, and ultimately in nonverbal contexts. The answer which resounds in the literature as a quasi-leitmotif is *coherence*. Corti (cf. above), in pinpointing "the constructive, interrelated function" typical of literary language but lacking "in everyday language at the spoken level," intends coherence. She is obviously referring to coherence of what van Dijk calls macrostructure, i.e., the semantics of the entire text is its domain. This is in opposition to what van Dijk (1977) properly calls connectedness, which refers to microstructures in which sentences are related through immediate, linear transitions. Whereas connectedness is an alias for linguistic syntax, coherence is held by Doležel (1976) as well as Corti (1978) to have no reflex in language structure (cf. Mathiot below). As samples of global incoherence, van Dijk (1972a: 308), following Labov, cites "the discourse of small children or seniles ..." and as samples of global coherence he cites "... a narrative, a coherent dialogue or proof." Apparently, coherence in fact does not disambiguate narrative from non-narrative.

The return to the term discourse (cf. above and Chapter 8 below) is in order here, since van Dijk speaks (in 1972a) of the incoherent discourse of small children and seniles. Five years later (1977: 153) he claims that the condition of semantic coherence in macrostructures "... characterize(s) any discourse of natural language." Discourse for van Dijk is no longer inclusive of all utterances, but only those utterances possessing coherence. Contrast, however, discourse in narratology proper, where it is the second arm of a complex sign function, the first being the story (cf. Barthes-Todorov above), which is subdivided into functions and actions. Here discourse refers to Hjelmslev's expression plane, Saussure's signifier, where the focus is on a set of relations of time, aspects, and modes which the narrator uses to inform the reader. Not surprisingly, Greimas sides with van Dijk in his broader use of discourse. considering it as the primary datum in every text. Greimas (Greimas and Courtés 1976: 445) can thus speak of scientific discourse, as in the case of a research proposal; interpretive discourse, for example, art criticism; persuasive discourse, advertising; or literary discourse, a poem, short story, or novel. (Compare Eco's [1990: 124] "double jeu" of story and discourse.)

Action Theory and Inferential Structure

What is surprising, however, is that van Dijk's *discourse* is parallel rather with Greimas's *narrative*. Consider Greimas' oft-repeated conviction that "every discourse entails a narrative dimension" (Nef 1977: 19), as well as his (Greimas 1977: 29) propositional formula for a minimal narrative utterance, $NU = F(A)$, which parallels van Dijk's (1972a: 307) "... textual deep structures ... presumably similar to the internal structure of proposition in a modal predicate logic." Not only do Greimas and van Dijk overlap in their natural language propositional base (function: actant, relation: argument, predicate : subject), but both are engaged in identifying global modalities, a cofundamental natural language parameter. In fact, Alan R. White, in his book *Modal Thinking* (1975: 1), quotes the medieval logician William of Shyreswood, who characterizes a modal statement as being one which "says how the predicate inheres in the subject." Van Dijk (1977) works with mental structures of action such as wants, desires, intentions. and purposes, and he exploits speech act theory to characterize discourse macrostructure, thus yielding macro speech acts or global speech acts. Analogously, Greimas (as quoted in Doležel 1976: 6) works with the global role of modalities in which "A modal category takes charge of the content of the message and organizes it by establishing a certain type of relationships [sic] between the constituent linguistic objects." For narrative structures he (Greimas and Courtés 1976: 443) postulates three "*modalities* of doing: volition-to-do, cognition-to-do, and power-to-do." Doležel (1976), building on Greimas's categories and employing the logical modal systems alethic (possibility); deontic (permission, obligation); axiological (goodness, badness, indifference); and epistemic (ignorance, belief), maintains that stories can be based on a single modality. Compare now van Dijk's (1977: 243) claim that "... one of the bases for distinguishing different types of discourse, such as narratives or advertisements, is the possibility of assigning one, simple or complex, macro-speech act to the production of such a discourse." In effect, then, van Dijk could identify narrative; he would achieve this ultimately through function, since speech acts are in a narrow sense language functions (cf. van Dijk above).

Van Dijk's narrative, then, is more felicitously called "story," while his use of discourse approximates Greimas' use of narrative. Greimas' instinct that narrative underlies all discourse should be understood as a component of discourse, not isolable in itself, but consisting of features such as propositional macrostructures and modalities. To these fundamental features we might add another global category of natural language which we call *inferential structure*. Inferential structure would hold that macro-structure emulates essentially the way we think, our basic tripartite thought process consisting of a general proposition, a specific proposition, and a conclusion. Thus a story's construction (orientation, complication, evaluation, and/or resolution) is inferential, just as is a research proposal's construction (introduction, problem, and solution).

Greimas's narrativity, by its ready inclusion of the use of "narrative" with respect to nonliterary discourse, i.e., a research proposal, can be seen to encompass a broader scope than Genette's "narratology" (cf. above); the two terms should clearly not be considered as being synonymous. As we proceed through narrative toward its possible application to nonverbal signs, Mathiot's provocation (1979; cf. "Defining Language—1," Chapter 3 above) that "discourse is not a part of language" appears less and less shocking. To be sure, discourse is not only a part of language, but of other phenomena as well. As van Dijk (1977: 245–246) observes: "... conventional organizations of discourse ... [parallel those] of the corresponding speech acts, *and of action in general*" (italics mine). There can be no doubt then that Greimas' narrativity as a "semiotique de l'action" (Courtés 1976: 15) will include nonverbal signs. Documented examples of action as narrative exist in the literature; consider, for example, the "micro-narrative act" of the circus pony that emulates a Lippizaner, as described by Bouissac (1977: 150). Narrativity is universal to action; it necessarily follows that a narrative: nonnarrative opposition (cf. above) is impossible.

We have not been concerned throughout our discussion with defining the term *nonverbal*. Sebeok (1977a: 1067) voices the general despair of delimiting this term when he writes:

> ... it would hardly be an exaggeration to claim that the range of the 'nonverbal' ... becomes coincidental with the entire range of culture exclusive of language yet further encompassing much that belongs to ethology. But this way of looking at 'nonverbal' seems to me about as helpful as the Kugelmass theories reported by Woody Allen ...

This chapter was written without insisting on a definition of nonverbal; Lange-Seidl (1977, cf. above) apparently assumes tacitly that her readers are able to recognize nonverbal signs. Analogous to the successful use of incompletely understood concepts in the natural sciences, e.g., the atom, the use of the concept of nonverbal sign in semiotics is productive without explicit definition. But more importantly, analogous to the atom, the nonverbal sign is fundamental to life, in this instance to communicative experience.

8

Narrative Configurated
with Text and Discourse

It is necessary to test whether *narrative* construed as action, specifically propositional macrostructure, modalities, inferential structure (cf. "Action Theory and Inferential Structure," Chapter 7 above), can be sustained in configuration with its oft occurring syntagmatic partners *text* and *discourse*. Not infrequently these three terms are found in commutation for one another. We test them empirically in reference to a citation from Wittgenstein.

Dictionary Definition

Wittgenstein writes in a letter to Ludwig von Ficker (von Wright 1969: 5): "My work consists of two parts: the one presented here plus all that I have not written. And it is precisely the second part that is the important one." Could this quotation be used successfully in the application of the words *text*, *discourse*, and *narrative*, which are current in the research of several disciplines including semiotics, linguistics, and literature? Confronted by this question we immediately appeal to *Webster's Third New International Dictionary of the English Language* (1964: 647, 1503, 2365–6) for possible clues in the disambiguation of these concepts:

> DISCOURSE n 1 archaic a: the act, power, or faculty of thinking consecutively and logically: the process of proceeding from one judgment to another in logical sequence: the reasoning faculty: RATIONALITY b: the capacity of proceeding in an orderly and necessary sequence 2 obs: progression of course esp.

of events: course of arms: COMBAT 3a: verbal interchange of ideas; often: CONVERSATION b: an instance of such exchange 4a: the expression of ideas; esp: formal and orderly expression in speech and writing b: a talk or piece of writing in which a subject is treated at some length usu. in an orderly fashion 5 obs a: power of conversing: conversational ability b: ACCOUNT, NARRATIVE, TALE c: social familiarity; also: familiarity with a subject 6 linguistics: connected speech or writing consisting of more than one sentence.

NARRATIVE n 1 Scots law: the part of a document containing the recitals; specif.: the part of a deed immediately following the name and designation of the grantor reciting the inducement for making it 2: something that is narrated (as the account of a series of events): STORY, NARRATION 3: the art or study of narrating 4: the representation in painting of an event or story or an example of such a representation.

TEXT n la (l): the original written or printed words and form of a literary work (2): an edited or emended copy of the wording of an original work b: a work containing such text 2a: the main body of printed or written matter on a page exclusive of headings, running title, footnotes, illustrations, or margins b: the principal part of a book exclusive of the front and back matter c: the printed score of a musical composition 3a (l): a verse or passage of scripture chosen esp. for the subject of a sermon or for authoritative support (2): a passage from an unauthoritative source providing an introduction or basis (as for an essay, speech, or lecture) b: something providing a chief source of information or authority c: TEXTBOOK 4a: TEXT HAND b: a type considered suitable for printing running text 5a: a subject on which one writes or speaks: THEME, TOPIC b: the form and substance of something written or spoken 6: the words of something (as a poem, libretto, scriptural passage, folktale) set to music.

We may conclude, but not with much conviction, that perhaps Wittgenstein's written words are primarily *text*, his unwritten words primarily *discourse*, and his letter a type of *narrative*. The immediate effect of this conclusion, however, is a mental jolt into the reality of the terminological pollution in which we find ourselves in the burgeoning field of an act of verbal behavior, regardless of our particular research discipline. In particular, text is interchanged with discourse, and discourse is confused with narrative. The problem of their distinction is not trivial, if it concerns relevant conceptual differences. The purpose of this chapter is to ascertain whether, in fact, there exist cogent reasons for maintaining these three terms as independent concepts; if there are such cogent reasons we are witnessing the rapid evolution of a semantic set.

Text and Discourse

It appears undeniable that at least at some time in the history of two of these terms they reflect European versus North American wording. Certainly the use of text in the "text linguistics" of Wolfgang Dressler (1973) rings with greater familiarity to the European ear, while the use of discourse in Zellig Harris's (1952) "discourse analysis" possibly accounts for the currency of the latter term in North American. In brief, there may exist a layer of purely English versus, in particular, German labeling of this discipline called variously text or discourse linguistics or grammar. With that disclaimer, we can turn to the definition of the first of these terms, text. Our working hypothesis is then that there is indeed a terminological distinction to be found in the set *text/discourse/narrative.*

Isenberg (1970: 1) defines text as "eine kohärente Folge von Sätzen, wie sie in der sprachlichen Kommunikation Verwendung finden." Petöfi (1973: 205) writes: "The term next will refer ... to a sequence of spoken or written verbal elements functioning as a single whole, which is qualified according to some (mostly extralinguistic) criterion as being a 'text.'" These two definitions rest on underlying coherence conditions in determining text. Alternately, Gülich/Raible and Hartmann understand text as a supersign. Gülich/Raible (1977: 40–1) write: "Ein Text, allgemein gesagt, ein sprachliches Zeichen, und zwar das primäre (bzw. originäre) sprachliche Zeichen. Dieses primäre sprachliche Zeichen ist seinerseits aus weniger umfangreichen, hierarchisch niedrigeren sprachlichen Zeichen aufgebaut ... Texte [werden] nicht in der Art einer 'linguistique de la parole' betrachtet, weil sowohl ihre konstitutiven Elemente als auch ihre konstitutiven Regeln auf der Ebene der Langue erfaßt werden." Hartmann's (1971: 10) definition reads: "Der Text, verstanden als die grundsätzliche Möglichkeit des Vorkommens von Sprache in manifestierter Erscheinungsform, und folglich jeweils ein bestimmter Text als manifestierte Einzelerscheinung funktionsfähiger Sprache, bildet das originäre sprachliche Zeichen."

The above definitions underscore two widely held parameters of text: *coherence* and *supersign*; however, they make no mention of discourse. In these definitions it is nonexistent as a separate entity. In fact Dressier (1973: 12) defines text as "die höchste sprachliche Einheit" equal to English *discourse*, French *discours*, Italian *discorso*, Russian *tekst*. We need then to turn to those discussions that utilize both words. Halliday (1978: 108–9) defines text as "the instances of linguistic interaction in which people actually engage: whatever is said or written, in an operational context, as distinct from a citational context like that of words listed in a dictionary." Halliday's use of discourse appears synonymous with that of text. The text is realized in the context of a theoretical sociolinguistic construct called "situation," which is identified in three parts: (a) what is actually taking place, (b) who is taking part, (c) what part the language is playing (109–10). In his 1964 *The Linguistic Sciences and Language Teaching*, Halliday, along with McIntosh and Strevens, calls the three components of the situation "field of discourse," "style of discourse," and "mode of discourse," respectively. In his 1978 book *Language as a Social Semiotic: The Social Interpretation of Language and Meaning*, Halliday does not insist on the use of field, style (now "tenor"), and mode in a collocation with discourse. Instead he emphasizes how they are determinants of the text (1978: 122, 110). Aside from the above collocations, Halliday has two instances in his 1978 book in which discourse is used in a rather general concrete sense: to explain that text is not a supersentence (109) and to attribute genre to each text (134). Consequently, the most we can perceive in Halliday's two unqualified uses of the term discourse is that discourse is the raw material of text.

Van Dijk in his 1977 *Text and Context: Explorations in the Semantics and Pragmatics of Discourse* quite clearly recognizes two separate entities in text and discourse. He writes (3): "utterances should be reconstructed in terms of a larger unit, viz. that of TEXT [which] denote[s] the abstract theoretical construct underlying what is usually called a DISCOURSE." Discourse, on the other hand, van Dijk (5) considers "as a sequence of linearly ordered *n*-tuple of sentences" constrained by semantic and pragmatic rules which differentiate it from composite sentences. For van Dijk then, text is a theoretical unit, while discourse has linguistic flesh and blood—an attitude which somewhat supports the supersign or *langue* concept of Gülich/Raible and Hartmann above. Instead of text linguistics, Gülich (1970) speaks of macrosyntax in dealing with the text, whereas Halliday (1978: 135) insists that text is a semantic concept, not merely a supersentence.

Evidence from psycholinguists points to no distinction in text and discourse, but to a division between syntax and semantics. Frederiksen, in an article entitled "Semantic Processing Units in Understanding Text" (1977: 66), distinguishes "between semantic units (such as events) and textual units (such as sentences)." Frederiksen seems to equate text production with discourse production. Frederiksen, who holds that text structure reflects knowledge structure (57), postulates three decision levels for what he labels alternately the process of text generation or discourse production. From the propositional network or the "message domain," a textual message is chosen. This message or propositional knowledge is selected through memory search and pragmatic decisions; it results in level one, the "message base." To the message base the speaker or writer applies decisions about sequence, topicalization, reference, and correspondence between semantic and textual units, yielding level two, the "text base." To the text base the speaker applies decisions of sentence structure to yield "a sequence of grammatical sentences (text)" (67). Similarly, Hurtig in "Toward a Functional Theory of Discourse" (1977: 101) holds unequivocally that "the sentence is the largest linguistic unit whose structure is syntactic." Hurtig uses the word text only in the equivalence "text or discourse" (99); he strongly favors the view that sentence grammars deal primarily with syntactic constituents, while discourse grammars are concerned mainly with semantic, logical, or cognitive constituents (102). The text or discourse itself is "a string of successive sentences ... (which] can be monologues, dialogues, or multiperson interchanges ... [and have] topical or logical structure" (90).

To summarize thus far, the two psycholinguistic studies employ text or discourse interchangeably to designate a physical set of related sentences which comprise a linguistic message. They hold that the explanation of text or discourse requires the so-called interactionist theory of linguistic behavior, which is based on the interaction of formal linguistic grammar with the principles of perception and production outside the grammatical system. This position is supported also by linguists such as Bever, Katz, and Labov in opposition to the so-called inclusive theory, which holds that the separation of grammatical facts from linguistic but nongrammatical facts is arbitrary and intuitively unmotivated. Halliday would support the psycholinguistic conventions. Van Dijk's notion of discourse approximates the psycholinguistic / Halliday attitude toward discourse or text, while his notion of text appears closer to that of Gülich/Raible and Hartmann's supersign.

The viewpoint of the *littérateur* opens yet other windows on our discussion of text. In particular our horizons are broadened by theories such as those of the Soviet School (e.g., Lotman, Uspensky), which consider texts as comprising a system of many and varied interconnected modalities that is tantamount to culture (cf. Shukman 1976, Baran 1976). However, within literature narrowing trends exist, for example, that of Marie-Laure Ryan (1979), who prefers to study a literary system in terms of rules instead of in terms of signs, maintaining that the linguistic sign is limited to the lexicon. Ryan is intent, as are most literary theorists, on determining the dichotomy between literary and non-literary texts. She is convinced that the opposition between literature and non-literature should be studied with a focus on typology, which includes genre theory. Her premises are that genre applies only to a text and a text is a self-sufficient linguistic utterance. She illustrates her thesis by maintaining that conversation, for example, is a type of discourse but not a type of text. Thus for Ryan (1979: 311) text must be governed by "global requirements and conditions of coherence" (cf. Isenberg, Petöfi above). Such coherence is lacking in the case of conversation since, Ryan (1979: 311) claims, "real-life dialogues" are comprised merely of "a loose linear concatenation of sentences ... not preventing speakers from changing topics and interrupting each other." The distinction here, then, between text and discourse is that the former always falls within genre theory. Observe, however, that Ryan's view of conversation is in stark contrast with that of Halliday; recall that in one of the two uses of discourse (above) Halliday states (1978: 134): "there is generic structure in all discourse, including the most informal spontaneous conversation." For Halliday conversation can qualify indiscriminately as text or discourse; for Ryan it can only be discourse, not text. In some anthropological circles the term text appears to be shunned altogether. Thus, for example, Butterworth (1978: 321) simply speaks of "a piece of conversational behavior," and Mathiot (1978: 203, 217) refers to language as but one possible ingredient of "communicative episodes" (cf. "Defining Language—1," Chapter 3 above).

Nevertheless, Halliday does consider the possibility of *non-text*. He postulates three factors to designate text in opposition to non-text. Besides generic structure and the commonly held cohesion principle, Halliday speaks of textual structure, that is, thematic and informational patterns which contribute to the well-formedness of the texture. He demonstrates (1978: 134) that the thematic structure is scrambled in the following, and consequently it is a non-text:

> Now comes the President here. It's the window he's stepping through to wave to the crowd. On his victory his opponent congratulates him. What they are shaking now is hands. A speech is going to be made by him. 'Gentlemen and ladies. That you are confident in me honours me. I shall, hereby pledge I, turn this country into a place, in which what people do safely will be live, and the ones who grow up happily will be able to be their children.'

Ryan (1979), in turn, identifies two sorts of texts in literature which do *not* have coherent logico-semantic representations; the one is nonsense poetry, the second is what *littérateurs* have come to label simply as "text," which refers to *avant-garde* literature well-formed at the sentence level, but ill-formed at the sentence concatenation level. If nonsense poetry and *avant-garde* "text" can qualify as text, then it would seem reasonable that sentence sequence sets of schizophrenics, seniles, or small children should likewise qualify as text. Van Dijk (1972: 308) would exclude these on the basis of lack of semantic coherence. Consider, for example, the following "representative of 'schizophrenic language'" as cited by Lorenz (1961: 604):

> Contentment? Well uh, contentment, well the word contentment, having a book perhaps, perhaps your having a subject, perhaps you have a chapter of reading, but when you come to the word 'men' you wonder if you should be content with men in your life and then you get to the letter T and you wonder if you should be content having tea by yourself or be content with having it with a group or so forth.

The passage appears less grammatically scrambled than Halliday's "non-text" citation above. Whether we would judge it as necessarily schizophrenic, had we seen it in isolation, is an open question. Lorenz would answer the question with a qualified affirmative; she writes (603): "We are faced with the paradox that while we recognize schizophrenic language when we see it, we cannot define it." But Brown (1973: 400) tells us "that only some of the linguistic productions of schizophrenics appear disorganized or deluded; very many do not" (cf. "Medicine and Linguistics," Chapter 9 below). In view of the qualifying of nonsense poetry and *avant-garde* literature as text and in view of the inability of linguistics to define satisfactorily pathological language, it appears that the coherence condition requires revision to embrace texts which do not pass the standard coherence test.

Returning to Lotman, non-text occurs "the moment when a simple fact of linguistic expression ceases to be perceived as sufficient for a linguistic message to become a text" (cited in Rewar 1976: 362–3) in its stead the cultural "text" emerges. Barthes (1971, 1968) prefers to speak of more or less text in which text represents the new. By text he means not so much a positive object with well-marked boundaries, but more a methodological field, a syntagm, a chain of meaning. Again text becomes a very broad concept in the hands not so much of the *littérateurs* Lotman and Barthes, but of the semiotists Lotman and Barthes.

Text = First, Discourse = Second, Narrative = Third

In chapter 7 (above), it became amply clear that the concept *narrative* is not bound to literary language, written language, or even to language in its ordinary sense. Let us now bring it into configuration with *text* and *discourse* by reverting to the initially quoted Wittgenstein statement and the *Webster's Third* definitions. Faced with having to pit the Wittgenstein quotation against the three dictionary entries, our initial intuitions yielded no strong prejudices in assigning Wittgenstein's written words, unwritten words, and letter. In fact, the original task appeared unfruitful since the dictionary senses of the three terms do not strike individually discriminating tones. As the dictionary compilers warn of their definitions (*Webster's Third* 1964: 19a): "The system of separating [the sense] by numbers and letters ... is only a lexical convenience. It does not evaluate senses or establish an enduring hierarchy of importance among them. The best sense is the one that most aptly fits the context of an actual genuine utterance." Yet the dictionary glosses of "ideas" for discourse may have influenced its assignment to unwritten words, namely, the whole world of Wittgenstein's thoughts, while text and narrative fell then to the more concrete written words and letter, the former having appeared more general and accordingly more appropriate to the seemingly wider latitude offered by the many dictionary glossings of text.

Such floundering in terminological uncertainty, however, is entirely absent in the evolving usage which we document in the cross-disciplinary applications of text, discourse, narrative for acts of verbal and verbal-like behavior. Albeit the parameters we are seeking are similar, the terms shift considerably. At its simplest the following distinctions hold to bind the emerging semantic set:

	text	**discourse**	**narrative**
physical	+	±	
abstract	+		±
	(*letter*)	(*written words*)	(*unwritten words*)

Compelling arguments for this evolving triad come from Peircean semiotics. Here all phenomena, including language, action, and thought, are signs; indeed man himself is a sign, to quote Sebeok (1977: 181): "man is ... a process of communication ..., or, in short, a *text*" (emphasis mine). Beyond this, however, the glue for cementing this semantic set resides in Peirce's phenomenological categories of *Firstness, Secondness*, and *Thirdness*, into which we can set *text* as a First, *discourse* as a Second, and *narrative* as a Third. Alternately, text is the sign proper, discourse is the object, and narrative is the interpretant within Peirce's classic definition (1: 339): "A sign [text] stands FOR something [discourse], TO the idea [narrative] which it produces or modifies." The qualities of the categories serve to reinforce the assignment of the terms. Thus, a letter is mere possibility and belongs to the past, written words exist in fact and are part of the present, while unwritten words have imputed existence and belong to the future thought. That these qualities interlace is to be expected, since that factor is inherent in all phenomena; nonetheless, their primary qualities serve to identify them distinctively. What remains of the features reviewed above such as syntax: semantics; sign: rule; genre: non-genre; coherence: incoherence; text: non-text; more text: less text; normal language: pathological, child and senile language is relegated to connotative senses in the evolving set of definitions within a study which is then most graphically (iconically) termed *text grammar* (cf. "narrative grammar" Bal 1997: 12). The reduction to the given set of binary features distinguishing *discourse* from *narrative* accords well with Eco's (1990: 124) "*discourse*" and "fabula," respectively, which he confirms are "difficult to isolate" (cf. Chapter 7 above).

9

Protosemiotic

The understanding of the language-inlay, the narrative inlay (cf. Chapter 6, 7, 8 above) in all semiotic modalities is, of course, most spectacular in the conceptualization of man as a "text" (cf. Sebeok 1977b: 181, cf. "Text = First, Discourse = Second, Narrative = Third," Chapter 8 above). The most fundamental and essential, indeed primeval, reading (meaning) of what we can term the human text, the "signifying animal," is based in medicine.

Medicine

Historically medicine has been synonymous with semiotic. Human beings themselves, i.e., their wellness/illness as signaled by signs, has always been a hermeneutic endeavor entailing a symptom, its object, and ill meaning. The behavior of and by the body of the human being, which includes the mind, thus signifies the well-being or equilibruim of the human and their ill-being or the non-equilibrium. Histories of medicine attest to a folklore in which the first doctors regarded the being of a diseased person without exclusivity for either physical or for the mental sign, i.e., the whole being, body and soul, was under diagnosis or interpretation; this speaks to "psychosomatic" medicine, in the truest sense of the word. Of course, it was not understood until Galen (second century BC) that the brain and not the heart was the seat of the soul. Still, what is crucial to note in speaking of the equilibrium of a human being is not only the felicitous integration of the mind/body dichotomy, but also the game strategies evoked by the concept of equilibrium which speak to a continuous interplay of many factors in the maintenance/breakdown of that equilibrium (recall the

Saussurean chessboard; (cf. "Physics' Law and Biology's Growth," Chapter 2 above).

These many factors which are in the purview of medicine are indicated by qualification of the medical leg of the semiotic tripod as the "admittedly uneven leg upon which semiotic rests, very likely the most deeply rooted" (Sebeok 1976: 181). Thus, Schwarz and Wiggens (1985: 352) are unable to incorporate medicine into their "hierarchy of pure sciences" which, on an ever ascending scale of "abstraction and precision" include the (1) social sciences (sociology, political science, anthropology, economics) (2) social psychology, (3) psychology, (4) biology, (5) chemistry, (6) physics. They write: "Doctors draw on the methods and conceptualizations of many sciences in order to develop those theories and techniques that are peculiar to medicine. Medical science remains, as a result, a multiplicity-in-unity that is forever fluid and subject to change and extension." (353) Clearly, medicine is not an even leg with philosophy and linguistics in a semiotic tripod. Medicine as protosemiotic represents a difference in kind; it is rather the notch joining multipods of which it is a part. However, it is not to be construed as the parent to all sciences. In the sections below, representative studies displaying the interchange of medicine as semiotic is presented, with but four of many related arts and sciences. Immediately, however, the focus is on the medical sign or symptom.

Symptom

Symptomatology, in some cultures designated "semeiology" (Sebeok 1976: 181) concentrates on the symptom as sign. It was Galen, as well, who recognized that a symptom in one part of the body does not necessarily signal that that specific part of the body is the diseased part. Accordingly, the chessboard metaphor (cf. above) is fitting (a move in one part of the system can effect a move in another part of the system) and the possible non-isomorphic, i.e., non-iconic fit between sign and object is thereby demonstrated. Indeed, symptoms such as irregular pulse or fever act indexically, i.e., they are indicative of a malady while not being the malady itself. If, however, a symptom is indicative of an array of maladies, it is polysemous, Finally, if the regulation between the symptom and the disease is arbitrary, the symptom is a symbol.

The symptom as a *terminus technicus* refers to subjective evidence given by the diseased subject, while sign as a *terminus technicus* is the objective evidence observed by the physician to corroborate the claimed symptom, the former equal to Baer's "introspective" sign and the latter to Baer's "intersubjective" sign (1975: 173). The composite signs are technically termed syndrome, which is integral to the patient disease history (anamnesis), patient disease determination (diagnosis), and patient disease prediction (prognosis). The three Galenian interpretive processes in symptomatology speak to Peircean *Firsts*, *Seconds*, and *Thirds*, i.e., past, present, and future, respectively. Although in the thinking of Freud (1926: 87) a symptom "actually denotes the presence of some pathological process," in today's medicine, which is attuned to wellness and preventive medicine, a sign such as a regular heartbeat also qualifies as a symptom. Similarly, the terminological subjective/objective distinction is frequently neutralized in current medical scenarios. A modification of this last point is offered by such counter-examples as discussed by Shands and Meltzer (1977), in which the subjective symptoms are corroborated by no apparent objective signs—a pathological sinsign in itself.

Meaning

The hermeneutic in medical semiosis is central (cf. "Medicine and Psychology," below). Throughout history Hippocrates' aphoristic insight that "Our natures are the physicians of our diseases" has stimulated far-reaching implications. We understand that the meaning of a syndrome is to be detected within the self through Thure von Uexküll's definition (1984: 27): "An organism is a system whose needs determine a code that enables it to interpret environmental (Umwelt) effects in a specific way and to act appropriately. Effects, interpretation, and reaction in the system-theoretic approach can be related to sign, interpretant and object in Peircean semiotics." Clearly, the illness/wellness scenario is one of the interaction of self/nonself, in that "the self and the universe are reciprocals" (Shands and Meltzer 1977: 89). This reciprocity for the "signifying animal" is aptly displayed by Uexküll's theory of autoambience (cf. "Medicine and Biology," below) and Thom's grip catastrophe (cf. "What is Language," Introduction above).

A symptom is a member of a communicative code or system just as linguistic sign; it has form and content, the latter subject to known semantic features such as ambiguity, polysemy, sense, and reference. Staiano (1979: 111) designates a symptom as "a form of cultural expression ... a behavioral act ... an interactional maneuver employed in a situation in which other forms of communication may have failed or are considered inappropriate." Thus, the meaning of an irregular pulse may refer to any number of coronary ailments, or, indeed, to other somatic or psychological abnormalities.

The hermeneutic task in psychological abnormalities frequently appears particularly non-iconic and non-indexical. Shands and Meltzer thus observe (1977: 80) that "the core of all the problems which human beings have in their relations with each other is to be found in the specific human method in which meaning is implicit in consensus—without being 'rooted' in any 'objective' context." Although Shands and Meltzer address psychiatric disorders, it is clear that their definition extends to somatic disorders as well, which can be medically, and/or culturally, and/or linguistically polysemous.

Self

The symptom unites the meaning of the self and the nonself. The discussion of self can actually not be divorced from that of meaning in symptomatology. It is a leitmotif of medicine that "the self and the universe are reciprocals" (Shands and Meltzer, cf. above). This refers unambiguously, as was said at the outset, to the main actor in medicine, the body and the mind. Earlier (1970: 250) Shands had written: "... the self appears to be a development, emerging in a particular epoch in time ... The eventual form of the self is that of a comprehensive symbol [sign] of the universe, reciprocally reflecting and representing the complexity of the universe." In point of fact, in Peircean terms, the triangulation of the self with the nonself shows the self to represent *Firstness*, the nonself *Secondness*, and the meaning that binds them, *Thirdness*. In the words of Baer (1982: 29) the *leitmotif* reads: "Self and world ... are mutual self-realizations governed by a single code. In other words: self and not-self together— and only together—are one sign ..." (cf. below).

A comprehensive definition of the self defies possibility. This is because many definitions of self appear deeply rooted in specific cultures. Yet, such a statement, on the nature of the Chinese self, as that of Chu (1985: 272) reads quite general. "The self is conceptualized as a configuration of roles expressed in self—other expectations and observable self-other interactions." Bharat (1985: 226) speaks of "a self that is 'dividual' rather than individual" in defining the Hindu metaphysical self or *atman*. This eastern focus of self is repeated in Devos' (1985: 179) observation: "The Japanese sense of self is directed toward immediate social purposes, not toward a process of separating out and keeping the self somehow distinct, somehow truly individual, as remains the western ideal."

Interestingly, the strong individualism imputed to the concept of the western self is not obvious in Johnson's (1985: 129–30) defining characteristic of self:

> (a) ... *self is a social construction which is symbolically and signally created* between and among social beings ... (b) ... *a phenomenological object which can be productively studied through a series of evanescent actions* ... (c) ... most of these theories of self are *situational and capable of study in naturalistic settings* ...

Note especially characteristic (d): "... *the self is no longer regarded as a unitary phenomenon* that is, as an encapsulated, individual variable." Remaining features of Johnson read:

> e) Since the self is *intersubjective and is seen in the phenomenological contexts of actual encounters,* its manifestations take the form of *communication* ... (g) The self is simultaneously *seen as a phenomenal and nonphenomenal* ... (h) ... self acquires substance according to *semantic* (definitional, etymological), *syntactic* (grammatical and logical), and *pragmatic* (extralinguistic and gestural) meanings present in communication.

We recognize here the Morrisean components of semiotics (cf. Posner on Morris," Chapter 10 below).

Johnson's deletion of his characteristic (f), "While the self is primarily a social (i.e., non-corporeal) concept, it is *intimately connected to bodily experience* ..." in his later (Johnson 1989) summary of these defining characteristics points to, in fact, the body/mind unity in medicine, in the truest sense of the term psychosomatic. The self, then, shares or partakes of features (at least some) not only from a universal somatic genetic code, but also from a universal psychological genetic code. Johnson's paradigm, in aiming at "communalities"

(1985: 129) reflects well possible characteristics of a semiotic self for medicine and its supporting arts and sciences.

Medicine and Biology

The semiotic paradigm of Jakob von Uexküll belongs to biology in a broad and unusual sense. It is his "Umweltforschung" or theory of autoambience, of which the principal presupposition holds that reality, made manifest in "Umwelten," appears as signs that are received and decoded by an organism's "Gemüt" or apperception, through natural laws. The self is psychophysically suited to its autoambience, the non-self, which, in turn, has its existence through the particular self, i.e., the autoambience is the sum of the self's own sensory perceptions. Uexküll explains by way of metaphor (1940: 61): "Das Körperhaus ist einerseits der Erzeuger der Bedeutungssymbole, die seinen Garten bevölkern und andererseits das Erzeugnis der gleichen Symbole, die als Motive in den Hausbau eingreifen." Fittingly, Uexküll's "Bedeutungslehre" describes the essential meaning, the psychosomatic signifying of a being.

For the functioning of the interchange in which the subject is also the object of its autopoietic world of meaningful signs, Uexküll hypothesizes a sensory motor model, his "Funktionskreis" (1940: 8–9). Central is meaning which unites two entities, the carrier of the object of the outer world, the nonself, and the user of the subject of the inner world, the self, into a sign. In this sensory motor model Uexküll shows how a meaning carrier consists of a perceptual feature carrier and a functional feature carrier, the function feature of the latter cancelling the perception feature of the former, and thus completing the cycle. A meaning user, in turn, consists of a perceptual organ and a functional organ. The perceptual organ transforms a perceptual sign, an elementary sensation of the receptor or sense organ, into a perceptual feature. Finally, the perceptual organ induces the functional organ to send a function sign to the effector, resulting in a function feature and the above mentioned completion of the cycle (cf. "Uexküll on Uexküll," Chapter 10 below).

Uexküll's biology, however, distinguishes plant from animal organisms; he claims that plants possess neither receptor nor effector organs (1910: 10). In view of the understanding of the genetic code , it is likely that Uexküll's paradigm requires modification. Indeed, Begley (1983: 72) reports the possibility of "a plant emitting a chemical signal that is perceived and acted upon by another ... ecologists believe that the trees' messages travel on the wind, although the chemical basis of the vocabulary has yet to be identified."

The essence of an Uexküllean view as a communicative system is, nevertheless, sound, and it is coherent with views such as Rubenstein's (1980: 102), that diseases can arise from "'faulty communication among cells." Rubenstein explains:

> Cells communicate with one another by releasing mediators that travel various distances, sometimes only to an adjacent cell and at other times through long journeys in the bloodstream to other parts of the body. The messages are picked up by the receptors, which relay the information to structures within the cell where the incoming signal triggers a biochemical response.

Certainly, the sophisticated communicative code with which the incoming signal (the nonself) and the cell (the self) interact represents most exciting insights in the composite field of biology and medicine today.

Medicine and Psychology

The interdisciplinary occupation with the self notwithstanding (cf. Johnson 1989: fn. 4), the self doubtless holds a very central place in psychotherapy. Since "psychiatry" is tantamount to "medicine" (recall that medicine is considered the protosemiotic, cf. "Medicine," above), psychotherapy, albeit through the eyes of the psychiatrist, Chinen, will here be subsumed under the rubric psychology, as a contributing field to medicine. More importantly, it is, in fact, the purpose of Chinen (1989: 227) to explicate "psychotherapy as a model of human understanding in general, using semiotic concepts for analysis." He notes "because both scientific and humanistic viewpoints converge so dramatically in it, the practice of psychotherapy offers an excellent, specific model of how the two perspectives relate."

Chinen holds that multiple modes of understanding are common to human experience generally, and that these modes each exhibit a differing logical modality indicative of a distinct relationship between a sign and its object. He concentrates in particular on four types of understanding, namely, diagnostic (or representational), empathic, instrumental, and intuitive. For his data, Chinen cites the case of a thirty-five year old teacher in therapy for depression pursuant to the collapse of an amorous relationship. The rejection/depression trauma may be exacerbated by childhood rejection and/or genetic sensitivity to depression.

According to Chinen, the diagnostic mode of thought is a scientific mode of understanding in which propositions are asserted to be true in an existential modality. Thus, e.g., the sign, in the case given, the teacher's depression, has reference to an actual situation or to occurrences in the teacher's life, e.g., childhood rejection. Since the proposition of the teacher's present depression (sign) represents a (previously) existing situation (object), the reference (interpretant) is of the diagnostic or representational mode. In ferreting out the symptoms of the depressed teacher, multiple signs can have the same referent, as *tokens* to a *type*. Since the representational mode of understanding is a scientific one, positivism would hold that it can be applied to any phenomenon, human and non-human alike.

Chinen's empathic mode, which he also calls hermeneutic, conveys the logical modality of possibility rather than that of existence. The sign, via the teacher's depression, is but possibly reminiscent of childhood rejection. *Firstness* is predominant in this semiosis, which Chinen demonstrates as coming about through daydream, game, free association. Unlike the representative mode, which aims at objective truth, the empathic mode in which (1989: 231–32) the "therapist endeavors to enter the experiential world of the patient" aims at mutual "consensus and agreement" in meaning, certainly less objective and more subjective (cf. "Meaning," above).

The instrumental mode of thought Chinen correlates with the logical modality of conditional assertion. It is pragmatic in that the truth (1989: 234) "is what 'works' in the long run in solving particular problems." Thus, e.g., at the risk of inciting further rejection, the therapist may attempt an assertion in which he suggests to the teacher that her depression results from the sense of her lover's rejection, which is reinforced by the sense of her childhood rejection. The attempt or conditional nature of the instrumental mode acts as instrument, in fact, to achieve a reaction on the part of the teacher in order to gain insight into the analysand's self. The pragmatic mode is humanistic and requires but one occurrence in contrast to the scientific representational mode of understanding, which requires multiple confirmation.

The intuitive mode of understanding is expressed in the logical modality of universal assertions. Such a universal about the teacher's syndrome is exemplified by Chinen in the proposition "All people feel depressed when rejected by their lovers, because that rejection reminds them of their parents' rejection." The sign refers to real, but indefinite objects in the intuitive mode. Indeed, Chinen holds that the intuitive mode of understanding takes place in an actual clinical speech situation, in which the therapist discerns no real sense of the analysand's self, his or her personal identity. In a state of suspended judgment and openness, the therapist intuits via a sign (kinesic, proxemic, verbal or a combination thereof) a subliminal feature of the analysand's experience that is crucial to the given psychotherapy. The intuitive mode of understanding is immediately cancelled by a switch to the representative mode of understanding. Since Chinen's tetramode paradigm refers to "human understanding in general" (cf. above), it applies to the cognitive processes of all humans at all times, i.e., in both the illness and the wellness states integral to medicine.

Medicine and Linguistics

In dealing with the field of linguistics vis-à-vis medicine, one would expect to study verbal scenarios between doctor and patient. This is, indeed, one facet of medical linguistics, found, e.g., in the work of Oksaar (1984). Linguistics also interacts with medicine in the investigation of pathological language. One of the relatively few studies of this latter type by a linguist is that of Chaika (1974), in which she concludes six linguistic features of schizophrenic language. They are (275):

> ... (1) sporadic disruption in the ability to match semantic features with sound strings comprising actual lexical items in the language (2) preoccupation with too many of the semantic features of a word in discourse ... (3) inappropriate noting of phonological features of words in discourse ... (4) production of sentences according to phonological and semantic features of previously uttered words, rather than according to topic ... (5) disruption in the ability to apply rules of syntax and discourse ... (6) failure to self-monitor, e.g., not noting errors when they occur ...

These features of schizophrenic language are refuted by Fromkin (1975), as not being specific to pathological language. Assessing the experimental work done in general in schizophrenic language and thought, Roger Brown observes (1973: 401–2; cf. "Text and Discourse," Chapter 8 above):

> There have been many attempts to describe the nature of the basic deviation in schizophrenia: concreteness, or overinclusion, or privateness in concept formation; overgeneralization in learning; paralogic in thinking; associative intrusions in language, a failure to filter what is irrelevant in attention, etc. ... The results seem to me generally disappointing in that they ... usually yield small, barely significant differences between schizophrenics and normals.

The humanistic interspersion of poetry amidst scholarly articles as can be found, e.g., in the journal *Perspectives in Biology and Medicine* 28 (cf. Schwartz and Wiggins 1985: 22.1; Engel 1985: 22.7) certainly is intriguing. As a type of anamnestic linguistic/medicine exercise (cf. "Symptom" above), let us consider the possibility of detecting evidence or symptoms in the language of a poet diagnosed as schizophrenic in 1933. The poet is the Swiss poet Robert Walser (1878–1956); the poem is "Van Gogh'" (1927; reprinted here from *Belege* 1978: 52–53; English translation mine):

        1 Der arme Mann
           es mir nun mal nicht antun kann.
           Vor seiner gröblichen Palette
           zerstreut in mir sich jede nette
        5 Aussicht ins Leben. Ach wie kalt
           hat er sein Lebenswerk gemalt!
           Er malte, scheint mir, nur zu richtig.
           Will jemand sich ein wenig wichtig
           vorkommen in der Ausstellung,
       10 so wird ihm bang vor solchen Pinsels Schwung.
           Schrecklich, wie diese Acker, Felder, Bäume
           einem des Nachts wie klob'ge Träume
           den Schlummer auseinanderreißen.
           Hochachtung immerhin vor heißen
       15 Kunstanstrengungen, beispielsweise

vor einem Bild, worin im Irr'nhauskreise
Wahnsinnige zu sehen sind.
Den Sonnenbrand, Luft, Erde, Wind
gab er ohn' Zweifel prächtig wieder.
20 Doch senkt man bald die Augenlider
vor so selbstquälerischer Stärke
in doch nur halbbefriedigendem Werke.
Zu grausen fängt's ein' an,
wenn Kunst nichts Schön'res kann,
25 als rücksichtslos ihr Müssen, Sollen, Wollen
vor schau'nden Seelen aufzurollen.
Wunsch, wenn ein Bild ich seh',
liebkost zu werden wie von einer güt'gen Fee,
geh, geh, adee!

1 The poor man
can't do that to me.
Before his coarse palette
every amiable view
5 of life is destroyed in me. Oh how coldly
he has pictured his life's work!
He paints, it seems to me, quite correctly.
Should someone consider himself a bit important
in the display,
10 anxiety overtakes him with such strokes of the brush.
Horrid, how these acres, fields, trees destroy
at night like boorish dreams
one's slumber.
Respect, nevertheless, for burning
15 artistic endeavors, for example,
for a painting, in which in an asylum
the insane can be seen.
Sunfire, air, earth, wind
he rendered without doubt beautifully.
20 Still one's eyes close
at the sight of such a tortuous force
in after all only half satisfying works.
One begins to shudder
when art can produce nothing better,
25 than its ruthless must, should, would

before observing souls.
Wish, whenever I see a painting
to be caressed as by a kind fairy;
go, go, adieu!

A well-known axiom of linguistic method states that the grammatical core of a text resides in its function words, or functors, and their relations to one another. Frequently the grammatical core is demonstrated by referring to the "Jabberwocky" of Lewis Carroll or the "Gruselett" of Christian Morgenstern, e.g., "Twas (brillig) and the (slith)y (tove)s did (gyre) and (gimble) in the (wabe)," and "Der (Flügelflagel) (grauster)t durchs (Wiruwaruwolz)," respectively, in which the non-bracketed items certainly convey relationships, not only meaningful, but necessary, i.e., obligatory (*Secondness*). Another group of words which contain functional elements are pronouns, since they may indicate case, gender, and number, but their relational power resides first and foremost in their deixis (*indexicality*). While the relationship of the functors is largely grammatical, that of the pronouns seems largely semantic, and, accordingly should be somewhat non-obligatory. In this way, pronouns would emulate content words or contentives, viz, those words with specific dictionary meaning, so, e.g., *Vogel* to follow *der* in the "Gruselett" fragment above.

Consider the opening sentence of Walser's "Van Gogh" *Der arme Mann es mir nun mal nicht antun kann.* The end-line rhyme aside. substitution of *Maler*, e.g. for *Mann.* or indeed of *Van Gogh* for *Mann*, or for as much as the entire phrase does not effect a relational change of the magnitude equal to that which occurs, let us say, when *mir* is replaced by *dem Dichter* or *Walser*. However, the change of *der arme Mann* to *Du* would be of equal magnitude. Obviously then, the person indicator of pronouns, although a function, represents a unique semantic force, and thus we can say it is obligatory to the semantic core of this particular text. It speaks to the self, to personal identity.

The hermeneutic of Walser's "Van Gogh" is self-referential. Walser's initial lament or quasi-accusation is very interpersonal (self and non-self at the outset) between *Mann* and *mir* (1. 2), less so between *seiner Palette* (1. 3) and *mir* (1. 4). With the shift of *mir* to *jemand* (1. 8), Walser conceals the fact that his "Van Gogh" poem is self-referential. He had written his editor that in composing the poem he was "conjuring up ghosts," naming Van Gogh "a terrifying magician." whose "repulsive, yet impressive, magnificent, yet painful manner" he sought to characterize (trans. from Machler 1971: 435).

Deepening interpersonalization via pronominal forms occurs with the continuation of *jemand* into *ihm* (1. 10) and *einem* (1. 12), *solchen* (Pinsels Schwung) (1. 10), and *diese* (Acker, Felder, Bäume) (1. 11). In addition the plurals (which are functors) of these last three nouns lead to a generalization of Van Gogh's paintings, and beyond, to nature and the cosmos as expressed in the unmodified *Sonnenbrand, Luft, Erde, Wind* (1. 18) disturbing and torturing the observer, him who regards the painting. Painting, artistic endeavors (*Kunstanstrengungen*) (1. 15), apparently limitless (plural, unmodified), have no personal object, no form of *man*. Painting, art (*Kunst*) (1. 24) becomes the absolute force (*ihr Müssen, Sollen. Wollen*) (1. 25). The *ich* reoccurs (1. 27) to close the poem by an escape of the subverted self into childlike fantasy. Van Gogh is last heard of, and sympathetically so, in line 19. By returning to *man*, i.e., *ein* in line 23, the painter is assimilated into the poet, indeed the observer. The self and nonself are indistinguishable as individuals. They lose their identity, subordinated by the ruthless demands of art (ll. 24–5).

The empathy-laden poem, Walser's vicarious experience with Van Gogh as artist, his "ability to 'be-with' a fellow human being" (Chinen 1989: 228), are confirmed independently in Walser's prose pieces which address Van Gogh's painting "Zu der Arlesierin von Van Gogh" (l912) and "Das Van Gogh-Bild" (1918). In the former, he refers to the *"Maler-Dulder"* ('painter-sufferer'), while in the latter Walser says *"daß man den Künstler zu bedauern habe"* ('that the artist is to be pitied') (Grevin 1971, v 6. 59, 337). Walser apparently speaks of several Van Gogh paintings in the poem, yet his identification of a *"Bild, worin im Irr'nhauskreise Wahnsinnige zu sehen sind"* ('a painting in which the insane are to be seen in an asylum setting') (ll. 16–17) presents the climax of his insights into the self of Walser and Van Gogh.

Particularly interesting for a linguistic reading of the Walser poem, in an effort to detect pathological speech symptoms is the work of Salinger, Portnoy, and Feldman (1978), who find that in experiments done on function words, in which they included English *and, but, of, for, to*, the language of schizophrenics is more predictable in low contexts then in high contexts, the reverse being true of the language of normals. They write (47):

This provides direct evidence for schizophrenic speech having interrelationships among words over short spans, although normal speech has such relationships over relatively long spans. Schizophrenic speech being more predictable than normal speech at low contexts suggests that those closer words are more closely related to one another than are the more remote words.

Coupled with the so-called Chapman Hypothesis which states that "... schizophrenics tend to rely on a word's strongest denotative meaning to the relative exclusion of its other, weaker meanings," a linguistic reading of the class *pronoun* is an ideal structure for understanding a short piece such as "Van Gogh" by a poet such as Walser. It hardly confirms, however, that Walser was schizophrenic.

Medicine and Anthropology

The search for biuniqueness, isomorphism (cf. "Peirce *qua* Linguist," Chapter 4 above) between a segment of speech and its meaning is no less the aim in the study of somatic symptoms than in the study of psychological symptoms. From the medically allied field of anthropology, Staiano provides fieldwork data which attest to the polysemy of symptoms (cf. "Meaning" above) in psychosomatic (body and mind) illness/wellness. The multiplication of meanings of medical signs is exacerbated by the non-commonality in the therapeutic enterprises of the doctors in the area. Staiano studied medical conditions in Punta Gorda in Central America's Belize (previously known as British Honduras). Among the Garifuna or Black Caribs of Punta Gorda, she identifies five types of doctors, all "'bush doctors' regardless of ethnic group or therapeutic role" (1981: 321–22: (a) A healer, a "herbalist or bush doctor or midwife who has learned his or her trade, almost always from a close relative." Healers make no claims to supernatural powers, although they are willing to treat patients who suffer from sorcery ("obeah"), (b) A dreamer-healer is a doctor (in the field case, a midwife) who, although she made no claim to supernatural powers, believes she receives inspiration in her dreams for the identification of medicine appropriate to a given malady. (c) A self-afflicted healer is a doctor who also dreams the appropriate medicine, but who herself suffers the illness she treats. (d) A gifted healer is a doctor who is ordained by birth to practice medicine. He is able to treat "obeah," and he is inspired by guiding spirits while awake and while dreaming. (e) A "buiai" is a healer who suffered illness as a youth, is possessed of supernatural powers "hiuruha" which, in fact, do the healing. Staiano notes (1981: 322): "Through the *hiuruha* of the *buiai* an individual may speak with his ancestors (*gubida*) and discover what it is they may desire. The *hiuruha* of the *buiai* may have information about past events no longer remembered by those living and they may be able to explain occurrences which otherwise appear inexplicable." The rite or ritual of healing, a "dogo," in preparation a year or longer, "lasts approximately three days with almost continuous dancing and drumming, [during which] the *buiai*, with the aid of his spirits, transmits the concerns and desires of the ancestors."

Beside the five healers, the Belize patient has the option to seek still another opinion from a biomedical doctor. The patient is not interested in reducing the possible readings of his symptoms; he is rather aiming at their proliferation This varies radically with the "intractable codes" (1981: 330) of biomedicine. Staiano writes. "... from the patient's point of view, the potential for negotiation, for a re-evaluation of symptoms and their meanings, or for a re-alignment of symptoms into different symptoms increases the likelihood of exploiting a resource which will be perceived as effective in the treatment of illness."

Of the several case studies Staiano offers, the scenario involving a diabetic, Juan Sho, may typify the Belize penchant "to negotiate a 'diagnosis'" (1981: 330). Mr. Sho consulted an American living in Punta Gorda "who had developed a reputation for accurately reading cards and analyzing dreams" (325). He further used bush medicine for his disease, and also saw a government biomedical doctor who prescribed pills. Staiano herself informed Mr. Sho of the effects of diet on diabetes and of self-monitoring of urine sugar content. A Mennonite farmer advised Mr. Sho to procure insulin. Mr. Sho could not obtain insulin in Belize and, not understanding the necessary relationship between his prescribed pills and his diabetic symptoms, let his prescription lapse, in favor of bush medicine ("sorocee"). Subsequently, Mr. Sho, rejecting pills and change in diet, obtained "bitters" (herbs and roots) from a Mayan bush doctor and later from a Carib healer, Staiano concludes (1981: 325): "He was hoping shortly for a cure [although she had told him that was not possible] and stated that he believed a cure was possible since, according to the government physician, the illness had reached his kidneys and his urine but had not yet reached his blood." In point of fact, multiple interpretation of the medical sign is not peculiar to a bush culture such as that of Belize, although the aim of the proliferation of interpretants certainly is less common in a culture with predominantly biomedically based medicine (cf. "Toward Isomorphism," Chapter 18 below).

Only four of the related sciences and humanities of medicine have been presented above. Certainly they represent but a fraction of the disciplines that feed into the protosemiotic, medicine. The most abstract and precise discipline, physics (cf. "Medicine," above) is repeatedly appealed to in the literature on semiotics and medicine (cf., e.g., Baer: 1982: 28–29, or Chinen 1989: 232, or Shands and Meltzer 1977: 80). Thom (1975: 323) explains: "... the dynamical situations governing the evolution of natural phenomena are basically the same as those governing the evolution of man and societies, profoundly justifying the use of anthropomorphic words in physics." Not surprisingly, Yates (1985: 356), in describing the overlap among the disciplines of physics, mathematics, and biology, suggests that "... semiotic studies can build the essential bridge between ... models of theory and models of data" (cf. "Compatibility of Paradigms," Chapter 1 and "Nineteenth-Century Science," Chapter 2 above).

It is not otherwise with disciplines that are also arts, such as music. While the acoustics of music reach into physics, certainly "the use of music as a therapeutic agent" (Ostwald 1989: 279) underscores once more the scope of semiotics and the position of medicine as protosemiotic. Undeniably, (Engel 1985: 363):

> ... the roots of both humanism and science draw their nourishment from the same human sources, that is, from what the phenomenologists have designated the lifeworld and the lived body [cf. "Medicine" above], and from the practical understanding that derives therefrom. Nowhere is the confluence more evident than in medicine.

10

Protosemiotists

If the confluence of the roots of both humanism and science is to be found in medicine (cf. end of Chapter 9 above), and if medicine can be characterized as a protosemiotic and as one leg of the semiotic tripod, the other two being linguistics and philosophy (cf. "Medicine," Chapter 9 above), then the progenitors of semiotics are to be found in medicine-related disciplines, in particular in philosophy and linguistics.

We have already been introduced to two modern protosemiotists, Saussure (cf. Chapter 2 above) and to Peirce (cf. Chapter 4 above). This chapter furthers our insight into the semiotic contributions of Peirce and Saussure and familiarizes us with other central figures galvanizing semiotics today. *Die Welt als Zeichen*, edited by Krampen *et al.* (1981), provides ready access to the "fathers of modern semiotics" (9; throughout the translation from German of Krampen *et al.* is mine).

Central Figures

In studying Krampen *et al.* 1981 the reader is led into eight rather autonomous chambers, or modules (1981: 12), "so that one can read this book not only forwards and backwards, but one can also start in the middle." We have then a semiotic structure by and large without connecting walls. The advantage to such a presentation, to use another familiar metaphor, is that although the glue or cement is not visible, the building blocks are laid eminently bare—an achievement in itself for, so to speak, a building which is frequently reputed to have no known blueprints, i.e., architectural plans (cf. "What is Semiotics?"

Introduction, "Compatibility of Paradigms," Chapter 1 above; cf. Chapter 11 below).

It is accordingly most fitting that the building blocks, in this case the cornerstones of the semiotic construct, are discussed individually in Krampen *et al.* to show precisely that semiotics is not simply an indiscriminate method or an undefined approach equatable with structuralism or any other intellectual persuasion (cf. "Linguistics/ Semiotics as Science," Chapter 2 above). Further, the building blocks do not represent an accumulation of any and all sciences or academic disciplines, but they provide (Krampen *et al.* 1981: 181) specifically "three fundamental semiotic traditions—the medical, the philosophical, and the linguistic." The medical is represented in Krampen *et al.* 1981 primarily, i.e., from the point of view of education, by Uexküll and Bühler, the philosophical by Peirce and Morris, and the linguistic by Saussure, Hjelmslev, Jakobson and Sebeok. What is fascinating in Krampen *et al.* 1981 is that we do indeed encounter creators of semiotics, but we do so through the eyes of semiotists who themselves are prime movers in semiotic theory. Thus it is that Sebeok is both a grammatical subject and a grammatical object.

Why do we deal in Krampen *et al.* 1981 with precisely these eight semiotists as the "fathers of modern semiotics" (12)? An expedient answer is that the forerunner, so to speak, of Krampen *et al.* appeared as the initial issue of the *Zeitschrift für Semiotik* (Krampen 1979) under the specially designated topic "Semiotische Klassiker des 20. Jahrhunderts." This delimits then the meaning of "modern" as appropriate to Krampen *et al.* 1981 and we understand why John Locke, for example, is not represented. While the inclusion or the exclusion of certain semiotists is not addressed in the foreword to Krampen *et al.* 1981, in his prologue to Krampen 1979 he is quite concerned with the fact that (7, trans. mine) "Many a reader will miss in this issue authors like Bühler and Cassirer, perhaps also contemporary representatives of semiotics such as Eco and Sebeok." To be sure, Bühler and Sebeok join the Krampen 1979 group consisting of Peirce, Saussure, Uexküll and Morris in Krampen *et al.* 1981. Further, Hjelmslev and Jakobson are added to the 1981 volume, whereas Georg Klaus of the journal group is not found in the book. Without allowing this discussion to degenerate into superciliousness, or into a kind of semiotic Who's Who, we need to realize that it is, in fact, a legitimate question to ask which contributors to semiotics can justifiably be considered modern progenitors of this discipline. Krampen (1979: 7) holds that space limitations somewhat influence the selection in the journal issue and promises to fill lacuna in future issues. Such an operation is not possible in a one-volume book; accordingly, the answer should not and cannot be deferred. It is crucial to the recognition of semiotics as a discipline in its own right. In order to address this question and its answer, we must inspect the life and work of the eight semiotists as presented by semiotists; for each of the latter, in turn, a biographical sketch is offered in Krampen *et al.* 1981. In the following sections particular attention is afforded to the definition of the *sign* as a hallmark of each of the eight protosemiotists.

Oehler on Peirce

Klaus Oehler entitles his thirty-two page (in Krampen *et al.* 1981: 15–49) treatment of Peirce "The Concept and Design of Peircean Semiotics." Oehler, himself a Professor of Philosophy at the University of Hamburg, is a past president of the Deutsche Gesellschaft für Semiotik, vice-president of the Peirce Society, a member of the Institute for Studies in Pragmaticism at Texas Tech University, as well as co-editor of the *Zeitschrift für Semiotik.*

Oehler highlights Peirce as "The principal founder of modern semiotics ... the most original and versatile thinker, whom America has as yet produced" (in Krampen *et al.* 1981: 17–18). The details of his physical life become one with the details of his mental activities (cf. Feibleman 1969), progress in his conceptualization of the sign and sign processes. Charles Sanders Peirce (1839 Cambridge, Massachusetts—1914 Milford, Pennsylvania) was a logician, mathematician, natural scientist, and philosopher. Degreed at Harvard, *summa cum laude*, Peirce held a position with the United States Coast and Geodetic Survey from 1861 to 1891. From time to time he lectured at Harvard, in 1865 on "The Logic of Science," and at the Lowell Institute, in 1866 on "The Logic of Science, or Induction and Hypothesis"—lectures that led to the production of his breakthrough "On a New List of Categories" of 1867, introducing the world of learning to the heart of Peircean semiotic theory, viz. his threefold division Quality, Relation and Representation, subsequently termed by Peirce *Firstness*, *Secondness* and *Thirdness*. Peirce conceived logic broadly as semiotics, and his efforts in learning all other fields were directed only and always with philosophy, specifically logic, as the ultimate goal. He wrote (cited by Oehler in Krampen *et al.* 1981: 22: "from the day when at age 12 or 13 I took up, in my elder brother's room a copy of Whately's 'Logic,' and asked him what Logic was, and getting some simple answer, flung myself on the floor and buried myself in it, it has never been in my power to study anything—mathematics, ethics, metaphysics, gravitation, thermodynamics, optics, chemistry, comparative anatomy, astronomy, psychology, phonetics, economics, the history of science, whist, men and women, wine, meteorology, except as a study of semeiotic." Peirce's lifelong love affair with learning, the astounding fecundity of his mind, his uncompromising convictions, all dim in comparison to the impact of how his semiotic changes irreversibly the intellectual life of anyone who has come in touch with it.

So revolutionary is the Peircean contribution to the doctrine of signs that Oehler predicts historians will necessarily bifurcate the story of the development of semiotics into a pre-Peirce period and a post-Peirce period (in Krampen *et al.* 1981: 27). Oehler (23) characterizes Peirce's definition of the *sign*: "a sign is something which stands for something else and is understood by someone or has meaning for someone" as a "common sense definition" which, however, loses the aura of obviousness as soon as one undertakes to reflect upon it. Reflection on the Peircean definition of the sign leads to the extraction of the three essential elements of a *sign*, viz. the sign itself, the object, and the interpretant, which correlate to Peirce's categories of *Firstness*, *Secondness*, *Thirdness* and, in turn, to a great many triadic relations, all in support of the three ways of thinking, viz. abduction, induction, deduction.

Posner on Morris

In the second of eight portraits of protosemiotists, Roland Posner writes on "Charles Morris and the Behavioral Foundation of Semiotics" (in Krampen *et al.* 1981: 51–97). Posner is Professor of Linguistics and Semiotics at the Technical University, Berlin. He is founding president of the Deutsche Gesellschaft für Semiotik, the general editor of *Zeitschrift für Semiotik,* and editor of "Grundlagen der Kommunikation" and "Approaches to Semiotics."

Posner scans the biography of Charles W. Morris (b1901 Denver, Colorado—d1979 Gainesville, Florida). A student of George Mead, Morris is degreed from the University of Chicago, where he subsequently held a professorship for most of his academic career. Posner (in Krampen *et al.* 1981: 54) pinpoints the rich, geographically diverse spheres of influence from which Morris's thought developed: "the North American tradition of Pragmatism ... the Anglo-American tradition of Empiricism ... the Middle European tradition of Logical Positivism. From the stance of each of these traditions toward empirical data, Morris ultimately (1934) derived his well-known threefold division of semiotics into syntax, semantics, pragmatics, distinguishing the relationship of the sign "to other signs, to objects, and to a person or persons," respectively (in Krampen *et al.* 1981: 55; cf. "Linguistic Semiotics," Chapter 3 above). However, Posner regards Morris's understanding of the three dimensions of semiotics as a "transitional stage" (in Krampen *et al.* 1981: 85 and fn. 9) in the development of his thought. Posner explicates Morris's semiotics as built on the behavior theory of George Mead. Behavior is conceptualized by Mead, and accordingly Morris, as "everything that can change in a living being in the course of time" (in Krampen *et al.* 1981: 56). Morris places his definition of a sign in juxtaposition to a framework of triadic characteristics of behavior: perception, manipulation, consummation as phases of an act, which correlate with designative, perceptive and appreciative signs, in turn with informative, valuative and incitive uses of the sign, and finally with a distanced, dominant, and domineered or receptive attitude on the part of the sign user or the actor. A sign then is (in Krampen *et al.* 1981: 60): "a preparatory stimulus which in the absence of an impulse-satisfying object induces the disposition to a response sequence, as the impulse-satisfying object itself would do."

Krampen on Saussure

Krampen, in "Ferdinand de Saussure and the Development of Semiology" (in Krampen *et al.* 1981: 99–142) makes allowance for the use of Saussure's own term, *semiology*, rather than the current *semiotics* in discussing Saussure. (Current usage of the term *semiotics* was determined by the International Association for Semiotic Studies; German and French have retained the singular, thus *Semiotik* and *sémiotique*, respectively [in Krampen *et al.* 1981: 196, fn. 1]. Compare Hjelmslev's use of both, cf. "Trabant on Hjelmslev" below. Following Benjamin H. Smart, Bühler, cf. "Sebeok on Bühler" below, often used the word *sematology*. *Symptomology*, alias *semeiology* was current with the Ancients, cf. "Baer on Sebeok" below.)

Martin Krampen is Professor of the Theory of Visual Communication at the Academy of Arts, Berlin. He is co-founder and past president of the Deutsche Gesellschaft für Semiotik, and also co-editor of the *Zeitschrift für Semiotik*.

In reviewing the biography of Ferdinand de Saussure (b1857 Geneva–d1913 Geneva), Krampen considers one of the central figures in a century characterized by assiduous linguistic activity and astounding breakthroughs in that field. (Cf. "Nineteenth-Century Science," Chapter 2 above). Even before the awarding of his degree *summa cum laude* from the University of Leipzig in 1880, Saussure published the *Mémoire sur le système primitif des voyelles dans les langues indo-européennes* (Leipzig 1879), in which he hypothesized the existence of Indo-European laryngeal sounds, a quarter of a century before the discovery of Hittite and half a century before the identification by Kuryłowicz in the Hittite data of actual reflexes proposed in Saussure's brilliant and masterful conjecture. This monograph also contained Saussure's concept of opposition of elements that "was to become the nucleus of his general linguistics" (in Krampen *et al.* 1981: 101) and, accordingly, one of the cornerstones of structuralism— probably the single most influential and widespread approach in the humane sciences in the twentieth century (cf. "Linguistics/Semiotics as Science," Chapter 2 above). From 1881 to 1891, Saussure taught at the École des Hautes Études in Paris and from 1891 until his death he held a chair for Sanskrit, Indo-European and General Linguistics at the Université de Genève.

The Saussurean bibliographical item that has world renown and is translated into Japanese, German, Russian, Spanish, English, Polish, Hungarian and Italian, the *Cours de linguistique générale* (first published in 1916 = *Course in General Linguistics* 1959), was not even written outright by Saussure; rather it is a reconstruction of his lectures by two students of Saussure, Charles Bally and Albert Sechehaye. Krampen (in Krampen *et al.* 1981: 103–104) speaks of a "new look" in Saussure interpretation, a Saussurean "renaissance" prompted by the publication of Saussure's own original notes, which Krampen claims yield insights other than those conveyed by the *Cours*. On the other hand, additional comparative study of the actual class notes of Saussure's students with the *Cours* offers the possibility of multiple interpretation of certain Saussurean concepts, not the least controversial being that of the relationships of linguistics and semiotics. Specifically, Krampen (in Krampen *et al.* 1981: 106–107) considers Barthes' renowned declaration that semiotics is a part of linguistics as a "perversion" which can be neutralized by reading the Saussurean designation for linguistics vis-à-vis semiotics, viz. "patron général," as "patron saint" rather than as "commanding officer"—a reading allowed by recourse to lecture notes of Saussure's students (cf. "Linguistics," Chapter 3 above).

In addition to treating the semiotics: linguistics association (above), Krampen (in Krampen *et al.* 1981: 108) introduces as "the most important notional mates" those of *parole* and *langue*. Langue "is a system of signs" which comprise a "signifier" and a "signified"..."an insoluble unity as two sides of a coin or of a piece of paper." A great many other familiar binary characteristics function in Saussure's systemic construct, such as arbitrary: motivated, paradigm: syntagm, synchrony: diachrony (cf. "What is Semiotics?" Introduction above)." Krampen displays part of the scholarly network for which Saussurean structuralism is held responsible, viz. the correlation of sign systems with the system of language in the theories of Hjelmslev, Barthes, and Lévi-Strauss. Through insistence on a necessary distinction between structural linguistics and structuralism, Krampen (in Krampen *et al.* 1981: 134) writes, while all languages are composed of signs, the false conclusion can be avoided that all sign systems are languages. By reaching forward to Hjelmslev (cf. "Trabant on Hjelmslev" below), a most intriguing early name within Saussure's sphere of scholars is that of his contemporary, Adolf Noreen, with whose work Saussure "certainly must have been familiar" (in Krampen *et al.* 1981: 111). Krampen emphasizes (112 and footnote 9) that Noreen used the expression "Semologie" before Saussure; he cites Noreen's tripartite division of grammar into phonology, semology, and morphology. Krampen's (in Krampen *et al.* 1981: 111 and footnote 8) source for the Noreen citation is De Mauro's "Notes biographiques" to his edition of Saussure's *Cours* (1976), which Krampen holds to refer to Noreen's monograph *Om språkriktighet.* The cited passage, however, properly belongs to Noreen's *Vårt Språk.* We have no indication that Saussure was familiar with the work of his American contemporary counterpart in semiotics, Peirce. (For a useful comparison of Peirce and Saussure cf. Singer 1978: 211–21.)

Trabant on Hjelmslev

Jürgen Trabant, who is Professor of Romance Linguistics at the Free University of Berlin and co-editor of the journal *Kodikas/Code,* entitles his study "Louis Hjelmslev: Glossematics as General Semiotics" (in Krampen *et al.* 1981: 143–171).

According to Trabant (145), Eugenio Coseriu of the University of Tübingen., "probably the most knowledgeable expert on the history of linguistics," places Hjelmslev on a par with Humboldt (cf. "What is Language?" Introduction, and "Language/Life," Chapter 2 above) as an originator of a theory of general linguistics. And Eco considers Hjelmslev to be "the only author [of Saussure, Morris, Hjelmslev, Buyssens] who could have set up a general theoretical framework for semiotics" (in Krampen *et al.* 1981: 177; cf. Eco 1995: 20–23). Hjelmslev (b1899 Copenhagen–d1965 Copenhagen) wrote his doctoral *dissertation, Études baltiques,* under the direction of Holger Pedersen in 1932. It was "good old traditional historical phonology, as it was required to be" (Fischer-Jørgensen 1965: vii), since Hjelmslev's 1928 *Principes de grammaire générale* had been considered too theoretical to be acceptable for a dissertation. Already we discern in the early Hjelmslev his unrelenting drive for theory. He studied in Lithuania (1931), Prague (1923–24), and Paris (1926–27). He was influenced (Fischer-Jørgensen 1965: v–vi) "by the Danish grammarian H. G. Wiwel ... by the Franco-Swiss linguistic school [cf. above for Saussure and Sechehaye; also Grammont] ... by Eduard Sapir, and particularly by his assertion that the essential fact of language is to be found in the formal patterning, and not in the sounds or the concepts ... by the Russian formalists ... who demanded a purely formal description of grammatical categories." In 1931 Hjelmslev founded the Linguistic Circle of Copenhagen, which he nurtured throughout his life, and in 1939, together with Brøndal, he initiated the *Acta Linguistica Hafniensia.* He was Reader of Comparative Linguistics at the University of Copenhagen.

Trabant exposes his readers to the elements of Hjelmslev's theory of Glossematics. Although also called by Hjelmslev "Structural Linguistics" or "Immanent Linguistics," Glossematics is "not a science of language at all" ... but it is "precisely a science of signs, a science of general semiotic structure" (in Krampen *et al.* 1981: 146). Hjelmslev's springboard is his extension of the Saussurean *langue* beyond merely *langue linguistique* also to *langue non-linguistique,* "semiotic structure in general" (149). Heavily influenced by Saussure, Hjelmslev borrows two further concepts of Saussure, his characterization of a sign as a *signifier* and a *signified*, termed by Hjelmslev the plane of *expression* and the plane of *content*, respectively, and his distinction between *form* and *substance*. Whereas Saussure considered language as consisting of two substances (one in each plane) with but one form, Hjelmslev holds that each plane has both form and substance. Trabant offers Hjelmslev's classic example from the content plane of a set of color terms contrasting English with Welsh. The color spectrum, specifically the formed areas expressed by the substances *green, blue, gray, brown,* is bifurcated, i.e., formed, differently in Welsh, where the same total areas are expressed but by only the three substances *gwyrdd, glas, llwyd.* What is the object of Glossematics is "solely the substanceless, pure form" (in Krampen *et al.* 1981: 152). Since there can be no doubt that language signs are in fact signs, Hjelmslev hypothesizes that the hallmark of signness is the double articulation of expression and content (150), in particular, only expression form and content form, yielding in Glossematics "the purely formal, dematerialized sign in and of itself" (in Krampen *et al.* 1981: 156) (recall the influence of Sapir and the Russian formalists, above; cf. also "Physics' Law and Biology's Growth," Chapter 2 above). Only entities that are structured like language signs are considered signs (in Krampen *et al.* 1981: 150). Indeed, for Hjelmslev "a language is a semiotic into which all other semiotics may be translated—both all other languages and all other conceivable semiotic structures" (1963: 109). While for Hjelmslev the term *semiotics* equals *sign system* equals *langue* (in Krampen *et al.* 1981: 146), the term *semiology* equals a *metasign structure* such as linguistics which, when it becomes the content of another sign system, becomes a metasemiology, at which stage Glossematics is able to accommodate more than form, viz. substance as well (in Krampen *et al.* 1981: 164–165; cf. also "Metalanguage and Object Language," Chapter 5 above). Yet Hjelmslev's Glossematics remains a highly abstract, algebraic construct, prompting Eco's designation of Hjelmslev as a man who "could have" hypothesized a general theory of semiotics (cf. above). But surely, Hjelmslev has the last word (that ironically expresses the *modus operandi* inherent in much of semiotic method); he holds that "For the scholar nothing is more beautiful than the sight of a science still to be created" (cited by Fischer-Jørgensen 1965: xxii).

Eco on Jakobson

In setting the scene upon which Roman Jakobson emerges, Eco provides an overview of the forefathers of contemporary semiotics. Umberto Eco is Professor of Semiotics at the University of Bologna. In 1969 he co-founded the International Association of Semiotic Studies, an umbrella organization for semiotic societies around the world. For many years he served as the International Association's General Secretary. Eco's 500-page award-winning first novel. a medieval mystery thriller, appeared in English translation as *The Name of the Rose* (1980); *Foucault's Pendulum* (1988) and *The Island of the Day Before* (1995) followed.

As mentioned above, Eco begins his exposition of "The Influence of Roman Jakobson on the Development of Semiotics" (in Krampen *et al.* 1981: 173–204) with a short integrating interlude which allows us to test the intellectual climate that produced the "fathers of modern semiotics" (cf. "Central Figures," above; cf. also Eco 1995). We are thus referred to the ancient pre-Socratic, Sophist, Hippocratic, Platonic, Aristotelian, and Stoic traditions with regard to sign phenomena. The interest in the study of signs by the Church Fathers, by the Modists to William of Ockham, thence by the Port Royal grammarians, to the "semaelogia" of Wilkins, the "semeiotiké" of Wallis, the "Sematologie" of Dalgarno, and the "semeilogia" of Kircher makes encouraging semiotic history indeed (in Krampen *et al.*: 1981: 175; cf. also "Krampen on Saussure" for varying terminology). Yet, in spite of the contributions to semiotics by Locke, Hobbes, Hume, Berkeley, Leibnitz, Giambattista Vico, "semiotics as such was ostracized by the scientific community during the succeeding centuries" (in Krampen *et al.* 1981: 176). The final and most significant casualty of this ostracism is, fascinatingly so, Peirce, whose failure to obtain a permanent academic chair resulted, according to Eco, in the extremely delayed discovery of much of his work. Eco calls Peirce the "father of semiotics" outright, i.e., not of ancient or of modern semiotics, but of all semiotics (in Krampen *et al.* 1981: 176).

However, Eco considers Jakobson "to have been the most important catalyst in the contemporary 'semiotic reaction'" (in Krampen *et al.* 1981: 178). Eco offers mainly a bibliographical sketch tracing Jakobson's mental life, which would justify a reformulation of his favorite motto from '*"linguista sum: linguistici nihil a me alienum puto"* to *"linguista sum: nihil a me alienum puto"* (179). Roman Osipovich Jakobson (b1896 Moscow–d1982 Boston) studied language at the University of Moscow and took his Ph.D. at Prague University. He was Research Associate at Moscow University from 1918 to 1920. In 1934 he became Professor of Russian Philology and in 1936 of Czech Medieval Literature at Masarykova University in Brno, Czechoslovakia. Jakobson was Professor of General Linguistics and Czechoslovak Studies at the École Libre des Hautes Études in New York City from 1942 to 1946. From 1943 to 1949 he was Professor of Linguistics at Columbia University and from 1949 to 1967 Jakobson was S.H. Cross Professor of Slavic Languages and Literatures at Harvard University. He was awarded numerous honorary degrees, appointed to many visiting professorships, and granted membership in linguistic and other scholarly societies around the world. Jakobson was co-founder of the Linguistic Circle of Prague and in particular bore, throughout his work, the stamp of Prague School phonology which he, together with Trubetzkoy, Karcevskij and others, revolutionized. Taking a radical departure from Saussure's relativism, Jakobson was not so much interested in the distribution of speech sounds as in the *how* and *why* for the universal distinctiveness of sounds. In 1952 (*Preliminaries to Speech Analysis*, Cambridge, Massachusetts), jointly with Fant and Halle, Jakobson identified twelve binary acoustic distinctive features to disambiguate human speech. Coupled with speech spectrography, the binarity principle correlated well with information theory, which studies the efficiency of communication quantitively. It is within this time frame for about a decade that Jakobson became "convinced of the possibility of a general semiotics;" in fact, with the 1961 publication of his "Linguistics and Communication Theory" "the semiotic plan [was] complete" (in Krampen *et al.* 1981: 180). Eco proclaims Jakobson the "catalyst, who, so to speak, granted other researchers the right 'to try out semiotics'"—semiotics now no longer a dream, but a reality (in Krampen *et al.* 1981: 181). Eco delineates "The [eight] Basic Assumptions" of current semiotic research prompted by the work of Jakobson: (1) A sign is something which stands for something, following the Scholastic *"aliquid stat pro aliquo"* (in Krampen *et al.* 1981: 181); (2) *Meaning*, signs other than verbal language, pervades the universe (182); (3) Accordingly, semiotics must work with an interdisciplinary transfer of: (a) the linguistic criterium of *relevance*, (b) the psychological concept of *frustrated expectation*, (c) the concept of speech functions, (d) the notion of binarity, (e) the concept of distinctive features, (f) the pair

code: message, (g) the pair selection: combination, (h) the principles
of Prague School poetics (183–186); (4) all semiotic systems can be
seen as *systems of rules* (186–188); (5) description of signs should be
based on their similarities and differences in referring, being received,
being stored (188–191); (6) a semiotic theory is semantic as well as
syntactic (191–192); (7) there is no semiotics without a semantics that
is both extensional and intensional (192–194); (8) semiotics consists
not only of syntax and semantics, but also of pragmatics (194).

Sebeok on Bühler

Sebeok , author of the essay on "Karl Bühler" in Krampen *et al.*
(1981: 207–232) is the subject of "Baer on Sebeok" (cf. below). In
discussing Bühler, Sebeok publishes (in Krampen *et al.* 1981: 228–29)
for the first time a vita, typed by Bühler himself on May 21, 1938 and
preserved in an archive in Vienna. Karl Bühler (b1879 Merkesheim
near Heidelberg–d1963 Los Angeles) studied both medicine and
philosophy, earning an M.D. from the University of Freiburg in
Breisgau in 1903 and a Ph.D. from the University of Strassburg in
1904. He studied further in Berlin under Erdmann and Stumpf, a
precursor of Gestalt psychology, and in 1906 at the University of
Würzburg he became assistant to Külpe, a student of Wilheim Wundt.
In 1907–1908 Bühler wrote his habilitation dissertation on experimental investigations of the (*Tatsachen und Probleme zu einer*)
Psychologie der Denkvorgänge. Bühler thus shared, indeed played, an
essential role in the vigorous intellectual activity and the galvanizing
conceptual trends of the time, viz. Wundt's introspective content
psychology and Gestalt psychology. His *Psychologie der Denkvorgänge* sparked Bühler's challenge to Wundt's associationistic
theory. Bühler's question-answer-introspection experiments found
that imageless thought, thinking, can be devoid of sensory qualities.
Accordingly, "thoughts appear to be independent of verbal manifestations" (in Krampen *et al.* 1981: 211)—a viewpoint that is also in
opposition to the Humboldt-Sapir-Whorf principle of linguistic
relativity, which holds that thoughts are, in fact, influenced by
language (cf. "Peirce before Sapir-Whorf," Chapter 4 above). Opposed as well to the Wundtian reduction of experience into atomistic
elements was the basic tenet of Gestalt psychology, viz. that the whole
can only be understood from the configuration of its parts. Temporally
intermediate between Ehrenfels' 1890 introduction of "Gestalt-

qualitäten" and Wertheimer's 1912 "phi phenomenon," Bühler's *Psychologie der Denkvorgänge* concluded that "understanding takes place between [among] integrated wholes;" therefore, e.g., "word meaning is subordinate to sentence meaning" (in Krampen *et al.* 1981: 210–211). By 1913 Bühler published his *Die Gestaltwahrnehmungen.* In 1909 he became Professor of Psychology at the University of Bonn and in 1913 at the University of Munich. During World War I he served in the medical corps and developed psychological aptitude tests. In 1918 Bühler became Professor of Psychology at the Dresden Institute of Technology. From 1922 until 1938, he was Professor of Psychology at the University of Vienna, where, through the efforts of Bühler and his wife, Charlotte Malachowski Bühler, the Institute for Psychology "flourished and attracted a great number of foreign students" (Bühler's *vita,* in Krampen *et al.* 1981: 229). He was also associated with the Pedagogical Institute of the City of Vienna, and, needless to say, he was very aware of the psychoanalytic work of his contemporary in Vienna, Freud. In 1938, having been incarcerated by the Nazis for about six weeks, he emigrated via Norway to the United States. From 1940 to 1945, he was Professor of Psychology at the College of St. Scholastica (Duluth, Minnesota), Clark University (Worcester. Masssachusetts) and the College of St. Thomas (St. Paul, Minnesota); he had been visiting professor at Stanford, Johns Hopkins, Harvard. and Chicago in the 1920s. Bühler held his final positions with the UCLA medical school until 1955, and with the Cedars-of-Lebanon-Hospital, where he served as consulting psychologist.

Sebeok speaks to the "somewhat neglected aspects of the Bühlerian concepts of *sign communication* or the exchange of messages" as displayed in Bühler's *Die Axiomatik (der Sprachwissenschaften)* (1933) and his *Sprachtheorie: (Die Darstellungsfunktion der Sprache)* (1934), the latter incorporating the earlier work. The first of Bühler's four axioms or basic principles of language holds "that every language is a system of signs, that the sounds of language are posited by the speaker as signs and received by the hearer as signs, that the phenomenon of language arises as the mediator between individuals in the exchange of signs" (translated by Innis 1982: 91). This indicates nicely Bühler's organon model of language as an instrument with three functions: (a) the expressive function "which relates the sign to the source of the information" to yield the mood or the attitude of the speaker or writer, (b) the conative or appeal function "which relates the sign to the goal of the information," to influence the hearer or reader or to effect something, (c) the cognitive or representative function "which relates the sign to its context," to transmit facts or information (in Krampen *et al.* 1981: 217). Bühler's tripartite distinction was inherited by the Prague School of Linguistics (cf. "Eco on Jakobson" above; cf. "Linguistic Semiotics," Chapter 3 above), that studied language in terms of function; indeed, both Trubetzkoy and Jakobson acknowledge this insightful contribution of Bühler to functional linguistics (in Krampen *et al.* 1981: 217, 213). The representative function derives directly from the principle of "abstract relevance," which implies that only certain features of the total material reality are abstracted as semiotically relevant by the sign user, who uses the sign to stand for something else (again, cf. "Eco on Jakobson" above, the formulation *aliquid stat pro aliquo*). Sebeok notes the analogue of the abstract relevance principle to Peirce's concept of ground, "sort of idea," not the object "in all respects" (Peirce 2: 228). In turn, the abstractness of the relevance derives from the fact that the language sign fulfills all three functions, although in a given semiosis one dominates while the other two are subordinate to the total speech-act (the *parole*). Although for Bühler language was a social phenomenon and a work or structure rather than an act, in particular an Husserlian subject-related act, he did borrow from the *Logische Untersuchungen* of Husserl (†1938) and suggested a four-place language matrix in which *ergon* (work) is paired with *langue* as subject-independent, *energeion* (act) is paired with *parole* as subject related, while *ergon* and *parole* are seen as less abstract than *energeion* and *langue,* respectively (in Krampen *et al.* 1981: 218–219; cf. also "Linguistics/Semiotics as Science," Chapter 2 above).

Bühler's *Axiomatik* and his *Sprachtheorie* having concentrated on the representative function of language, the expressive function became the focus of attention in his book of the same year as the *Sprachtheorie*, viz. *Ausdruckstheorie (Das System an der Geschichte aufgezeigt* (1934). His distinction between representation and expression hearkens back to the Scholastic formula *ordo et connexio rerum*, in which representation is manifest in order signs, relations of equivalence, and expression is manifest in indicational signs, relations of dependencies. Further, "an expression signifies or also contains an inferential process from one existent to another, a movement of inference, therefore, *quo ad existentiam* from one given to another ... a representation ... contains the same process of inference *at most secondarily*, and ... relates one thing to another according to a structure common to both or, ... *quoad essentiam*" (translated by Innis 1982: 156–157). Expression behavior, as Sebeok points out, encompasses "functionally quite diverse phenomena" including quasi-personality traits, physiognomic characteristics, those of mimicry, and pathognomic features such as are reflected in lie detector tests, that are integral to both verbal and nonverbal semiotics (in Krampen *et al.* 1981: 220–221).

In his *Ausdruckstheorie*, Bühler also addressed the steady-state concept of Bernard, "the milieu concept ... that a genuine signal device is contained in the area of body internal regulation," five years prior to Cannon's coinage of the term *homeostasis* in his book, *The Wisdom of the Body* (in Krampen *et al.* 1981: 223–224). On the other hand, Bühler did not succeed in establishing the "isomorphy between the logic of the subject ... and that of the logician" (225). In fact, with regard to Bühler's life-long occupation with "the creative nature of thought" (225), Bühler concluded that "thought and reason, gestaltic and holistic experience ... is independent of the machine, or mechanical principle, and also independent to some extent of what is merely biological in the animal kingdom" (Wellek 1968: 201; cf. "What is Language," Introduction above). Still, in Bühler's posthumous *Die Uhren der Lebewesen* (1969), he considered that "biological clocks and 'cognitive maps'" are experienced alike in both man and animal— the "exciting and burning" consideration of an octogenarian semiotist (in Krampen *et al.* 1981: 226).

Uexküll on Uexküll

Thure von Uexküll writes on "The Semiotics of Jakob von Uexküll" (in Krampen *et al.* 1981: 233–279), his father. Thure von Uexküll was Director of the Medical Policlinic at the University of Giessen and Professor and Director of Internal Medicine and Psychosomatics at the University of Ulm.

Thure von Uexküll gives a few essential facts in the life of Uexküll, setting the stage for the latter's *Umwelt* theory. Uexküll (b1864 Keblas, Estonia–d1944 Capri) studied zoology in Dorpat, worked at the Physiological Institute of the University of Heidelberg and at the Zoological Station in Naples. He was awarded an honorary doctorate from the University of Heidelberg in 1907. Uexküll "founded a particular research method that he called '*Umwelt*-theory'—a theory that hypothesized how animate objects subjectively perceive their environment and how this perception determines their behavior" (in Krampen *et al.* 1981: 235). Sebeok, who first discovered Uexküll, so to speak, for the interests of modern semiotics in 1968, succinctly conveys the essence of this theory in the sentence "Uexküll investigated the sensory capacities of animals, how the world is pictured in their mind, and how organisms conduct their life from within the prison of their senses, circumscribing their *Umwelt*, or *subjective environment* [emphasis mine], with which their behavior stands in an overall homeostatic (feedback) relationship" (1979: 9). The Institute for *Umwelt* Research at the University of Hamburg was established by Uexküll in 1926.

Uexküll's semiotic paradigm cannot be relegated to physiology, ethology, or psychology; nor will it allow itself to be assigned outright to the Natural Sciences or to the Humanities. Rather, Uexküll conceived of his discipline as belonging to biology *in a broad or unusual sense* (in Krampen *et al.* 1981: 235). Thure von Uexküll explains separate presuppositions, a distinct method, and a unique goal for *Umwelt* research. The principal presupposition holds that reality, made manifest in *Umwelten*, appears as signs that are received and decoded by our *Gemüt*, i.e., apperception (in Krampen *et al.* 1981: 237 and 273–74 fn. 4), through natural laws. Our *Gemüt* is an organ of nature to perceive nature: nature creates man, man creates nature (236–237). While Uexküll characterizes his method as one of "participatory observation" (in Krampen *et al.* 1981: 237), the goal of his *Umwelt* research is a "theory of the composition of nature" analogous to the composition "of a score for the 'semantic symphony' which nature performs on the inestimable diversity of numberless *Umwelten* just as on a giant keyboard, on which our life and our *Umwelt* are but one key" (in Krampen *et al.* 1981: 238).

Thure von Uexküll considers the possible extension of the reciprocal interchange between nature and man, to the postulate that "man created language, language created man" (in Krampen *et al.* 1981: 238–239)—a most provocative analogue in view of the Humboldt-Sapir-Whorf hypothesis (cf. "Sebeok on Bühler" above). Uexküll himself addressed other questions of primary concern to linguistic research in the final quarter of the twentieth century, e.g., whether the rules of language are inborn or culturally transmitted (in Krampen *et al.* 1981: 240, 269; cf. "Object Language," Chapter 5 above), indeed, in how far the signs of human language are meaningful in the *Umwelten* of animals (238), and what "dialect(s)" and "language

famili(es)" exist in animal communication (in Krampen *et al.* 1981:
274–75, fn. 6; cf. also "Illation and the Signifying Animal," Chapter 6
above). Interestingly, the laws of nature which show an analogy to the
laws of language are valid only for living beings that, as Thure von
Uexküll explains, are alone endowed with "'specific life energy'" to
enter into what Sebeok identifies as "'*semiosis*'" (in Krampen *et al.*
1981: 240–42, 276, fn. 8). From this specific energy it follows that the
most elementary sign process, a "'semiotic atom," is a code that regu-
lates the life of a cell to distinguish the *self* from the *nonself* (in
Krampen *et al.* 1981: 243; cf. also "Self," Chapter 9 above). Integral
to the opposition *self : nonself* is the insight that "A living cell
possesses its own ego-tone," so that, in fact, semiosis is a subjective
process, for "the attributes of all things, so Kant teaches us further,
belong not to them, but are solely sense impressions transferred by us"
(in Krampen *et al.* 1981: 244–245, 267).

Thure von Uexküll discusses two types of elementary ego-tone sign
processes, order signs (so-called temporal and spatial signs) and content signs (so-called sense signs) (in Krampen *et al.* 1981: 246–248).
He sees in Uexküll's codes or regularities for elementary sign processes a strong analogue to Morris' triple "aspects" of semantics,
syntactics, and pragmatics (in Krampen *et al.* 1981: 248–255; cf.
"Posner on Morris," above). The pragmatic aspect allows for the distinction between perceptual feature and perceptual sign; the first is
external and belongs to the physical world, the object, while the last is
internal and belongs to the ego-tone of the sense cell of the subject (in
Krampen *et al.* 1981: 241). The perceptual feature and perceptual sign
are integral to Uexküll's understanding of the sign process. For
Uexküll a sign equals "meaning carrier + meaning (and meaning =
reference to the meaning user)" (in Krampen *et al.* 1981: 260, 258,
265). Thus meaning unites two entities, the carrier of the object of the
outer world and the user of the subject of the inner world, into a sign.
This is the point: counterpoint relationship which illustrates Uexküll's
"functional cycle." In his sensory motor model, Uexküll shows how a
meaning carrier consists of a perceptual feature carrier and a functional feature carrier, the function feature of the latter canceling the
perception feature of the former and thus completing the cycle. A
meaning user, in turn, consists of a perceptual organ and a functional
organ. The perceptual organ transforms a perceptual sign, an elementary sensation of the receptor or sense organ, into a perceptual feature.
Further, the perceptual organ induces the functional organ to send a

function sign to the effector, resulting in a function feature and the above-mentioned completion of the cycle (in Krampen *et al.* 1981: 264–266). The task of Uexküll's biology is first to study the semiosis of human *Gemüt*, then in our role as observer to study the semiosis of animals and plants (245, 256). In the case of animals man alone can observe an object as neutral ("Gegenstand") and transfer it into a non-neutral object ("Objekt") as encountered by the animal. Plant life differs again in that while animals possess *Umwelten* as do humans, plants possess merely space shells or envelopes since the meaning carrier and the meaning user are commensurate in plants, i.e., there is no specialized organ for each (in Krampen *et al.* 1981: 262). (This is now open to challenge by recent findings, such as those of Begley [1983: 72], pointing to the possibility of "a plant emitting a chemical signal that is perceived and acted upon by another ... ecologists that the trees' messages travel on the wind, although the chemical basis of the vocabulary has yet to be identified.")

Baer on Sebeok

"The Semiotics of Thomas A. Sebeok" in Krampen *et al.* 1981: 281–321) by Eugen Baer presents Sebeok's both well-seasoned and entirely new insights. Eugen Baer is Professor of Philosophy at Hobart and William Smith Colleges. He is co-founder and past president of the Semiotic Society of America.

Baer recounts factors in the life of Sebeok which make understandable the latter's position as the prime mover in the present world of semiotics. Thomas A. Sebeok (b1920 Budapest) came to the United States in 1937 and became a citizen in 1944. In 1941 he was graduated from the University of Chicago, where he had studied with Charles W. Morris (cf. "Posner on Sebeok" above), and in 1945 he received his Ph.D. from Princeton, where, via New York, he was influenced by Roman Jakobson (cf. "Eco on Jakobson" above). Sebeok joined the faculty of Indiana University in 1943; he is Distinguished Professor of Linguistics and Semiotics, Professor of Anthropology, Professor of Folklore, and Professor of Uralic and Altaic Studies. At Indiana he established the Research Center for Language and Semiotic Studies. Away from the Indiana campus, Sebeok is ubiquitous as a visiting professor, a consultant to national and international organizations, and an advisor at-large to the scholarly world—both on a personal level and on an institutional level—stimulating a virtually endless array of learned endeavors. In this role Sebeok served as president of the Linguistic Society of America in 1975 and as its secretary-treasurer from 1969 to 1973. He was co-founder of the Semiotic Society of America, its first secretary-treasurer in 1975, and from 1975 to 1980 its executive director, and served as its President in 1984. In 1994, Sebeok was Honorary President of the Fifth Congress of the International Association for Semiotic Studies.

The semiotics of Sebeok, the linguist, is biologically based or perhaps more insightfully, one might say that the linguistics of Sebeok, the semiotist, is biologically based. Ultimately, too, the philosophy of Sebeok is biologically based. This brings out clearly that essentially all semiosis in the "logic of life" is analogous to that of the genetic code, "the most fundamental [code] of the entire semiotic network" (in Krampen *et al.* 1981: 284). In fact, the genetic code and the language code are in many ways homologous. Thus, e.g., *discreteness* is a common characteristic. For a concrete linguistic instance consider the following (Rauch 1979a: 22):

> Nevertheless, it remains a fact that the discrete elements within the continuum cannot become nondiscrete without scrambling the linguistic code. We may seek a model in the DNA genetic code, where change in a code takes place not by change in discrete elements but by addition or deletion of discrete elements. Applying this model to the linguistic code, we may accordingly observe, e.g., the Indo-European resonants, which are [+ vocalic] and [+ consonantal], but which in the code which is in phase, i.e., not scrambled, must be either the discrete element [consonantal] or the discrete element [vocalic].

Sebeok's semiotics leads to a broad understanding of a "definition of life" (in Krampen *et al.* 1981: 285) which has developed and seasoned, withstanding the test of troublesome implications such as the question of the possession of language by animals. "Life" takes place wherever two energy systems interact, a self and a non-self system, an organism and its *Umwelt* (cf. "Uexküll on Uexküll" above), a sign bearer and a sign object meaningfully united by a code. The definition of life is thus a definition of semiosis; the two are commensurate.

Sebeok, by his appeal to biology, effects a full circle in the development of semiotics—from medicine to philosophy, to linguistics, and into a new biology of semiosis. The semiotic paradigm has then just now found completion as an independent discipline (cf. Chapter 9 above). In this sense it is at once very old (Hippocrates 460–370 BC, Galen 130–200 AD) and very new. Sebeokian semiotics embodies the insights of the forefathers and the "'fathers of modern semiotics" (in Krampen *et al.*: 12), Sebeok himself being both the father and child of his newly accomplished paradigm, the latter by viewing other paradigms (cf., e.g., "Sebeok on Bühler" above) through his own. To be sure, Sebeok had at his disposal over two millennia of rich resources upon which to draw: for medicine also Locke and Uexküll (cf. in Krampen *et al.* 1981: 288–289; cf. also "Uexküll on Uexküll" above), for philosophy most immediate but probably also the single most decisive and catalytic of all time for semiotics, Peirce, (cf. "Oehler on Peirce" above and Chapter 4 above), together with a broad spectrum of philosophical semioticists over the millennia (in Krampen *et al.* 1981: 289–290, cf. also "Eco on Jakobson" above), and for linguistics, Saussure (in Krampen *et al.* 1981: 290, cf. also "Krampen on Saussure" above and Chapter 2 above). However, the final link in the circle of the semiotic paradigm, the refinement and inspired systematization of its biological (genetic) base, is unquestionably Sebeok's own. One of the crucial steps in this systematization is Sebeok's formulation of zoosemiotics, in particular in the juxtaposition of "Anthroposemiotics and Zoosemiotics" (in Krampen *et al.* 1081: 291). His very incisive statement with regard to this relation reads: "Because I now consider it increasingly doubtful that any sign system that is not manifestly language-related belongs with man's repertoire of anthroposemiotic devices, I provisionally conclude, as a heuristic tactic, that all other systems used by man are to be construed as zoosemiotic until demonstrated to be otherwise" (1979: 40; in Krampen *et al.* 1981: 294). Thus, in a stunning reversal of the classic focus, Sebeok speaks to "Zoosemiotic Components of Human Communication" claiming, by means of a linguistic notion, that "Anthroposemiotic systems are always marked, in contradistinction to the zoosemiotic systems that comprehend them" (1977a: 1060).

Baer points out that central to zoosemiotics are the two concepts of ritualization and morphology (in Krampen *et al.* 1981: 291). As one of "four varieties of semiosis," ritualization is gene-dependent and stands in diachronic relationship to the synchronic interdependent communication and to the synchronic ego-dependent signification, which, in turn, is relative to the diachronic alter-dependent infancy, senescence, incapacitation (1979: 30; in Krampen *et al.* 1981: 292, fig. 1). Other Sebeokian classifications of signs are presented by Baer according to sign sources, emanating from the bifurcation organic: inorganic (296, fig. 2); sign channels, following from the bifurcation matter: energy (298, fig. 3); and sign production resulting from the bifurcation silent: sounded (298, fig. 4). A fourth classification of signs follows from a division into instrumental and somatic. No one has surpassed Sebeok in the identification and application of the Peircean sign classification of *icon*, *index*, and *symbol* to animal behavior. His examples of the trophobiosis between ant and aphid for the icon, the symbiosis between the black-throated honey guide and man for the index, and the copulation ritual of balloon flies for the symbol have already become established as widely recognized classic examples in zoosemiotic literature (in Krampen *et al.* 1981: 300–302).

To explain the other concept central to zoosemiotics, that of morphology, Baer discusses the place of René Thom's morphogenesis in Sebeok's paradigm, a place undoubtedly confirming its biological dimension. Linguists and non-linguists alike throughout this century had made the claim that language is the premier sign system (cf. "The Sign System Par Excellence," Chapter 3 above). In the mid-seventies Sebeok made the claim that genetic copying is the semiotic process *par excellence*' (1979: 120), since "Sebeok sees in biological reproduction the foundation of semiotics, insofar as it becomes basically clear here, that a sign realizes itself only through replication in another sign" (in Krampen *et al.* 1981: 286). Baer now writes (293) that "for Sebeok ... morphogenesis ... is the semiotic function par excellence." To be sure, Thom's "catastrophes," archetypal morphologies which display a change in the equilibrium of an entity or force, underlie both language and genetic copying. Following Peirce, Sebeok identifies the decisive mark of the sign as *Thirdness*, uniting the *sign* with its *object*, which can be displayed as a loop with a curve in which the inside of the loop is turned outside and vice-versa, demonstrating, in fact, that an organism is the "interpretation of his *Umwelt* and, the reverse, the *Umwelt* [is] ... the interpretation of the organism" (in Krampen *et al.* 1981: 306; cf. "Uexküll on Uexküll" above). Signs within an organism are termed "endosemiotic" while signs without, i.e., in the *Umwelt* of an organism, are called "exosemiotic" by Sebeok. These two semiotic processes, which *Thirdness* translates from one into the other, are "the semiotic self." The equilibrium of the semiotic self is regulated by the immune system and the signal anxiety system that are complementary (in Krampen *et al.* 1981: 303–304). In complementarity too, are the "Forms of Life and of Language" (311), laying to rest the problem of the primacy of one over the other (by extension, cf. again the Humboldt-Sapir-Whorf hypothesis, "Sebeok on Bühler" above). "Sebeok shows very nicely, how the mutual condition of anthroposemiotics and zoosemiotics, similar to Thom's catastrophes, presupposes an interplay of autonomy and mutual heteronomy" (in Krampen *et al.* 1981: 314).

Baer clarifies further the essential Peircean-Sebeokian contention whereby a sign has its life in another sign. Sebeok's definition of sign holds then that "A sign consists in the sign synthesis of self and other; it is therefore internally metaphorical, since its meaning is in each case imported (imputed) from that which it is not" (Baer 1979: 362; in Krampen *et al.* 1981: 314). Freud's thesis of totemism and Lévi-Strauss' approach to totemism bear witness to this conception of the metaphorical nature of the sign and to the "mutual containment of nature and culture," respectively (Baer 1979: 363; in Krampen *et al.* 1981: 315). The mutual containment of nature: culture, body: soul is particularly scrutinized by Sebeok in the mutual containment anthroposemiotic: zoosemiotic where the so-called "Clever Hans" and "Clever Daisy" semioses illustrate that the sign transmitted by the human sender effects a sign in the animal receiver which is but a "return" of the sign of the sender (in Krampen *et al.* 1981: 316). Sebeokian zoosemiotics, indeed, conceals "the true wealth and the true mystery of semiotics" (318), in which the principal question remains, how we are plugged into our world, i.e., "how endosemiotics becomes exosemiotics and the reverse" (317).

Semiotic Architectonic

We return now to our initial query in the section "Central Figures" above, viz. is our semiotic architectonic in balance or askew with the design of these eight paradigms, no more and no less. Interestingly, after abiding for a time with the thoughts of each one of the eight semiotists, the reader leaves them reluctantly. (S)he wishes that (s)he were at one and the same time a philosopher, a linguist, and a biologist. The reader can actually experience these roles vicariously through the encyclopedic writing of Sebeok, who has achieved the colossal synthesis that semiotics is. Sebeok alone can provide the cement for joining the various approaches while simultaneously contributing to its massive structure (cf. "Baer on Sebeok" above). All paradigms are somehow derived, yet that of Peirce (cf. "Oehler on Peirce" above), Saussure (cf. "Krampen on Saussure" above), and Uexküll (cf. "Uexküll on Uexküll" above) give an impression of independence that might have warranted their order in Krampen *et al.* 1981 to be that of its forerunner, Krampen 1979, where these three semiotists immediately follow one another. On the other hand, Kant clearly pervades semiotic thinking, while Thom provides an indispensable dimension.

Yet, the question nags us: Why are these eight semiotists ordered the way they are in Krampen *et al.* 1981? Let us recall their respective definitions of the sign: Peirce—"a sign is something which stands for something else and is understood by someone or has meaning for someone" (cf. "Oehler on Peirce"); Morris—"A sign then is 'a preparatory stimulus which in the absence of an impulse-satisfying object induces the disposition to a response sequence. as the impulse-satisfying object itself would do'" (cf. "Posner on Morris"); Saussure—"Langue 'is a system of signs' which comprise a 'signifier' and a 'signified' ... 'an insoluble unity as two sides of a coin or of a piece of paper'" (cf. "Krampen on Saussure"); Hjelmslev—"the hallmark of sign-ness is the double articulation of expression and content ... in particular only expression form and content form, yielding 'the purely formal, dematerialized sign in and of itself'" (cf. "Trabant on Hjelmslev"); Jakobson—"A sign is something which stands for something, following the Scholastic *'aliquid stat pro aliquo'*" (cf. "Eco on Jakobson"); Bühler—"the sign user ... uses the sign to stand for something else" ("Sebeok on Bühler"); Uexküll—"a sign equals 'meaning carrier+meaning (and meaning=reference to the meaning user)'" (cf. "Uexküll on Uexküll"); Sebeok—"A sign consists in the synthesis of self and other; it is therefore internally metaphorical, since its meaning is in each case imported (imputed) from that which it is not" (cf. "Baer on Sebeok"). Quite simply then, the order of semiotists in Krampen *et al.* 1981 follows from philosophical orientation, to linguistic orientation, to biological orientation. This is not to imply that these orientations are clean-cut; they cannot be in genuine semiotics, so, for example, Peirce's exquisite sensitivity to the fact that "every symbol is a living thing" (2: 222). On the other hand, "the refinement and inspired systematization of its [semiotics'] biological (genetic) base" ("Baer on Sebeok") is not achieved until Sebeok.

Within the framework of this biological semiotics, we pose the question: What then is the beginning of life for a sign; when, so to speak, does it draw its first breath? The answer, in itself not simple, is, nevertheless, now surprisingly simple to obtain, since "all morpho-genesis" is a "conflict, a struggle" (Thom 1975: 323), whether this be the spiral in the helix, the ebb and flow of the tide, or the heartbeat of the sign. We look accordingly, to Peircean *Secondness* that allows for the classical *aliquid* and *aliquo* of the above definitions of the sign. The instantiation of the meaningful juxtaposition of these two entities, however, requires *Thirdness*. Peirce's definition holds; it is univer-sally valid not only everywhere, but at all times. Sebeok's biosemi-otics demonstrates this.

11

Semiotics: At the Turn of the Millennium

In closing off Part One of this book, Chapter 11 returns to the pervasive question of the identity of semiotics, first encountered in the Introduction, amplified in Chapters 1 and 2, and seen to recur as an essential leitmotiv, whether subliminally or overtly, throughout all of the preceding chapters.

State of the Art

The *Bibliography of Semiotics 1975–1985,* edited by Eschbach and Eschbach-Szabo (1986), is one of several indicators reflective of the vast, seemingly non-integrated efforts which feed into the semiotic enterprise. The *Bibliography* compilers (1986: 7) describe this harried state of semiotic affairs, a near-frenzy in semiotic research as a

> ... world-wide intensification in the field ... National semiotic societies have been founded all over the world; a great number of international, national, and local semiotic conferences have taken place; periodicals devoted to semiotics have increased ... book series devoted to the subject have increased as have the number of books and dissertations in the field.

Writing a "Prolegomena of a possible historiography of semiotics," Eschbach (1983: 27–28) reinforces the reality that

> ... current views on the definition of the subject-matter of semiotic study range from narrowly linguistic and logical to the broadly pansemiotic, bound only by the universe. The working methods of those who claimed to be engaged in semiotic re-

search are just as varied, the only common denominator being the claim itself.

To be sure, semiotists appear to be intellectually frolicking in an unfettered fashion in a veritable Garden of Eden. Linguists can draw an analogy to allophonic swarming, which, however, is a stage prior to eventual systematization or reconstruction. The conceptual/ methodological free-for-all in semiotic research is a healthy condition, indeed characterized by *Firstness* and accordingly exceedingly creative. But the disregard for designated confines set for research is only a passing mirage, since for most semiotists the disregard must cohabit with a nagging need to search for a paradigm.

Obsession with definition and virtual paradigm paranoia are, however, self-reflective signposts of the maturation of semiotics in the waning years of the millennium. In a farsighted question posed to some ninety-one semiotists in 1986, Thomas A. Sebeok inquires (1986a: 369) as to the identification of "principal goals for semiotics to achieve during the final decade of this century." The overwhelming majority of the thirty-four replies encourage the conventionalization of a semiotic paradigm—e.g., Bettetini (Sebeok 1986a: 371): "very clear principles to be referred to;" Bremond (372): "la délimitation du territoire qui lui revient dans le champ des sciences humaines;" Gardin (374–75): "to clarify its epistemological foundations and methodological requirements, on a par with, though allegedly different from, those of Science;" Greimas (376): "élaboration de la théorie sémiotique à vocation scientifique;" Kevelson (378): "establish a model or prototype for semiotic investigation;" Koch (379): "it may grow at least into a 'science on probation;'" Rector (385): "establish a coherent framework;" Swiggers (386): "The construction of a unified model;" Watt (387): "further development of the 'scientific' ... side of the field."

In stark contrast, Baer (in Sebeok 1986: 369) boldly encourages that "Semioticians should continue the endless discourse on the sign and the signless in which everyone can participate and which cannot readily be identified." This counter-balance to rigid conventionalization is, it seems, inherent in the "lingua franca" (Lanigan in Sebeok 1986: 381) that is semiotics. Lanigan maintains: "semiotics is the most appropriate theory and praxis to ground the full range of arts and sciences that will account for the *post-modern condition of discourse* at the end of this century." The simultaneous expansion and narrowing of the semiotic focus is endemic to the semiotic enterprise; thus Gandelman (in Sebeok 1986: 374) advises against "extending its activities to new provinces of science, or consolidating its position in newly 'conquered' fields," while Poyatos (in Sebeok 1986: 385) urges "a further search for applications of semiotic thought and frameworks in many areas where they are not yet used as concretely and productively as they could be." Gandelman proposes a turn to "in-depth reflection," but Poyatos urges "some turning away from too abstract speculation." This difference in viewpoint is not simply the "general" versus "particular" controversy common to intellectual pursuits; it is the peculiar attraction of semiotics that it continues to defy comprehensive special as well as comprehensive universal study of signs.

Perhaps Eco's 1973 statement (in Eco 1975: 17) *"we hope there never will"* (emphasis mine) with regard to the observation that "there does not yet exist a single unified theory [of semiotics]" (cf. "Linguistics/Semiotics as Science," Chapter 2 above) will prove prophetic—in spite of the statement in Eco's Preface (1979: v) to the Proceedings of the First Congress (1974) of the IASS designating as one of the IASS-approved tasks of the Congress the discussion of "the possibility of providing the discipline with a unified methodology and a unified objective." By the time of the Second Congress (1979) of the IASS, Borbé (1983: v–vi) prefaces the Proceedings as "a representative collection with regard to a uniform methodological instrument ... [However] semiotics is not one binding paradigm." Ten years later, with regard to the Third IASS Congress papers, Herzfeld and Melazzo (1988: v) continue to speak to "the complex intertext that this semiotic enterprise represents." And, Pelc (1989: 3), referring to IASS congresses, declared "a uniting of efforts in turning semiotics into a science as well as into a set of academic disciplines." We, of course, find similar sentiments outside the IASS and its congresses. To cite but one example, consider Lange-Seidl's (1981: 3) declaration on the concept of a "sign constitution": *"Ob das Ergebnis einer Konstitution immer ein 'Homogenes Ganzes' ist, sei bezweifelt."*

A Canon and Theses for Semiotics

The pluralism of semiotic thought appears to belie the existence of a paradigm with a canon and theses, yet individual metasemiotic writings continually attest to a canon (or canons) and theses. Let us look first at canon-formation. Kenner (1984: 374) attributes (Modernist) canon-formation to "readers ... later writers choosing and inventing ancestors; chiefly though ... [to] the canonized themselves who [are] yet to be aware of a collective enterprise, and repeatedly acknowledge(d) one another." We thus understand that there is no time constraint delimiting candidates. So, for instance, Sebeok is chosen both as a canonized and a canonizer in the set of eight biographies composing *Die Welt als Zeichen* (Krampen *et al.* 1981; cf Chapter 10 above). On the other hand, the comprehensive *Encyclopedic Dictionary of Semiotics* (Sebeok 1986) does not enjoy entries on such contemporaries as Sebeok and Eco, albeit both are contributors to the work. Nevertheless, the *Encyclopedic Dictionary* offers a wide array of canonical entries, from Plato to Jakobson. Still another fecund source of canonization is the popular semiotic trope "Forgotten" or "Neglected Figures" in semiotics created by Sebeok (1979) and reaching number thirty-three in Watt 1990.

Even less codified appears a set or sets of theses for semiotics. The vastness of semiotic writing is essentially theoretical and metatheoretical (cf. chapter 5 above). Thus, a set of theses can be extracted from, e.g., Jakobson's (1979) initial address to the First Congress of the IASS or from any number of contributions to that Congress, or from the published proceedings of the Second Congress (cf. Borbé 1983) or of the Third Congress (cf. Herzfeld and Melazzo 1988). The search for one paradigm appears to be the recurring particular burden of these international semiotic congresses, although they by no means hold the monopoly on concern for the integration of a set of axioms for semiotic method (cf. "State of the Art" above).

The question which still lingers and continues to challenge the international community of semiotists as the millennium closes is whether, in fact, we should realistically expect and, indeed, attain a canon and a set of theses for semiotics, the latter on the model of something like the ten multi-pronged Prague School theses. (The venerable "Theses presented to the First Congress of Slavists held in Prague in 1929" enjoy a new English translation by Vachek (Vachek and Dusková 1983: 77–120; cf. also Rauch 1990b). We are faced with the possibility of supplementing the existing fourteen-article organizational statutes of the IASS (reprinted in Bernard *et al.* 1989: 5–8) with a finite set of theses formally postulating axioms which speak to the semiotist's focus toward axiomatic treatment of the sign act, arbitrariness, autoambience, inference, and other starkly fundamental tenets of semiotics. Should we, at long last, rid ourselves of this nagging onus of concern for semiotics without canon, without theses (and institutionalize both for the record)? Or is this burden's existence, after all, the semiotist's *raison d'être*—i.e., is the best canon indeed no (conventionalized/delimited) canon; are the best theses indeed no (conventionalized/delimited) theses?

Tolerance and Openness

At the beginning of this volume, Chapter 1 displayed the current openness of science generally. Surely this is a reflex of a socio-cultural trend reflective of worldwide radical changes socially, politically, economically, and, accordingly, intellectually. It is not necessary to enumerate details in the diverse cultures of the human community which have brought our consciousness to the point of, in one word, *openness*, certainly at the least more openness, in which we now find ourselves. Thus, e.g., Tarnas (1990: 23; cf. "Compatibility of Paradigms," Chapter 1 above) speaks of a "holistic and participatory world view, visible in virtually every field," while Yates (1986: 359; cf. loc. cit., Chapter 1 above) tells us that "Science has been softened up ... and seems to be open to new dimensions," and in popular rhetoric Strobe Talbott (1992: 71) proclaims "Humanity has discovered that differences need not divide." Nor do we attempt to analyze the myriad factors and forces that have led us to this new tolerance in the waning years of the second millennium. What is impressive is that toleration is an inherent attribute of semiotic method, i.e., it is not superimposed by researchers in given eras or given loci. It is in the nature of the semiotic paradigm to shun a conventionalized/delimited canon and a conventionalized/delimited set of theses—a fact that has long exasperated semiotists with its Sisyphean challenge (as discussed in the section above).

Another source for gauging the state of semiotics at the turn of the millennium is Nöth's 1990 *Handbook of Semiotics*; it may serve as a bible for the present state of the art of semiotics. The description-deviant nature of semiotics is amply and immediately overcome by Nöth in his "Introduction" (1990: 4) with such remarks as "it is impossible to give a comprehensive survey of all implicitly semiotic research." The old ghosts of whether semiotics is a "science," "movement," "fashion," "revolution," "project," "doctrine," "theoretical," "applied" (1990: 4–5) are also expeditiously felled and demoted to quasi-moot questions by Nöth's reference to Kristeva's view of semiotics as "'an open path of research, a constant critique referring to itself in autocriticism'" (Nöth 1990: 5). Although we highlight "open" of the Kristeva citation, the *"autocriticism"* characterizes the semiotic endeavor extremely well. It is precisely the autocriticism which universally exacerbates the openness of the paradigm, and Nöth's presentation is no exception to this sensitivity. Nöth's *Handbook* represents a premier research tool of enormous value to global semiotics.

Eco's Hope

Eco's hope that there "never ... exist a single unified semiotic theory" (cf. "State of the Art" above), not only uncannily answers the question whether the best canon and the best theses for semiotics are non-conventionalized, non-delimited (cf. "A Canon and Theses for Semiotics" above), but his hope inexorably sets the tone for the future of semiotics. Eco's statement undoubtedly reads very post-modern (cf, Chapter 1 above) and reflects well the remarkable diversity in both semiotic method and cultural provenance which emerged in the final decade of the twentieth century. In preparation for the 1994 Fifth Congress of the International Association for Semiotic Studies, held at the University of California, Berkeley, semiotists around the world were polled in the Summer of 1991 for themes at the current pulse of the semiotic paradigm. The reply of "retrospective ... evaluating" within the framework of "prospective ... perspectives" for semiotics (Lucia Santaella Braga, São Paulo, Brazil) echoes the continual self-critical feature of semiotic research (cf. Kristeva quote above). Similarly, Ivan Mladenov (Sofia, Bulgaria) appropriately proposes a discussion of "Semiotics Beyond Definitions (The Survival of Semiotics Despite Numerous Attempts to Dissolve it in Definitions)," while Solomon Marcus (Bucharest, Rumania) stresses viewing semiotics "from inter- to transdisciplinarity." On the one hand, Eugen Baer (Geneva, New York) calls for "Semiotics as *organon* for all inquiry;" on the other hand, Peter Haidu (Los Angeles, California) speaks of "renewed examination of alternative forms of semiotic theory."

Other themes singled out by semiotists in the poll included: "musical Semiotics" (Eero Tarasti; Helsinki, Finland), "literary discourse" (Michael Riffaterre; New York, New York), "metaphors we live by" (Linda R. Waugh; Ithaca, New York), "theatre semiotics" (André Helbo; Brussels, Belgium)' "theology" (Gayle A. Henrotte; La Verne, California), "index, icon, symbol" (Charls Pearson; Atlanta,

Georgia), "marketing Semiotics" (Jean Umiker-Sebeok; Bloomington, Indiana), "sémiotique de l'espace" (Pierre Pellegrino; Geneva, Switzerland), "semiotic of the unconscious" (John Deely; Dubuque, Iowa), "semiotic of culture" (Nurith Gertz; Tel Aviv, Israel), "semiotics and communication" (Gila Safran-Naveh; Cincinnati, Ohio), "semiotics and analytical philosophy of language" (Umberto Eco; Milan, Italy), "semiotics" and "feminist theory" (Thaïs Morgan; Tempe, Arizona), "medical and psychiatric ... semiotic studies" (Frank A. Johnson; San Francisco, California), "mathematical semiotics" (Mariana Net; Bucharest, Rumania), "time, memory and history" (Thomas G. Winner; Cambridge, Massachusetts), "semiotics and natural sciences" (Eleanor Donnelly; Indianapolis, Indiana), "cognitive Science" (Jackson G. Barry; College Park, Maryland).

The above themes certainly reflect the present thematic richness and diversity of semiotics. Several replies to the 1991 poll spoke to the currently changing "topography of semiotics (Nöth 1990: ix) explicitly in accord with several, some quite abrupt, global changes (cf. "Tolerance and Openness" above). Thus, e.g., Vilmos Voigt (Budapest, Hungary) observes that "... the current events in East Europe and elsewhere show the importance and dynamics of 'New Signs Replace Old Signs;'" Daniel Brewer (Irvine, California) suggests "'The Subject in/of the State.' Especially in view of the reemergence of nationalism as a means of expressing identity, how might one review contemporary theoretical constructs relating to subjectivity, ideology, power and knowledge, etc.;" and Xiankun Li (Wuhan, China) notes that:

> ... exchange of information on semiotic studies between East and West is a special topic of importance. Semiotic studies in the East has its own characteristics from either the historical or the realistic point of view. The characteristics of Chinese writing, for instance, have influenced the cultural ideology of the Chinese people. Traditionally speaking, the Chinese semantic theory is so rich that I consider it worth tapping and exchanging.

The general concern evident in the written responses of most pollees with the rapidly changing semiotic topography or "landscape" (term from title of the First IASS Congress, cf. Eco 1979), and that landscape's need for new grooming, growing, and even mutating represented a challenge well met at the Berkeley Congress, not the least of which because of the University of California's celebrated tolerance for creative and open interchange. To be sure, the theme of the Sixth IASS Congress entitled "Semiotics Bridging Nature & Culture," held in Guadalajara, Mexico (July 1997) continued to stress "an *open* debate to increase our knowledge about ourselves in our relation with nature" (from the "Call for Papers," emphasis mine).

Indeed, Eco's hope of a non-unified, non-single theory of semiotics was upheld at the Berkeley Congress by the robust offering of hundreds of scholarly papers from among the seven hundred semiotists representing forty-nine countries (cf. Rauch and Carr 1996). Strikingly, Eco's hope acts as a beacon into the twenty-first century, reminding semiotists that pursuit of the study encapsulated by the Peircean aphorism "Symbols grow" (2: 302) requires intellectual tolerance and openness in the future.

Part Two

12

Spelling of Sounds and Iconism

The principal evidence which the reader of a historical text utilizes in cognizing the text is the written data. This is particularly the case in Old Saxon (cf. "Drawl in a Dead Language," Chapter 13 below) because of the richness of the variations in spelling, both for consonants and vowels, and both in root and affix syllables in the data yielded by the ninth/tenth century biblical epics entitled *Heliand* and *Genesis*.

Variant Spellings

Variation between and among graphs is rampant in all syllables of an Old Saxon word. The variations may be free, i.e., not influence meaning, for example the adverb *simlon ~ simblon ~ simnon ~ sinnon* 'always,' showing variations which represent common *phonetic iconisms* or assimilations. In addition they may be phonologically significant, for example graph lowering of the strong masculine dative singular <e> desinence to <a>, indicative of an open *e* sound, perhaps also indicative of end-syllable weakening. They may be iconically produced in the syntagm, for example *te gidruogi dādi* 'as a deception might have done,' in which the <i> of the noun copies the <i> of the verb, or *reginugiscapu* 'fate,' where the final <u> iconically induces medial <u>. Finally graphic variation may be meaningful, signifying distinct morphemes, e.g., accusative singular *hell* 'hell' with affective meaning alternating with *hellia* (cf. Rauch 1987b). Graphic variation in the Old Saxon inflectional syllable appears particularly volatile. Consider the title and main character of the Old Saxon epic data, *hēliand*, in the nominative singular (cf. Table A):

Table A

> hēlandi
> hēlandeo
> hēlendi
> hēleand
> hēland
> hēleando
> hēlendio

Both in medial and inflectional syllable, graphic variation abounds. Once the base has been recognized, the reader concentrates on disambiguating the desinence, i.e., the inflectional suffix. Sehrt (1966: 245) lists the base form as "*hēliand, hēleand, hēland* substantiv partizip *Heiland* (nur von Christus)" without discriminating the desinential variations in the nominative singular. The standard Old Saxon grammars characterize the noun *hēliand* as a member of the consonant *-nd* stems, genetically present participle, which inflect as short *a*-stems in the genitive/dative singular, and which can use a pronominal genitive plural in *-ero*. Thus, Gallée (1910: §338) *Altsächsische Grammatik* offers the paradigm word 'friend' for the set (cf. Table B; Sg. = Singular, Pl. = Plural, N. = Nominative, A. = Accusative, D. = Dative, G. = Genitive):

Table B

Sg	N.A.	friund	Pl. friund
	G.	friundes, -as	friundo
	D.	friunde, -i, -a	friundun, -on

Holthausen (1921: §320) shows similar, although not identical endings. (according to Holthausen <;> indicates analogical variants to the *a*-stems.) Cf. Table C:

Table C

		Singular	Plural
	N.A.	*friund*	*friund; -os, -a*
	G.	*friundes, -as*	*friundo*
	D.	*friunde, -a*	*friundun, -on*

The set identification of Gallée and Holthausen may suggest to the reader of the syntagmatic *-eo*, *-io*, or *-o* forms of the nominative singular *hēliand* a possible paradigmatic genitive plural, while the -i desinence might be read as a rare dative singular in which *e* is raised to *i* (cf. Table A). However, the word *hēliand* shows an expanded *-ero* genitive plural; additionally the syntax of the data in which these non-zero forms occur requires subject, that is, nominative meaning, e.g., lines 2277–8 (cited from Sievers 1878: 158): *thoh im simla ferah for-gaf hēlendi Crist* glossed by Genzmer (1956) "Ihm gab zurück seinen Sinn Krist, *der Heliand*," and by Scott (1966) 'Yet Mighty Christ always, *the Healer*, gave him back his life.' Notice that both the German and English rendition of OS *hēlendi* are nouns, *der Heliand, the Healer*, this, in spite of its collocation with another noun. The interpretation of the *hēlendi Crist* syntagm as epithetic noun + noun compound (as witnessed in both translations above) by the second language learner of Old Saxon and indeed by the native speaker of Old Saxon is not out of the question. Surely, the naive reader is not cognizant of the fact that *hēlendi* embodies the ø-inflection of strong *ja*-stem adjectives to which present participles are susceptible. Relative to the base form, *hēliand*, *hēlendi* can be read at best as a synchronic syncope or as an excrescence relationship. Relative to the *-Vo* desinence as in *hēlandeo* of manuscript M, *hēlendi* of the identical citation in manuscript C can be read synchronically as a syncopated ending. The *-Vo* morphemes themselves bespeak the weak *n*-stems, both of nouns and adjectives, again allowing a noun interpretation. Although the *-i* form varies freely with the *-Vo* form in syntagm, the ø-desinence form does not—strong evidence that Sehrt's implied restructuring of the adjective forms has not yet occurred in the Old Saxon data. Yet the cognition of the three genetic sources synchronically viewed by the naive reader of the syntagm remains open to the question, because of the syncopes, epentheses, graph lowerings, and graph raisings which inform the Old Saxon inflectional data.

Hermeneutics and Phantom Icons

Due to this seeming graphemic rummage, the standard grammars, Gallée (1910) and Holthausen (1921), appeal not infrequently to scribal error. Thus, e.g., Gallée (§ 314.5) writes of the genitive plural *lidu* 'limb': "ist wohl fehlerhaft." This <u> desinence (instead of expected <io>) can be accounted for by <i> syncope and raising of <o>

to <u>. Accordingly, on the basis of extant forms, *lid* could be assigned synchronically to strong masculine *i*-plural nouns and not to genetic *u*-stems as Gallée and Holthausen do.

The genitive singular strong feminine noun *bedu* 'prayer' is attributed by Holthausen (1921: § 283.3) to analogy with the dative singular desinence. Such *iconism* may be a causal factor; however, dialect and/or scribal habit may also be factors: ms. C uses the *bedu*, ms. M *bede*, the latter considered Old Frisian habit compared to the expected *beda*. Ms. M also attests to a *bede* dative singular which can be iconic with the genitive singular; or it can be viewed as graphic lowering of <u> to <o> to <a>, often interpreted as weakening of end syllable plus graphic raising of <a> to <e>. In fact, both the genitive and the dative singular desinences of strong feminine nouns vary the graphs <u, o, a, e> (cf. Table D from Holthausen 1921: §282; according to Holthausen <;> indicates analogical variation from dative in the singular and form other noun classes in the plural.) Table E from Gallée 1910: § 307:

Table D

	Singular	Plural
N.A.	geƀa, -e	geƀa
G.	geƀa; -u, -o	geƀono
D.	geƀa, -o, -a	geƀon; -um, -n

Table E

Sg.			Pl.		
	N.A.	geƀa, -e		N.A.	geƀa
	G.	geƀa, -e, -u		G.	geƀono, geƀo
	D.	geƀa, -o, -a, -e		D.	geƀon, -un

These graphic variations heighten the degree of probability in decision making for the hermeneutic task facing the reader of Old Saxon. To be sure, such decisions are resolved in the traditional grammars by appeal to genetic origin or reconstruction. A case in point is the description of the Old Saxon weak masculine/neuter, genitive/dative, singular desinence which occurs as -*on*, -*an*, -*en*, -*un*. Holthausen (§308) comments: "Die alte Endung des G. und Dat. Sg. -*en* ... muss als *Merkmal der Sprache des Heliand und der Genesis* gelten." To be sure, the hypothesized Indo-European morpheme for the given desinence is *-en*, certainly an unknown fact to the native speaker of Old Saxon. With regard to *Table* D, notice that Holthausen quite unambiguously differentiates a genitive singular <-a> and a dative singular <-u/-o> from all other graphic variants (notice his use of the semicolon) in this strong feminine noun paradigm, which he labels genetically "ō-Stämme." The somewhat facetious question which presents itself is how the ongoing communication of the native Old Saxon was possible without the benefit of genetic language insights. Rauch's *Introduction to Old Saxon* (1992c) assumes that it, indeed, was possible; her grammar, accordingly, takes the viewpoint that the second-language learner of Old Saxon can read the Old Saxon data successfully without recourse to genetic facts, and that s/he is, in fact, engaging in "historical interlanguage" learning (cf. "Interlanguage and Historical Text," Chapter 18 below).

Framed another way, the challenging question speaks to what the native Old Saxon, and by implication the second-language learner of Old Saxon, cognizes when confronted with an array of graphic variations. A few additional cases in point will serve to prioritize the descriptive/explanatory options facing the Old Saxon linguist. The strong feminine *i*-plural noun *tīd* 'time' also shows a nom.pl. *tīda* which can be genetically linked with the strong genetic ō-stem feminine nouns as *geba* (cf. Tables D, E). Alternatively, the -a of *tīda* can be linked with Old Saxon graphic lowering from <i> to <e> and from <e> to <a>. The decision requires a judgment as to whether the reader (native Old Saxon or second-language learner) cognizes the noun as belonging to a paradigmatic class or whether s/he perceives the graphic and/or phonological variation, and thus *iconism*, in the inflection. The answer is quite independent of the teleological explanation offered by Sievers (1878: 503 n. 106) of the scribal iconically produced <-a> embedded in syntagm with *(Ne sint) mīna (noh) ... cumana*, "my times (are not yet) come." Remarkably, Holthausen (1921: §283.4) maintains that the <-i> variation, *thiedi*, for the dat. sg. strong ō-stem feminine *thiodu* 'folk' follows the genetic "*i*-Deklination," while the <-a> variation, *thioda*, belongs "wohl zu einem mask. oder neutr. a-Stämme" (cf. Tables D, E again). Such statements represent the construction of phantom icons and they directly impute to the Old Saxon native speaker trained linguistic etymological abilities. Nor is it the case that for the most part the current second-language learner is etymologically sophisticated. Moreover, Holthausen overlooks the fact that a feminine gender paradigm is unambiguously targeted by the preceding determiner in the noun phrase syntagm, which in Indo-European languages generally play the role of servitude. Thus, we read, e.g., *thesaro thioda, theru thiedi* 'these, the people,' with tell-tale feminine inflection of the article. The dative singular variant *thioda* also occurs with the feminine article *thesare*.

To be sure, the single, anomalous dative singular *theson thioda*, with masculine/neuter determiner, is, according to Gallée (1910: §308.2) either scribal error or indicative of nascent gender change to neuter, in accord with Middle Low German and Middle Netherlandic. Appeal to future linguistic history on the basis of one form is as tenuous as appeal to genetic history in a grammar focused on *diachronic synchrony*. This is not at all to deny that some Old Saxon nouns straddle gender types and/or noun paradigm types. It does, however, speak directly to the immediate perception of graphic variants by the reader of the Old Saxon text. Although the reader may gradually extrapolate from the confusion of desinential graphs, neutralizations, and syncretisms in noun inflectional morphologies of the diachronic (that is, dynamic) synchrony, his most immediate and productive icon construction is simply cognition of the graphic lowering phenomena of, most commonly, <i, u> to <e, o>, and in turn, to <a>, which, for its part, can be found raised to <e, o> in the Old Saxon data. Phantom icons of genetic history are thus destroyed by the empirically based abductions of diachronic synchrony.

13

Accompanying Sound: Paralanguage

Not all of the sound of a chunk of speech is visible in the spelling or writing of words or sentences. The invisible sound parts of written words, that is, those not reflected in writing segments, e.g., alphabets, hence called segmental systems, belong to suprasegmental systems, e.g., stress and pitch, or to paralanguage (cf. "[L] in Paralanguage," chapter 6 above).

Delineating Paralanguage

If language is the many children of several disciplines (cf. "The Language Inlay," Chapter 3 above), then paralanguage is also; but paralinguistics is to linguistics, unfortunately, a neglected stepchild at most (cf. Poyatos 1993: 1–6). George Trager's admonition, over several decades ago, to the linguist that "communication is more than language" (1958: 1) and that in using language we are ultimately dealing with and dependent on what he (4) terms the

> ... voice set ... the physiological and physical peculiarities resulting in the patterned identification of individuals as members of a societal group and as persons of a certain sex, age, state of health, body build, rhythm state, position in a group, mood, bodily condition, location,

expresses a viewpoint with appeal to a growing number of contemporary scholars. One would certainly expect to find a receptive audience for it in today's pragmatic linguistics; however, David Crystal, in his 1974 overview of paralinguistics, reports (267): "Most linguists were—and are—of the opinion that paralanguage is at best of marginal significance to linguistics, and equally well or more appropriately studied by other disciplines." Indeed, Lyons (1995: 14) still notes: "As the term 'paralinguistic' suggests, these [paralinguistic features] are not regarded by linguists as being an integral part of the utterances with which they are associated."

Crystal's study shows that linguists as a group do not appear to know what, precisely, paralanguage encompasses. In part, the responsibility for this ignorance resides with the twentieth-century progenitors of paralanguage. On the one hand, Sievers' postulation of the physiognomic curves (1924), or Jakobson's (1971b: 682; cf. "Eco on Jakobson," Chapter 10 above) recognition that, "In addition to the multiform intentional information, our talk carries inalienable and unalterable characteristics which are generated chiefly in the inferior part of the speech apparatus, from the abdomen-diaphragmal area to the pharynx," as well as Trager's conviction (quoted above), act as certain fulcrums in the linguistic inquiry of paralanguage. On the other hand, such certainty is by far outbalanced by a range of attitudes including complete rejection for linguistics, qualified inclusion, and equivocal assignment. Thus, for example, Trager's attitude is somewhat Janus-like in that it relegates paralanguage to metalinguistics and consequently to the periphery of language proper. Sapir (1921: 47), whose influence pervades the entire century, believed that :

All that part of speech which falls out of the rigid articulatory framework is not speech in idea, but is merely a superadded, more or less instinctively determined vocal complication, inseparable from speech in practice. All the individual colour of speech—personal emphasis, speed, personal cadence, personal pitch—is non-linguistic fact ...

And finally, Archibald Hill, the creator of the term paralanguage, held kinesics and paralanguage to be one and the same field of communication activity (1958). In short, the seeds for obscuring the domain of paralanguage were inherent in its twentieth-century rebirth for linguists by linguists.

And yet, Trager's "first approximation" of a paralanguage system still represents in essence all that the linguist has. Furthermore, it remains not without attraction for the linguist, because Trager employs the usable and familiar binary feature framework in (1) identifying *voice qualities* of pitch range, vocal lip control, glottis control, pitch control, articulation control, rhythm control, resonance, and tempo, and (2) isolating *vocalizations* consisting of (a) vocal characterizers such as laughing, crying, yelling, whispering, moaning, groaning, whining, breaking, belching, yawning, (b) vocal qualifiers such as intensity, pitch height, and extent, and (c) vocal segregates such as the onomatopoeic sequence in English *uh-uh* for negation or the hushing hiss *shhh*.

Crystal wrestles with alternatives such as human and nonhuman vocalization, vocal and nonvocal human communication, segmental and nonsegmental features or suprasegmental features alone, in an attempt to delineate the boundaries of paralanguage. He proposes for linguistic analysis "a scale of linguisticness" to approach the nonsegmental sound system. One of the distinguishing characteristics of his approach (1974: 281) is the constraint that "Vocal effects lacking any semantic force would ... be considered nonlinguistic ..." It seems, however, that the determination of "semantic force" recycles the problem, since the field of linguistic semantics has an analogous problem of delimitation. A more fruitful enterprise, for the time being at least, would be to free ourselves of the compulsion to contain the field, and to seek simply the identification of paraphonological features on the basis of their necessary interdigitation with hard linguistic features. In the second part of this chapter, a data-based case is considered, in an effort to use cofeatures to determine a paralanguage feature. The case offers several added challenges, not the least of which is that it deals with a language void of live data, and thus brings to the immature field of linguistic paralanguage the further insight that the field is able to identify and to isolate a paralanguage feature setting the basis of articulation in a historical language.

Drawl in a Dead Language

The language chosen for the demonstration of paralanguage in a dead language is Old Saxon (cf. Chapter 12 above), once spoken in the northern part of the present primarily German speech area, and attested most fully in the two major ninth and tenth century manuscripts of the *Heliand,* an epic work of approximately six thousand lines. Old Saxon, among the historical German dialects, shares with Gothic the puzzling position of being extended in time without immediate predecessors or descendants. Preceding Old Saxon is only a reconstructed proto-language, West Germanic, and succeeding is Middle Low German, not attested until some four hundred years after the *Heliand* data. That the provenience (date, place, author) of the *Heliand* manuscripts is unknown, on the one hand, stimulates linguistic investigation in search of philological answers and, on the other hand, leads to degeneration into circular argument, whereby the data are considered impossible to interpret because they have neither locational nor temporal identification.

The manuscript data are popularly held to be ambiguous due to the preponderance of orthographic variation. This has stimulated the development of many theories, which range from those that hold Old Saxon to be an indigenous koiné albeit hybrid (e.g., Wolff's [1934] double-faced, original English-German characterization of Old Saxon), to those theories which advocate Old Saxon as a lingua franca or pidgin language, used for literary purposes in the case of the *Heliand*, for example, Mitzka's (1948/50) supradialectal business language.

Among the many debated Old Saxon linguistic data, the key vocalic issue is the determination of the sounds represented by the digraphs <uo>, <ie> and their variations, primarily the monographs <o>, <e>, respectively. *Heliand* manuscript M (ninth-century Monacensis in Munich) exhibits approximately 1460 <ō> spellings as opposed to 34 <uo> graphs, while *Heliand* manuscript C (tenth-century Cottonianus in London) attests to some 1750 <uo> graphs against 119 <ō> spellings. Assorted scattered spellings include <ŏ, u, v̊, ó, oo, ou>. (The data for the <ie, e> distribution are parallel to those for the <uo, o> tabulation.) Obviously, the graphic evidence in these two major manuscripts is in direct conflict. In generative studies such as Voyles (1971), an optional diphthongization rule is posited, which may occur under primary stress, as in *guod* 'good,' or under secondary stress, as in the derivative suffix *-duom* in *kuningduom* 'kingdom'. The optionality designation thus completely sidesteps accountability for the fact that manuscript C tends to use digraphs, whereas manuscript M uses monographs. Voyles posits this optional diphthongization rule without any manuscript or dialect constraint. In so doing, he follows those Old Saxonists who exploit the manuscript material in continuous search of a common Old Saxon, that is, archetypal forms (e.g., Rooth 1973), even though it appears that he is interested in synchronics while the others are generally aiming at reconstructed language. The two generative dissertations, Barnes (1971) and Woods (1975), disappointingly contribute no insight into the diphthongization problem. Barnes (52) dismisses the orthographic evidence by writing: "The actual phonetic value [of ie, uo, e, o] is not important as far as this dissertation is concerned." Woods chooses to study the language of manuscript M only, for the reasons of text length, availability, and authenticity. The first two reasons are unfounded, if not erroneous; the third reason is a moot question, precisely the sort of question which a solution to the diphthongization problem could help answer. By studying M exclusively, Woods too, then, can avoid concern with digraphs for Germanic *ô, of which there are only thirty-four in manuscript M, and consequently with a possible diphthongization in Old Saxon.

Taxonomic studies such as Moulton (1961) serve to reinforce the dominant theory regarding the <uo> and <ie> graphs in Old Saxon scholarship of the past quarter to half century, namely, that the digraphs are prestigious orthographic borrowings from Old High German. Thus. Moulton's (18) statement that <ie> and <uo> are "... nur als fränkische Orthographie für phonemisches [<ê, ô>] zu beurteilen" is reminiscent of Rooth's (1973: 211–12) conviction that "Als Sachse sprach [der Helianddichter] ô, und die uo-Schreibungen müssen als solche, Schreibungen, gedeutet werden, die unter dem modischen Einfluss des Fränkischen standen."

It would seem that evidence such as the appearance of supposed High German orthography in manuscript M in a word such as gilîk 'like' (adverb), which occurs as gilih and gilîch, but its complete absence with High German Sound Shift spellings in manuscript C, should already weaken the researcher's faith in the orthographic borrowing theory. However, by and large, Old Saxon scholarship has been so mesmerized by the seemingly enigmatic orthographic data that attention has not been paid to phonological maneuvers within the total system, a failing which is rather surprising in view of the fact that linguistic structuralism was coterminous with the rise of Old Saxon studies in the nineteenth century. Van Ginneken (1956: 576) posits as one of Jakobson's "sworn-comrades" rules that of "the tendency towards diphthongization of the main syllable and that towards apocope of the accompanying syllable." If we look at the end syllables in the digraph-producing manuscript C, stunned by the fact that their weakly stressed vowels are far better preserved than those of the monograph-producing manuscript M—a fact which has long been disputed and judged incongruous by researchers working with a correlation in which glided vowels if not full diphthongs, are compatible with full vowels, which then requires a rule that is the converse of the Jakobson-van Ginneken rule (van Ginneken 1956). The converse rule is possible if it is paralinguistically conditioned by the Tragerian vocal qualifier feature of extent, which opposes *drawl* to *clipping*. The drawl conditioner finds its substantiation not only in the preservation of weakly stressed vowels and diphthongs, but also in the cofeature of vowel epenthesis in the neighborhood of resonants (e.g., *burug* 'city'), which abound in manuscript C compared to manuscript M. Obviously, this view is not meant to disparage the orthographic data; that would be a false impression, since its premises rely heavily on orthographic evidence. What is rejected here is the outright simulation of foreign orthography, what we might call the parasite view, which should have been challenged all along, if for no other reason than that the *Heliand* manuscript C does not, in fact, mimic the Old High German diphthongization orthography. Consider, for example, manuscript C *nuon* 'none, the ninth hour', which reads *non* in manuscript M as well as in Old High German. Consider further that Old Saxon *hie* 'he' and *thie* 'that, who' (demonstrative, relative pronoun, masculine, nominative singular), with the digraph spelling <ie>, are words foreign to Old High German; and therefore, Old High German absolutely could not serve as a model for these Old Saxon words.

As can be expected, the implications of the converse Old Saxon diphthongization rule with its paralanguage conditioner *drawl* are many and stimulating. Within Old Saxon, the language specific social function of the paralanguage feature is of interest, while the transcultural mapping of a northern-southern isogloss may be suggested. A cursory examination yields indications of corroborating evidence from such Old Saxon allied languages as Middle Low German, Dutch, English, and High German, which could serve as a point of departure. This, in turn, certainly argues for a further search for possible northern-southern drawl or drawl-like isoglosses beyond the languages immediately involved here.

In a sense, the introduction of the paralanguage feature *drawl* into the Old Saxon phonological system represents a missing link in the breaking of the Old Saxon code. But, beyond this, it bespeaks the richness of linguistic paralanguage, the twilight zone between semiotics and linguistics, that awaits our investigation.

14

Causality

As observed in the previous chapter in the section "Delineating Paralanguage," linguists appear to shy away from paralanguage. Yet, we found in Chapter 13 above that the paralinguistic feature of *drawl* may well be reconstructed as the catalyst in effecting diphthongal <uo> and <ie> for a language of a millennium ago, Old Saxon. In this chapter on *causality*, we confront the question of exactly what sort of catalysts for language change/growth are commonly pursued by linguists. The question as to what cause is has for linguistics the position of, let us say for the sake of analogy as well as impact, the question posed by Parzival to his mother, Herzeloyde, "What is God?" In other words, when linguists address the question of cause they unwittingly join the ranks of metaphysicists, to quote the philosopher Joseph Owens (1961: 421) "... the long scholarly tradition that (goes) back through Aristotle ... regarded ... deepest causes. It (is) the highest type of scientific knowledge, that is, of knowledge through cause."

Exhilarating though the fact may be that we are rubbing elbows with philosophers, it is quite a sobering experience to be told by Akmajian, Demers and Harnish in their 1979 *Linguistics: An Introduction to Language and Communication* (216) that "The reader may be surprised to discover that linguists currently have little idea what causes language change." Their second edition is hardly more encouraging; Akmajian, Demers and Harnish (1984: 356) write: "surprisingly perhaps, linguists currently have little understanding of the exact causes of language change." As linguists, we realize that a great deal has been written by linguists about language change, including causation either explicitly or implicitly, so that, in fact, we can claim a venerable tradition of research dealing with causality in linguistic change. How are we then to interpret the quasi-agnostic

stance of Akmajian, Demers and Harnish? Do we linguists really not
know "What is cause?" Or, have our considerations of causation
advanced to a point where we are indeed ready to contemplate and
question cause philosophically?

Causation in Linguistics

The paradigm data for causation in linguistic change have come from
phonology. Throughout contemporary linguistics the phonological
component has shown itself to be the most amenable to laboratory
observation and, accordingly, it is expected to be more easily acces-
sible for insight into the *actuation of change*. In the phonological
component the mutual interaction of sounds in the syntagm as well as
in the paradigm have been considered causal. Thus, Paul (1966),
Bloomfield (1933; cf. "Linguistics," Chapter 3 above), Hockett (1965;
cf. "Object Language," Chapter 5 above), to an extent de Saussure
(1959; cf. "Krampen on Saussure," Chapter 10 above), Jakobson (cf.
"Secondness Driving Physiological Fact" below; cf. "Eco on
Jakobson," Chapter 10 above) and Martinet (1955), among others,
hold that so-called conditioned sound change, at least, originates
physiologically in the speech chain. Paul's understanding for this
event is syntagmatic ease of articulation. On the other hand, the
interaction of sounds in the paradigm, paradigmatic ease, forms the
rationale for Jakobson (1962b), van Ginneken (1956), de Saussure
(1959) and Martinet (1955), among others. Martinet, e.g., visualizes
the dynamics within the paradigm in terms of push chains, drag
chains, and functional load.

The details of syntagmatic and paradigmatic phonological interaction are many and varied. Among those for syntagmatic interaction is,
e.g., speaker or hearer faulty perception, due in turn perhaps to such
physiological factors as moisture in the vocal tract, wax or dirt in the
ears, as held by Hockett—a viewpoint to which Martinet could also
subscribe as a possibility. Thus, e.g., in the rise of the uvular *r* "dans
une langue où n'existe pas d'ordre aussi profond," Martinet (1955:
176) considers the imitation of usage in which a physiological-
pathological trait may be involved. As a functionalist, however, he
explains the merger of IE *p and *k^W in Oscan-Umbrian as an extension of the tendency of the Indo-European labio-velars to be
reduced—a tendency readily understandable, of course, in the case of
the merger of Indo-European labio-velars with labials, which also

occurs in Oscan-Umbrian. On the other hand, paradigmatic ease and syntagmatic ease combine in Martinet's explanation of the merger of Indo-European voiced stops with voiced aspirated stops. While he maintains that two voiced stops cannot occur in the same root, that IE *b is practically non-existent, and that the voiced stops rarely function as derivational elements, Martinet (1955: 186) holds that these "… neutralisations, c'est-à-dire les confusions limitées à certains contextes et pour lesquelles, par conséquent, il existe un conditionnement dans la chaîne …" For morphology Kuryłowicz (cf. "Nineteenth-Century Linguistics," cf. Chapter 2 above) presents elaborate paradigmatic changes. In the case of the merger of suffixes, e.g., he suggests (1964: 52) that the processes display a "phenomenon (which) may be partly reduced to the tendency to generalize redundant features."

The work of Kuryłowicz and of Mańczak on so-called tendencies in language change and in particular his formulations for *analogy* are generally known (cf. "Linguistic Analogy and Semiotic Abduction," Chapter 2 above; cf. Trask 1996: 112–15). Analogy as unmitigated cause appears to be hardly a viable discussion in today's linguistics; it no longer holds a step-child relationship to sound change as it had in the wake of the Neogrammarian hypothesis. For those paradigmatists who hold that linguistic change is grammar change, e.g., King (1969), Postal (1968; cf. "Abductive Processing of Features," Chapter 6 above), Klima (1965), among others, analogy is simply grammar change. On the other hand, those who cross the threshold from linguistics to philosophy for teleological reasoning in cause, as do Anttila (1972) and H. Andersen (1974) (cf. "Linguistic Analogy and Semiotic Abduction," Chapter 2 above; cf."Analogy in Linguistics," Chapter 15 below) consider analogy as an inlay to the various mechanisms of linguistic change. It is well understood in the Humboldt-Vennemann universal (cf. also "Peirce *qua* Linguist," chapter 4 above) which states (Vennemann 1972: 184): "Suppletion is undesirable, uniformity of linguistic symbolization is desirable: Both roots and grammatical markers should be unique and constant." There is, then, *analogy* within the greater context of every cause, and, accordingly, analogy is a phenomenon of a different kind from cause *per se* (cf. "Secondness Driving Physiological Fact" below; cf. Chapter 15 below).

This observation of the universal ingredient which is analogy in no way implies that *linguistic universals* cannot come under consideration as cause. Characteristic of paradigmatists who advocate linguistic change as grammar change are the principles of *rule ordering.* Kiparsky's (1968) principle that rules tend to reorder in the least marked order was actually understood as cause. So. e.g., Kiparsky (1965: 61) explains the effect of the Cluster Reduction Rule which eliminates aspiration directly before obstruents and the effect of Grassmann's Law in Greek and Sanskrit as "... a consequence of the two rules and their ordering, if we assume that their initial and final stops are both aspirated in the underlying representation." The universal nature of rule ordering for explaining the phonological as well as syntactic facts of natural language culminates in the Koutsoudas, Sanders, and Noll (1974) universal of "proper inclusion precedence," whereby, in the case of Greek and Sanskrit, both the cluster reduction rule and the rule eliminating aspiration before a following aspirate will apply to whatever representations satisfy the structural descriptions of the two rules.

The reordering of rules is a manifestation of imperfect learning in language acquisition, according to Kiparsky (1965). Children learn the grammar of their elders only partially, resulting in a simplified grammar in the next generation. In fact, the transmission of a grammar from one generation to the next as proposed by Halle (1962), building on Meillet, is postulated as the primary mechanism of language change by *grammar change* paradigmatists. Weinreich. Labov, and Herzog (1968) modify this model by claiming that change is not necessarily caused within a generation's time nor by parental influence to the exclusion of peer influence. They claim change takes place in social contact among speakers of heterogeneous language systems as a speaker learns an alternate, more highly valued form. Paul and Bloomfield explain change as imitation of the speech habits of others in contact—an imitation which Bloomfield makes accountable to the *prestige* of the source language. Alternate forms are seen by Hockett as random free subemic variation with consequent change as a matter of taste. Postal (cf. "Abductive Processing of Features," Chapter 4 above) writes (1968: 283): "It seems clear ... that there is no more reason for languages to change than there is for automobiles to add fins one year and remove them the next, for jackets to have three buttons one year and remove them the next ... the 'causes' of sound change without language contact lie in the general tendency of human cultural products to undergo 'nonfunctional' stylistic change." Postal's comparison of language change to consumer style changes may, in turn, impress as a matter of taste only. Moreover, his view is actually not trivial to a discussion of cause since it is diametrically opposed to that view which would compare language change to organic change, thus, e.g., Stevick's (1963) *ordered chance* in linguistic change as well as in biological change or Lees (1980; cf. "What is Language," Introduction above) genetic code in biological evolution parallel to language in the evolution of the mind (cf. section below).

Similar, yet distinct from the *generation transmission* model are the considerations of *natural phonology*. Donegan and Stampe (1979), e.g., hold the mind of the first-language learner to be non-tabula rasa, as it were, i.e., by nature endowed with a system of linguistic processes which, if they are not suppressed to conform to the linguistic processes standard to the speakers surrounding him, will produce language change. Appeal to *innate ability* as cause is an appeal to psychological/biological factors. Although a confirmed syntagmaticist, Paul too conceded that psychological factors are involved when he wrote (1966: 216):

> ... es (gibt) in der Sprache überhaupt keine absichtliche zur Bezeichnung eines Funktionsunterschiedes gemachte Lautdifferenzierung ..., dass der erstere immer erst durch sekundäre Entwickelung letzteren hinzutritt, und zwar durch eine unbeabsichtigte, den sprechenden Individuen unbewusste Entwickelung vermittelt natürlich sich ergebender Ideenassoziation.

Secondness Driving Physiological Fact

What impresses most in skimming considerations of cause of language change in the recent history of contemporary linguistics is the fact that in the long run we witness a sizable, uninterrupted and rich, hut rather homogeneous tradition of causation theories in linguistics. In the short run, we may have viewed one or the other approach as revolutionary, but they have not proven to be so. Perhaps this is why Akmajian *et al.* (cf. section above) charge that we have little idea of what exactly causes language change. On the other hand, the rich tradition does represent a cumulation of causes. Are these causes not valid?

Without entering into the history of thought on causality, it is relatively clear that this recent tradition of cause in linguistics, in particular *paradigmatic ease*, is strongly influenced by causality theories in the mathematical sciences which represent cause in terms of law, i.e., as explaining a phenomenon in terms of the laws it obeys. Exact description takes the place of explanation of cause; the answer to *how* instead of *why* is sought. In the theoretical sciences any set of generalizations or laws that saves a phenomenon is held to be valid, provided it is mathematically simple, comprehensive and has predictive power. Certainly then, our rich linguistic heritage contributes to the answering of the question, "What causes language change?"

If, for the most part, the *actuation of language change* is viewed as occurring subliminally, i.e., not at will, the type of cause that we are most commonly dealing with in linguistic change is probably what is referred to in philosophy as Sense III. Both Sense I and Sense II of cause assume conscious, deliberate human choice in producing an effect. In Sense I that which is caused is a human action; in Sense II that which is caused is an event in the physical or natural world. Sense III is characterized as a cause which produces an effect independently of human will; Sense III functions generally in explanations in the theoretical sciences of nature, e.g., physics, chemistry. Accordingly, Sense II of cause requires for the production of its effect intermediate conditions, while Sense III directly produces its effect (cf. further Collingwood 1940). Suffice it to say that understanding language essentially as an organism, so, e.g., Stevick and Lees (cf. section above), rather than as an artifact, e.g., Postal (section above), appears to coincide with the view that *cause in language change* is largely subconscious in its inception (cf. Chapter 19 below).

By the above modifications herein, e.g., "essentially, largely," it is obvious that monism of cause is not tenable; it is unlikely that any linguist nowadays would disagree with John Stuart Mill's concept of *pluralism* which reads (1851: 339–40):

It is seldom, if ever, between a consequent and a single antecedent, that this invariable sequence subsists. It is usually between a consequent and the sum of several antecedents; the concurrence of all of them being requisite to produce, that is, to be certain of being followed by, the consequent. In such cases it is very common to single out one only of the antecedents under the denomination of Cause, calling the others merely Conditions … The real Cause is the whole of these antecedents; and we have, philosophically speaking, no right to give the name of cause to one of them, exclusively of the others.

Not precluded by pluralism of cause is the vital concept of differing *necessity* or compulsion within cause (cf. "Mutual Scientific Influence," Chapter 16 below)—a factor proceeding immediately from the differing cause senses. In Sense III the cause is absolute, direct, in "a one-one relation" (Collingwood 1940: 313) with the effect. Interestingly, Henning Andersen, who reintroduced a strong philosophical stance in linguistic causation theory, does not exploit this essential factor. In his article "Abductive and Deductive Change" (1973), Andersen explains the replacement of the sharped labials /pbm/ by the dentals (/tdn/ in the Litomyšl dialect of Czech during the fourteenth century, with their subsequent reversion to plain velars in the nineteenth century. (For convenience he refers to the innovators as Tetak speakers with initial *t* for Czech *pjet* 'five,' as contrasted then with the Petak speakers.) Andersen, rejecting all previous explanations for the actuation of these changes, claims that the Peircean model of *abduction* and *deduction* underlies both transformations. In the fourteenth century, Tetak speech evolved through indeterminacy in the production and the perception of the sharped labials. As Andersen says (1973: 789): "The source of abductive innovations (in evolutive change) is to be found in distributional ambiguities from which the new grammar is inferred." In addition, the language learners (younger generation) with underlying dentals accommodate the gradually receding surface labials by means of an adaptive rule of $t > p$ in formal style or older-generation style. Gradually the adaptive rule is lost. For Andersen the loss of the sharped labials through *perceptual ambiguity* is a mental process wherein the minor premise is derived from the major premise and the conclusion, resulting in an innovation. This is, in essence, abduction. Similarly, Andersen appeals to abduction in explaining the nineteenth-century return of the dentals to plain labials. The triggering mechanism is not phonological ambiguity, but rather borrowing or influence from the neighboring prestigious Petak dialects. In this instance, an adaptive rule of the sort $p > t$ would compensate to retain doublets at least until that time when the socially preferred labials limit the Tetak peculiarities to the older and finally passing generation.

The nineteenth-century change has absolutely no structural effect on the Tetak phonological component. It amounts to a few more labial occurrences in the labial inventory. Many linguists would not consider it as linguistic change *per se*. Concerning the fourteenth-century abduction, Andersen himself writes (1973: 778): "We have seen above that the conception of language acquisition assumed for our model of phonological change involves processes that are basic to all activities of the human mind." Obviously processes which are fundamental to all activities of the human mind are a necessary ingredient in linguistic cause; indeed, this is the status of *analogy*, as discussed in the section above. However, such processes cannot then be decisive in identifying cause in a given linguistic innovation.

If we pursue the ingredient of direct, absolute *compulsion* in cause for the fourteenth-century evolutive change, we can find it within the minor premise of the abductive inference, namely the Tetak sharped labial was at least 51% dental acoustically and physiologically, i.e., the sharped labials were, so to speak, more acute than grave. Spectrographically the second formant was raised from the first, the mouth cavity was narrowed by the advancement of the tongue toward the alveolar ridge and the teeth with the accompanying dilation of the pharyngeal cavity. In the light of this phonological reality and related facts such as *vowel palatalization*, which is more common to Czech than any other Slavonic language, it is all the more surprising that Andersen dismisses outright Jakobson's (1962a: 275) consideration of the Tetak change as a case of regressive assimilation. Be that as it may, Andersen's abductive model is only of value as causation in this particular change if we require the dynamic of direct compulsion within the abduction and seek to identify it (cf. Savan 1980, for another critique of Andersen 1973).

Finally, we look to a definition of Mill's (1851: 121) in which he maintains "... the cause of a phenomenon, to be the antecedent, or the concurrence of antecedents, on which it is invariably and unconditionally consequent." Coupled with Hobbes's (1839: 121) insight that "The cause, therefore, of all effects consists in certain accidents both in the agents and in the patients; which when they are present, the effect is produced; but if any one of them be wanting, it is not produced ...," it is clear, that an event will not occur if any factor in an aggregate of factors necessary for the production of that event is absent. In consideration of the fact that linguists are beginning to contemplate ever more seriously the elegant philosophical question of *why*, in fact, certain possible linguistic changes (events) do not occur, we may confidently conclude that linguistic method has, to be sure, succeeded in identifying a substantial array of valid causal factors leading to a linguistic theory of causation.

15

Analogy

In linguistic causation, analogy has a venerable history. To be sure, analogy is a case of abduction (cf. "Abductive Processing of Features," Chapter 6 above), and hence *Firstness*; as such it is fallible yet creative. This chapter traces the development of analogy in contemporary linguistic thought and its nondiscriminate application to language change/growth (cf. "Linguistic Analogy and Semiotic Abduction," Chapter 2 above).

Analogy in Linguistics

"Nothing shows quite so clearly that 'language is a form of life' as does our recourse to analogous expressions." This sort of statement implies that *analogy* is user-oriented, and as such the statement could be found in a current linguistics book concerned with pragmatics or with sociolinguistic factors in language change. This provocative statement, however, comes from the field of philosophy (Burrell, 1971: 274), which refreshes our memory to the fact that the burden of understanding linguistic analogy resided originally with other disciplines, preeminently philosophy (as with causation theory, cf. Chapter 14 above), and later, also psychology. In linguistics, analogy is one of the concepts which evolved out of the golden era of the comparative method in the early nineteenth century (cf. Nineteenth-Century Linguistics," Chapter 2 above), and which found strong confirmation in its assignment as a corollary to the Neogrammarian Hypothesis later in that century (cf. "Language Grows," Introduction above). Thus, we witness, for example, Whitney's (1869) early use of Aristotle's four-part geometric proportion in discussing the analogy of the preterite to the preterite participle in the case of English *sung*, as well as Fick's

(1883: 583) somewhat visceral attack on what he calls the "Mode- und Kinderkrankheit der Analogisterei," notwithstanding the fact that he himself employs analogy in his work.

Interestingly, a century later the analogy controversy is once again in the limelight of linguistic method. Perhaps it is singled out as one of the high priority casualties in antitransformationalism. However, one cannot help but get the impression that the controversy of the preceding century was never even provisionally resolved with regard to analogy, and that, in fact, from 1876 (the Neogrammarian dictum) to the present, analogy simply hobbled along rather aimlessly, by and large under the aegis of sound change.

The question of all or none, that is, outright acceptance or rejection of analogy again appears to characterize the twentieth-century analogy controversy, but its implications are extremely sophisticated. Thus, we read, for example, in Anttila (1972: 180; cf. "Linguistic Analogy and Semiotic Abduction," Chapter 2 above), that "The different mechanisms of change share a common analogical core," as though in apparent contrast with King's (1969: 128) assertion: "As historical linguistics is treated in generative grammar, grammar is enough ... 'analogy' is grammar change." To be sure, the aim of both quotations is radically different, but it is equally true that in both positions analogy is generalized as integral to grammar. And this is the line of thinking which ought to be exploited. It does not imply that we should not pursue those questions, frequently posing binary possibilities and often hearkening back to the first analogy controversy. For example: Is analogy a primary or a secondary process? Does it belong to competence or performance? Is it sporadic or is it regular in every component of the grammar? Nor does this line of thinking imply that we might ignore the valuable results peculiar to competing methodologies. It does, however, stress that we might also seek to raise novel questions, perhaps even shift the axis of our study with regard to analogy. This is why viewing the Anttila/King citations as a synthesis, rather than as an opposition may be fruitful. For the same reason, it is worthwhile to observe that Henning Andersen, in his presentation to the First International Conference on Historical Linguistics (Edinburgh, 1973), assimilated analogical changes into his "Typology of Change" without the use of the word "analogy" or its congeners. Thus, for example, he types the case of Middle English *cheri*, a paradigm sample of analogy, as a "deductive innovation" (cf. "Secondness Driving Physiological Fact," Chapter 14 above). Can

Andersen therefore be accused of rejecting analogy, or of equating analogical change with sound change? The answer is unequivocally in the negative, and we are reminded that yet another approach to analogy may be the acceptance of the implicit use of the concept in research, without insistence upon an explicit definition, a technique familiar to the linguist with regard to the concept "sentence," or to the physicist with regard to the concept "atom."

Secondness Driving Analogy

Certainly analogy is abduction, but not all analogy is alike, that is, *iconic analogy* can be distinguished from *indexical analogy* as shown in two cases of linguistic change, the first chosen because it is prehistoric and morphosemantic, the second because it is historical and phonological. Since these changes, namely the evolution of the Indo-European perfect tense and the development of the Old High German diphthong /eo/ in South Rhenish Franconian, are completed changes in familiar languages with plentiful data, against a background of known external history, they are ideal for extracting analogical elements.

Kuryłowicz (1964; cf. "Causation in Linguistics," Chapter 14 above) and Meid (1971) have developed intricate hypotheses concerning the evolution of the perfect tense in Indo-European from a verbal adjective in analogy to the present active system, not only in analogy to the completed system but also in analogy to the stages of its development. The earliest active indicative of both present and aorist stems are tenseless, moodless injunctives with secondary endings. The minus tense, minus mood injunctive of the present stem builds a present tense by means of an *i*-suffix, thus producing the opposition *root plus i* (present) versus *root plus zero* (non-present), the latter form signaling the emergence of the imperfect tense. In some Indo-European languages the function of the *root plus zero* form is taken over by an *e-augment plus root* form, thus yielding a three-way opposition in which the bare root is again minus tense but now plus mood. Analogously the perfective stems of the active system take on an *e*-augment yielding a two-way opposition, since a present from by *root plus i-suffix* is impossible according to the rules of natural semantics.

Now, the emergence of the perfect tense emulates the development of the present active system, which has just been described. The proto-perfect form is semantically a medial present or a medial aorist, distinguished purely lexically in its earliest stage. We note immediately that, parallel to the active present and the active aorist, *medial* here becomes correlated with perfect, so that the category perfect impresses less as an *aspect* than as a voice. As stated above, the primeval form of the perfect is a verbal adjective; it is in either of the two ablauts, -*e* or -*o*, and combines the meanings of the three aspects imperfective, state, perfective. Parallel to the history of the active, the proto-perfect restructures itself by splitting off a new present stem in -*i* with medial stative meaning, while the original perfect form in -*e* or -*o* ablaut now serves only to signal the secondary meaning of an old perfect, still reflected for example in the history of some preterite-present verbs, namely in tenseless, intensive, iterative features. The earliest form of this intensive, iterative, medial perfect is again injunctive. This injunctive develops further by splitting off a new medial present by means of a dental suffix, thus *t* plus *o* plus *i*, and secondly by retaining its own meaning, either through a parallel form in dental, thus *t* plus *o*, or through the original bare stem in -*e*.

This original bare stem in -*e* is the form leading to the perfect in the historical languages. It is incorporated into the verb conjugation by a set of personal endings and by alternation of the root ablaut (root accent in the singular, suffix accent in the plural and dual) in analogy to the conjugation of the present active system. These *phonological and morphological analogies* to the present active system are claimed to induce semantic analogy, whereby we witness the metamorphosis in which the perfect, originally medial and tenseless, comes to signal past tense by changing from a medial to an active, that is, by assuming also the voice of the present active. The intermediate semantic step is considered to be the "resultative perfect," in which the verb exerts its effect not on the subject as in the case of the medial, but on the object as is found in transitive relationship. Consequently the perfect, which had represented a present medial state resulting from past action, with the change from medial to active concomitantly favors the feature completion of the action over the feature present, thus signaling past tense.

The phonological-morphological analogies posited for the split of the perfect into the present passive and the perfect active seem fairly clear and plausible. However, it does not seem reasonable to view the semantic change from medial to active as an automatic consequence of these formal paradigm analogies. The *semantic change* can be reconstructed by a series of independent analogies or correlations somewhat parallel to, for example, the case of "sell" in Contemporary English. The middle or quasi-passive occurs in such a sentence as "The house is selling well." This correlates with the outright passive in the sentence "The house is being sold." In the latter instance "sold" is a transitive which accordingly correlates with "sell" in the active sentence "He is selling the house." Thus, an intransitive correlates with the passive of a transitive, a passive correlates with an active, thereby an intransitive correlates with an active; consider also "appears, is seen, sees" and many similar sets (cf. "Linguistic Analogy and Semiotic Abduction," Chapter 2 above).

In linguistics we would hold these phonological, morphological, and semantic analogies all to be of the same type, in this case specifically, the motivation of the verbal adjective (the proto-perfect) into a verb conjugation according to the rules of the present active verb conjugation, and the motivation of the medial to an active whether as a result of those analogies in form and their semantic similarities, or due to the semantic analogy of the medial with both the passive and the active. However, the semiotic model of Peirce allows us to distinguish at least two different types of analogy at work here. The first type is represented by the phonological and morphological analogies, for example, the *factual similarity* of the endings, as well as by any semantic analogies which share like features, for example the factual similarity of semantic simultaneity (durativity-state) between the present and the perfect paradigm. These are all *iconic analogies* which are motivated through the possible rules in the grammar. The simple correlations of the medial with the passive and the active likewise represent iconic analogy, but only superficially. If we go a step further to uncover the strategy underlying those correlations, we find that the crux of the relationships resides in the *indexical analogy* between the active and passive, which is motivated through a *necessary* rule in the grammar. This means that the correlation between the active and passive proceeds from the inference that the category passive has existence only because of the existence of the active, that is, they are in mutual dependency. In effect then, we arrive at the startling conclusion that it is ultimately not factual similarity of any sort between the present active and the perfect systems, but it is rather the *factual contiguity* between the active and passive, whereby one is meaningless without the other, that activates the perfect paradigm. Perhaps equally startling here is the realization that the *indexical* principle deals a severe blow to the reality of the unambiguous primordial linguistic form.

A similar dynamic can be uncovered in the analogies posited for the second case of linguistic change chosen for this paper, namely, the historical development of the Old High German diphthong /eo/ in South Rhenish Franconian. The data for South Rhenish Franconian come in the main from the well-known Otfrid (ninth century), who is credited with introducing end-line rhyme into Germanic verse. Van Coetsem (1975) has brought back into prominence the early merger of Old High German /eo/ from Germanic *eu and Old High German /ie/ from Germanic $*\bar{e}_2$, into South Rhenish Franconian /ia/. The three major dialects of Otfrid's time keep these diphthongs distinct. A raising principle operates in all Old High German dialects, though at differing intervals, whereby the first element of all diphthongs is raised. But for /iu/ and Early Old High German /eo/, the Old High German diphthongs can be assigned to one of two sets: a set of opening diphthongs (*ie, uo*) (cf. "Drawl in a Dead Language," Chapter 13 above), or a set of closing diphthongs (*ei, ou*). When Early Old High German /eo/ was influenced by the *general raising rule* of the first element of the diphthong, it joined the set of opening diphthongs. In two of the major dialects, Old Alemannic and Old Bavarian, a rule lowering the second element of the opening diphthongs is in effect, thus yielding *ea, oa*, since it operates prior to the raising rule. However, in neither of these two dialects, nor in the third principal dialect, Old Franconian, is Early Old High German /eo/ changed by this *lowering rule*. Consequently, when /eo/ becomes /ia/ in Otfrid's South Rhenish Franconian, it is explained as *orthographic analogy* to Old Alemannic /ia/ from $*\bar{e}_2$, bordering to the South, or a combination of *phonological analogies* to the Old Alemannic early lowering of the second element of opening diphthongs (*ea, oa*) and to the Old Franconian early general raising of the first element of diphthongs, bordering to the North, or as an indigenous union.

In Peircean terms these analogies are again purely *iconic*, mirroring the orthographic or phonological processes of neighboring dialects. Otfrid, however, gives evidence of another type of analogy at work. Besides introducing end-line rhyme, Otfrid is credited with other rhythmic conventions such as the insertion of metrical accents and subscript dots to mark vowel elision; he made use of acrostics, and he also rhymed vowels word-initially, that is, he made use of vowel harmony, either at least to some extent or at some time in his history.

This last convention, rhyme within a word as well as rhyme between words, is often adduced as evidence for the *merger* of Old High German /eo/ with Old High German /ie/ in South Rhenish Franconian. However, if we view rhyme not just as an *iconic analogy*, that is factually similar in sound, but as an *indexical analogy*, the rhyme pairs assume teleological significance, acting more as a cause than as after-the-fact evidence. This means that, for example, the *ia* of *gibiatan* "to order" from /eo/ or of *miata* "reward" from $*\bar{e}_2$ is induced by vowel harmony with the following *a* in each word, and that, for example, the *ia* of the rhyme pair *riaf* : *sliaf* "it called : he slept" from /eo/ and $*\bar{e}_2$ respectively, induce each other. The development of the merger of Old High German /eo/ with /ie/ in South Rhenish Franconian is then motivated, at least in part, by an analogical strategy wherein a necessary relation or factual contiguity unites two elements. The identification of *Secondness* driving the analogy lends certainty to analogy and thus to linguistic causality which invokes analogy.

16

Linguistics and Semiotics Juxtaposed — 2

We have seen in the two cases of linguistic change, delineated in the previous chapter (15), that the Peircean distinctions of index and icon which obtain between the sign and its object allow us to treat linguistic analogies as discrete relational strategies, rather than as unmotivated generalizers. Peirce's *icon, index,* and the third member of this semiotic triad, *symbol,* derive directly from his three pervasive elements or categories inherent in all phenomena, namely *Firstness, Secondness,* and *Thirdness* (cf. "What Is Semiotics? Introduction above). Particularly fascinating in the two linguistic changes are the indexical analogical relationships which represent the phenomenological category *Secondness.* They have been pinpointed as the mechanism of change, because they represent necessity, existence, what Peirce calls "blind compulsion" or "associational compulsion" (1932: 305–06), which evolves from "otherness" (1931: 296), that is, existence through necessary relationship with something else.

Complementary Tools

In this chapter we examine the dynamics of another linguistic change, the development of alternate forms of the past tense in a small group of American English verbs. We use these data not only to display once more the enhanced explanation which the Peircean categories contribute, but to demonstrate how these semiotic tools cooperate with distinctively linguistic tools, in particular the time-honored principle of *minimal opposition.* The linguistic principle of minimal opposition disambiguates members of a set by one distinctive feature, thus, e.g., in phonology the feature of voicing of the initial consonant in the English word *bin* which distinguishes it from the English word *pin.* In

linguistics such minimal opposition is termed "emic;" thus, we consider the phonemes /b/ and /p/ to comprise a set disambiguated by
voicing of one of its members. As observed in "Object Semiotics"
(Chapter 5 above), semiotic method borrows from linguistics the *emic*
principle in various semiotic modalities with such concepts as proxeme, videme, cademe, edeme (cf. "Linguistic Semiotics," Chapter 3
and "Object Semiotic," Chapter 5 above).

On the side of semiotics the phenomenological principle of *Secondness* can again be demonstrated to be a decidedly semiotic tool.
Although Peircean *Firstness*, *Secondness*, and *Thirdness* are found in
linguistic treatments under the cover of *icon*, *index* and *symbol*, the
pure dynamics of the three phenomenological categories are not exploited fully by linguistic method. Once more we uncover *Secondness*,
but also *Firstness* in the contemporary American English discussed
here. In his 1970 *Language* article, "Aspect and variant inflection in
English verbs," Randolph Quirk discusses the results of a series of
tests intended to substantiate his hypothesis that in both British and
American English the so-called irregular weak verbs display, on the
one hand, a voiceless dental inflection to signal perfective (momentary) aspect and, on the other hand, a voiced dental inflection to signal
imperfective (continuous) aspect, for example *spilt* in "When I
shouted, he *spilt* his coffee" versus *spilled* in "The water *spilled* out all
day until the ceiling gave way." Quirk is convinced that the results of
his experiments corroborate a speaker distinction between perfective
-*t* and imperfective -*ed* which are associated with the past participle
and preterite respectively, and that, in fact (1970: 310) "we might infer a corresponding direction of analogical influence," that is, the participial -*t* penetrates the preterite paradigm. Anyone familiar with
Quirk's article is aware of the tenuousness of his results, which
prompts him to invoke even diachronic Middle English data, lending
some support to the claim of analogical influence of the participle
upon the preterite.

It is surprising, however, that Quirk's experiments consider only
written data and only the *dental suffix*, to the complete neglect of the
accompanying *vowel alternation* which occurs in three of the eight
verbs included in his results: *dreamt, leapt, knelt*, beside *spoilt, spilt,
learnt, spelt, burnt*. (Quirk 1970: 307 excludes *smell* and *lean* on the
basis of poor test design.) When Quirk's data (1970: 305 Fig. 2a, 2b ;
309 Fig. 4a, 4b) are studied with a view toward the vowel alternation,
a clear-cut correlation between non-alternating root and suffix -*d* and

alternating root and suffix *-t* emerges. This correlation is particularly strong in American English in which, using Quirk's statistics, *dreamed, leaped, kneeled* can be found to be more objectionable than *spoiled, spilled, learned* and *burned* in the *-ed* perfect (Fig. 2a: most objectionable: *kneeled* 20%; *dreamed* 18%; *leaped* 12%; *spelled* 12% and all others less than 12%). In the *-ed preterite, dreamed* and *kneeled* are the most objectionable while *leaped* joins the non-alternating group (Fig. 4a: most objectionable: *kneeled* 15%, *dreamed* 12%; all others less than 12%, *leaped* 4%). Conversely, *knelt, dreamt,* and *leapt* are, but for *spoilt,* the least objectionable of the eight verbs in *t-perfect* (Fig. 2b: least objectionable: *knelt* 27%, *dreamt* 39%, *leapt* 51%; except *spoilt* 47%, all others more than 51%); and, with the exception of *burnt,* the verbs *knelt, dreamt,* and *leapt* are also the least objected to in the *t*-preterite (Fig. 4b: least objectionable: *knelt* 17%, *leapt* 38%, *dreamt* 51%; except *burnt* 40%, all others more than 50%).

Of the three root alternating verbs, the order of objection to *-ed* suffix from least to most in both the perfect and preterite is *leaped, dreamed, kneeled*; correspondingly the reverse order might be expected for the *-t* suffix, and this is, in fact, the case in the perfect, thus least objectionable *knelt,* then *dreamt,* and most objectionable *leapt.* In the *t*-preterite, *dreamt* and *leapt* change places, thus least objectionable *knelt,* then *leapt,* and most objectionable *dreamt.*

Two conclusions can be drawn from these observations. Firstly: the iconic association of the *-t* suffix with the alternating root regardless of whether the suffix signals tense or aspect, or both, is accountable at least in part for the spread of the *-t* suffix (thus e.g., *knelt* is a relatively late alternate, nineteenth-century, as compared to the fourteenth-century *dreamt* and *leapt*). Secondly, the *-t* suffix relative to the verb *leap* is in an *indexical* relationship, that is, regardless of the spelling, the voiceless dental alone is possible, contiguous to a root in voiceless consonant by *general phonological rule.* The *neutralization* of the *-ed* and *-t* suffixes with *leap* accounts for *leap* joining the non-alternating roots in the perfect, *have leaped, have leapt,* as well as in the preterite imperfective *leaped.* At the same time, the strong alliance of *leapt* in the preterite perfective (where *leapt,* in fact, is less objectionable than *dreamt*) corroborates the neutralization of *-t, -ed* by showing that the onus of the distinction between *leaped* and *leapt* in the preterite resides in the alternating root alone.

Mutual Scientific Influence

In observing the occurrence of the irregular *-t* preterites in contemporary American English, we witness the effect of a *Firstness* association identifying the alternating root with the *-t* suffix, and the effect
of a *Secondness* association *compelling* the *-t* suffix alone to be joined
to a voiceless root final consonant. Linguistic method sorts out the
minimal opposition between voiceless and voiced dental; it also shows
voice as automatically constrained by environment. Semiotic *Secondness*, however, identifies the automatic constraint as *compulsory* in
contrast to the *similarity* between the alternating root and the *-t* suffix
(Firstness), which is only *possible* and not compulsory. Without doubt
then, the potency of the *Secondness* correlation is strongly predictive
and explanatory. From this point of view, it is difficult to understand
why Anttila (1972: 95) describes the paradigm of Latin *wōk-* / *wōkw-*
'voice,' which regularizes in favor of *wōk-* (nominative), instead of
the oblique cases according to Latin habit, as an example of "... the
irregularity of analogy (one cannot predict the direction) ...," while
maintaining that the change is regular in itself, since Latin prohibits
interconsonantal *w* which would result in **wōkws*. It must be admitted
that one can predict this particular Latin analogy after all.

Semiotic method provides a tool for strengthening the long-sought
predictability factor in linguistics, which, in turn, strengthens the position of linguistics as a science (cf. "Linguistics/Semiotics as Science,"
Chapter 2 above). Wells (1947: 24) notes: "When it [linguistics] becomes predictive not only of the past but also of the future, linguistics
will have attained the inner circle of science." In terms of Kuryłowicz'
(1949) well-known simile of analogy to the rain which is not in-
evitable, but whose paths are predictable once it does rain, *indexical*
analogies contain predictability. The fact that rainwater will seek its
lowest point is indexical, compulsory, just as the fact that grammatical
voices, rhymes of rhyme pairs ("Secondness Driving Analogy," Chapter 15 above), as well as contiguous devoicing of sounds necessarily
engender one another. Semiotic method demonstrates its explanatory
power—a characteristic of any scientific theory. Cohen (1975: 25)
writes: "One criterion of appraisal for a semiotic theory ... is its ability to assist the impartial resolution of ... controversies." And lastly,
semiotic method is acquitted of the frequent charge that it does not
have distinct working tools, but rather a tool box containing an accumulation of tools from the other sciences (cf. Moravcsik 1975: 112:

"It is senseless that there should be one unitary science"). Accordingly, language data, while enjoying crossfertilization by semiotics and linguistics, nevertheless require the individual treatment of each discipline.

17

A Language Evolves

The previous chapter (16) displays well that language yields some compulsory features which override all other features configured in causation for a given instance of language change/growth. That the compulsion is in the phonological, i.e., phonetic component (a voiceless consonant engenders a contiguous voiceless consonant; cf. Chapter 16 above), is not surprising since *sound* is produced by the physiological sound tract and is physically acoustically perceived. Phonology, i.e., phonetics, is accordingly the most physical component of the grammar of a language, and it is subject to the *laws of physiology and acoustics.*

The present chapter (17) will demonstrate again the struggle between and among causation forces. As with the development of the English past tense verbs in *-d* and *-ed* (Chapter 16 above), we will again uncover a compulsory phonological feature, which will, however, not be so absolute that it cannot be subverted by other (competing) compulsory features in the language.

At issue is the coming of age of Modern or New High German. The tale of its evolution or recognition as New High German is readily told on the basis of facts external to the language. Heretofore the pinpointing of the fascinating facts internal to the development into New High German has been considered futile. Peirce's categories will shed new light on the innermost factors motivating the growth of the language into Modern German. The hallmark sign of its internal development is the Modern German *-e noun plural.*

External Signs

A large number of standard reference sources dealing with the history of the German language yield phonological provenance grids which show the *periodization* of the German language from Indo- European (IE) to Proto-Germanic (Gmc.), to West Germanic (WGmc.), to Old High German (OHG), to Middle High German (MHG), and to New High German (NHG). Such periodization without Early New High German (ENHG) can be witnessed, e.g., in Horacek (1958: 42) or in van Dam (1961: 240f.). The division resides in the model of Jacob Grimm (1831) which, in turn, is based on number symbolism of 3. To be sure, division of the history of the German language predates Grimm, so, e.g., Schottel (1663), who judges the spread of the vernacular over Latin and Luther's era as the third and fourth periods, respectively. Similarly, Adelung (1781) speaks of a fifth period from the mid-fourteenth century to the Reformation and a sixth period to his own time. The first scholar to speak specifically of an Early New High German, however, is Wilhelm Scherer in the second edition of his "Zur Geschichte der deutschen Sprache" (1878). Scherer sees the sixth epoch of the history of the German language as (13) "Die Uebergangs- oder frühneuhochdeutsche Zeit ... (1350–1650 oder um 1500)." He describes (14) the well-known "Roheit und Verwilderung" of the sounds and forms of ENHG grammar, and concludes: "Gegen Ende der Uebergangszeit finden wir im Gefolge der Reformation die hochdeutsche Schriftsprache allgemein anerkannt, auch auf niederdeutschem Gebiete." Eggers, while maintaining more recently (1985: 1295) "... die meisten Sprachhistoriker ... sind sich ... darin einig, das Frühnhd. nicht mehr als Übergang, sondern als eine eigenständige Sprachperiode zu betrachten," nevertheless speaks of (1304) " ... die mit vielerlei Unsicherheiten belastete Periodisierung der Sprachgeschichte." So also the perspicuous schema of Reichmann (1988: 120–21), summarizing the periodization of the German language depicts well the scholarly extent of the skepticism surrounding not only the question of an ENHG period, but also the delimitation of its possible chronological parameters.

Although *non-linguistic factors* for delimiting the ENHG periodization are plentiful and datable, e.g., the Black Death (1348), the election of Charles IV of Prague (1347), the Golden Bull (1356) for a *terminus a quo* and the end of the Thirty Years War (1648) for a *terminus ad quem*, the pinpointing of linguistic factors specifically to delimit ENHG, and thus to legitimize the term ENHG, is highly controversial. The principal reason for this has already been mentioned in quoting Scherer above, viz., the "Roheit und Verwilderung" of the ENHG data, reflective of a socio-cultural, political, economical, dialectal free-for-all. The irony herein lies in the fact that it is precisely the *rummage in the written data* which lends definition or credence to an ENHG period. Thus, Penzl (1984b: 12–13) writes: "Ich halte die Aufspaltung in Schriftdialekte für das wichtigste Merkmal der frühnhd. Periode" (cf. also Erben 1970: 400). Most scholars recognize an end to this rummage in, as Scherer (cf. above) wrote, "(einer) allgemein anerkannt(en) hochdeutsch(en) Schriftsprache." As Behaghel reminds us (1901: 661): "Die Kennzeichen des Nhd. sind im wesentlichen nur solche der Schriftsprache und werden von einem verhältnismäßig kleinen Teil der Mundarten geteilt."

Internal Signs

Granted, then, that there is a recognizable ENHG period, are we to be content with the characteristic sign of general *orthographic instability* in the written language or are there discoverable internal linguistic hallmarks to define the period as well? Repeatedly, sources enumerate linguistic characteristics in comparison with Middle High German. These features can, however, also be understood as signs of New High German since they are, in fact, carried through to Modern New High German. So, for example, Brooke (1955: XXXIX) presents a representative treatment of such an indistinguishable focus on the ENHG period: "If we undertake a descriptive analysis of representative MHG texts of the early thirteenth century, and of ENHG texts of, say, 1580, it is easy to enumerate the principal changes which affected the body of the German language during the period of transition." The problem is, as stated above, that the principal changes are seen as internally transcending the external delimitation of the ENHG period. Brooke lists some fourteen phonological changes (XL–XLVI) as well as fourteen characteristics of ENHG noun and verb morphology (p. XLVII–XLVIII, L–LVII). He deals tangentially with adjective, adverb, and pronoun morphology (XLVIII–XLIX), as also with a few "notes" on syntax (LVII–LVIII) and vocabulary (LVIII–LIX). However, in the general literature, the spotlight for delimiting the ENHG period remains on phonological characteristics. Indeed, Jacob and Wilhelm Grimm (1854) determined their three periods, OHG, MHG,

NHG, mainly by *phonological changes*. This is also the case for identifying ENHG dialects. Thus, Piirainen (1985), for example, divides
ENHG areally into East and West Upper German and East and West
Middle German purely on phonological criteria. Similarly, Penzl
(1984b) points to the ENHG diphthongization and merger with existing diphthongs, the ENHG monophthongization, the ENHG lengthen-
ing of short vowels in open syllable, and the ENHG merger of Gmc.
and OHG *s* to pinpoint the beginning of the ENHG period around
1350. However, Penzl's (1984a: 23) astute observation "Das Frühnhd.
kann zwar vom Mhd. auch innersprachlich als Periode abgegrenzt
werden, aber schwer so vom eigentlichen Nhd." encapsulates the
challenge facing historical linguists and inadvertently answers in the
affirmative the question posed at the beginning of this section.
(Observe, however, as recently as 1987 the conviction of Szulc (122):
"man [kann] Anhaltspunkte für die Periodisierung der dt. Sprachgeschichte kaum der Sprache selbst entnehmen," in his rejection of
Scherer's designation ENHG.)

Tracing a Hallmark Sign

Despite rampant variation in all components of the ENHG grammar at
differing points in time, it is indeed possible, albeit "schwer," to reconstruct a relative time for the closure of the ENHG period. In this
chapter, I choose but one characteristic sign, among other possible
signs, which evinces enormous *restructuring* dynamics and consequences in the morphological component but is effectuated by all
components of the grammar of ENHG. This characteristic sign is the
noun plural marker. Certainly, the massive destruction of the genetic
stem classes in the MHG noun desinences is a startling reality. Thus,
e.g., in the OHG strong masculine, Gmc. *ă, ja, wa, ĭ, ŭ, r, nt,* and root
stems—fully eight stem classes—merge in MHG to a plural in -*e* or ⌀,
plus or minus umlaut. Such stem class merger is hardly otherwise with
the neuter and feminine nouns. For the purposes of argument, this paper concentrates primarily on the strong masculine paradigms. In view
of this neutralization of the genetic stem classes and the consequent
simplification of the noun plural, the subsequent proliferation or fan-
ning out of the noun plural marker into NHG is even more startling. In
addition to the ⌀ and -*e* plural markers, plus or minus umlaut, found
also in MHG, masculine nouns in NHG further admit an *er*-plural
morpheme, plus or minus umlaut; the -*er* was formerly constrained as

a neuter plural only, representing the IE neuter *s-stems. Thus, e.g., umlaut plus -er is extended to the ancient *n-stem (∅-grade of the suffix) *man* 'man,' which acts historically as a root stem with ∅ plural; in MHG it shows influence of the *ă-stems so that a plural in -e also occurs, thus *manne*. The proliferation of the umlaut plus -er plural begins in the fourteenth century and thrives by the time of Luther. Entering the NHG period, an -n plural marker, genetically weak, has crossover to such strong masculine nouns as *See* 'lake' (MHG *sēwe*). Finally, the seventeenth century -s plural further expands the morphological pool of plural markers. In effect, the MHG strong masculine plural marker has then doubled (from four to eight) in possibilities into NHG. (For analogous proliferation and apportionment of the plural morphs in feminine and neuter nouns see August 1975, van Dam 1963, Geschke 1979, Werner 1969.) How can this be, considering the Germanic *drift* of phonetic weakening of end syllables or of weakly stressed syllables?

The role of the Indo-European/Germanic adjective (article) has always been one of servitude. Indeed, it marks gender, number, case where the noun is incapable of doing so. However, the ENHG nominative/accusative plural adjective (strong *gut(e)*/weak *guten* 'good') and article (*die*) can obliterate a number as well as a gender distinction, so that the noun itself must bear a number function previously borne by an attributive. The rise of a *plural noun suffix* is prompted thus by systemic necessity, i.e., it is semantically distinctive, in distinction to, e.g., the -e dative singular masculine/neuter noun suffix or the inorganic -e 1. and 3. person singular preterite indicative suffix of strong verbs which can be found in ENHG, but is lexicalized in only one NHG verb, *wurde* 'became.' In both the dative form and the preterite form the suffix is semantically redundant, since for the former the determiner signals case, while for the latter *ablaut* signals tense (cf. further below). Consider now the strong masculine noun *tag* 'day' enroute to seeking a uniform NHG plural. Its NHG plural -e desinence, *Tage*, is susceptible to apocope, so that it appears also as ENHG *tag* beside *tage*. Further, whether with or without the e-desinence, the root vowel is shown both without (cf. above) and with an ahistorical umlaut, thus *täg* and *täge*. There are in addition occurrences of an n-plural for *tag*, e.g., *tagen*, but also *tǎgen*.

With a view to delimiting the ENHG period, let us concentrate wholly on the e-plural sign. Its amazing spread across the ENHG noun morphology runs contrary to the -e *apocope drift*, which peaks in the sixteenth century, as witnessed in Lindgren's (1953: 151–167) statistics for the first person singular present indicative verb desinence in -e, which gradually wanes from 1300 to 1500 regardless of dialect. The ENHG e-plural is found not only in all vowel plurals coming out of Old High German (e.g., in the OHG masculine *tagā*, the OHG feminine *krefti* 'powers'), but also as the plural marker for genetically ϕ plural nouns, e.g., neuter *ă-stems, OHG/MHG *wort* 'words', MHG *gebe* 'gifts', the latter (although an *ō-stem) homophonous with its singular due to *end-syllable weakening*. Indeed, the productivity of the -e plural is of such a magnitude that it redundantly marks er-plural nouns, thus, *heusere* 'houses', an OHG/MHG ϕ plural *hūs*. (Note that *heusere* is actually marked three ways for plural: besides the two suffixes, it also evinces umlaut.) The e-suffix, however, on words in -er, whether genetic (e.g., *wazzer* 'water') or not (e.g., *heuser* above), is subject to the apocope drift and is totally lost by the sixteenth century in the ten dialects for which statistics are provided by Wegera (1987: 189).

Observe, however, the statistics for the chronological survival of the -e plural on monosyllabic nouns. For the masculine and feminine genetic -e plurals, i.e., Gmc. *a and *ĭ stems (Wegera 1987: 184): In the fourteenth century, seven dialects (Alsatian, East High Alemannic, East Franconian, Hessian, Ripuarian, Thuringian, Upper Saxon) show at least more than 50% e-plural; the other three dialects (Middle Bavarian, East Swabian, Swabian) prefer ϕ or apocope. By the time of the fifteenth century, only four of the ten dialects show more than 50% -e plural, the rest preferring an apocopated plural. In the sixteenth century only Thuringian and Upper Saxon clearly prefer the e-plural marker; Ripuarian has half -e, half ϕ; and the remaining dialects have overwhelmingly the apocopated desinence. Three dialects, in fact, show 100% apocope: East Swabian, Alsatian, East High Alemannic.

The situation has parallels in the e-plural where it is ahistorical, on the neuter *ā-stems with genetic ϕ plural (cf. Wegera 1987: 187). In the fourteenth century only Ripuarian uses the -e neuter plural more than 50% compared with the ϕ-plural. In the fifteenth century only Hessian shows a better than 50% -e neuter plural and Ripuarian, for example, has reduced its use of -e plural from 62% to 38%. By the sixteenth century none of the ten dialects shows at least 50% use of the -e plural for neuter *ă-stem nouns; all prefer the ϕ-option. The *apocope law* is in full force.

The startling fact is that for all genders, whether with or without genetic reflex, the apocopated -*e* makes a dramatic seventeenth-century return to signal the plural. Thus, in the neuter **ā*-stems with historical ϕ plural sign, the non-genetic -*e* plural appears in East Franconian 100% and in Alsatian and Old High Alemannic 41% und 43%, respectively. This is in distinction to its total non-occurrence in these three dialects during the immediately preceding century. In Hessian the -*e* desinence increases from 5% in the sixteenth century to 70% in the seventeenth century. The sixteenth-century Thuringian 31% -*e* plural is increased to 75% by the seventeenth century, and the Upper Saxon 35% -*e* plural of the sixteenth century grows to 100% in the seventeenth century.

Returning to the genetic *e*-plural of the masculine and feminine *i*-stems, it occurs 100% in seventeenth-century documents of East Franconian, Hessian, and Thuringian as compared with 48%, 10%, and 81% in the respective dialect documents of the preceding century. Alsatian and East High Alemannic, which knew no *e*-plural in the sixteenth century, show -*e* 90% and 57%, respectively, by the seventeenth century. Indeed, even the -*e* agglutinated to nouns in -*er* in the plural tenaciously returns, albeit slightly: 15% in East Franconian, 65% in Alsatian (Wegera 1987: 189–90).

Competing Signs

We turn now to the question posed above: How is the proliferation of the plural desinence, in particular the reemergence of -*e* sign possible in spite of the *drift of end syllable weakening and/or loss*? There is general agreement on a broad cause-effect answer to this question. Indeed, the weakening itself leads to homophony; thus, e.g., Werner (1969: 114) notes: "Durch diese Enttonung sind, vorerst noch allgemein gesprochen, viele phonemische Unterschiede innerhalb der Substantivflexion aufgehoben worden."

Accordingly, the resultant phonological neutralizations are untenable for required semantic distinctions, as Augst (1975: 9) writes: "Der Grund für diese vielen Morpheme für den Plural liegt, synchron gesehen, darin, daß alle genannten Möglichkeiten gleichzeitig auch polysem sind, d.h. andere sprachliche Funktionen erfüllen." Both of these observations are codified by Natural Morphology. The *apocope* of -*e* leads to damaged or unstable inflectional classes, a condition which runs counter to the system-dependent naturalness principle of class stability defined by Wurzel (1987: 92) as favoring "inflectional systems whose inflectional classes are independently motivated and whose paradigms follow implication patterns that are as general as possible." On the other hand, the *polysemy* of which Augst speaks refers, among other morphemes (cf. *-er* below), to plurals which are homophonous with their singulars, such as ENHG *tag* (cf. section above). Universal Grammar discourages homophony, synonomy, polysemy by the principle of *isomorphism/invariance*, which underlies all linguistic *iconism* (cf. "Language Grows," Introduction; "Peirce *qua* Linguist," Chapter 4 above). From this principle Universal Grammar derives the requirement that plurality "be encoded by means of 'something' not just by 'nothing'" (Mayerthaler 1987: 28), which requirement accedes to the system-independent naturalness principle of *constructional iconicity*, in that a marked *semantic* feature such as plural (in distinction to singular) exhibit corresponding additional morphological material. Thus Werner's relatively early observation (1968: 116): "Es ist verständlich, daß schon im Laufe des Alt-hochdeutschen das—unhörbare—N.Pl.-Zeichen ∅ häufig durch andere—hörbare—Allomorphe ersetzt wird" receives corroboration in naturalness theory, itself supported by sophisticated insights from biology and psychology (cf. Mayerthaler 1987, Wurzel 1987).

To be sure, *phonological* drift is subverted by *semantic iconism* in the restoration of the ENHG *-e* plural sign, yet we must ask why specifically this "apocopated" *-e* (cf. section below) rather than umlaut, *-er, -en*, or combinations thereof, proves so productive? Again, we find some sort of general consensus, with, however, incomplete specific and convincing systemic insights. Thus, for example, in pitting the ENHG *-e*-desinence against the ENHG *-er* plural, Gürtler (1913: 84) observes: "Ich erblicke den grund für die ablehnende haltung mancher der ... wörter dem -er-plural gegenüber ... vielmehr in der wirkung des *a*-plurals," i.e., Gmc. ǎ-stems, viz., ENHG *-e* plural. Natural Phonology, too, would judge the ENHG *-e d*esinence as tending toward stability, in which "dominant paradigm structure conditions tend to effect a strict linking of inflectional class membership to the phonological and/or semantico-syntactic properties of words," as Wurzel (1987: 81) writes. The polysemy of the *-er* desinence is well-known; besides serving as a noun plural suffix, it functions also as a derivational noun agent suffix, the adjective comparative suffix, and as an adverb-building suffix. Nevertheless, the *-e* suffix sign itself is not unambiguous. Phonological constraint is invoked by Gürtler (1913: 83): "Es ist zuzugeben, daß bei neutralen stämmen mit auslautendem -*r* (*jahr, rohr* u.a.) der -*er*-plural möglicherweise nur aus gründen des wohllautes vermieden wurde." Yet in exhaustive research on the -*er* plural theory through the centuries of ENHG and on reflexes in earlier centuries, Gürtler (1912, 1913) is able to document ample data of stems in -*r* which attest to an -*r* plural, e.g., OHG *harir* 'hair,' OHG *tiorir*, MHG *tierer* 'animals' (1912: 502, 509); ENHG *feurer* 'fires,' *röhrer* 'reeds' (1913: 71). Most interesting, but susceptible to challenge, Molt (1906: 348) suggests a counter-iconicity, counternaturalness explanation for the low functional load of -*r* plural for stems in -*r* attributing it to "das bemühen, seltenere wörter durch die pluralische form nicht zu sehr von dem sing. zu trennen."

Upon taking into consideration the wealth of ENHG data, as well as labyrinthine theories concerning the proliferation, in particular the intricate paradigm structure conditions of the ENHG plural morpheme, Wegera (1987: 283–4) appeals to the *prestige* of the *Lutheran -e* sign propelled by socio-political factors of the East Middle German speech area.. (The prestige dynamic of the perceived Lutheran -*e* sign as a factor is particularly noteworthy in instances where the -*e* tends to be inorganic and redundant, but also non-indigenous. Wegera (1987: 284) observes for the plural of ENHG nouns in -*er*: "In einigen Fällen führt dies im Obd. zur Wiedereinführung eines vermeintlich obersächsischen -*e* auch bei mehrsilbigen Lexemen bes. auf -*er*, wo es im Omd. gar nicht mehr erscheint.") Admittedly such teleological explanations are but one of Wegera's foci, yet they are reminiscent of extralinguistic approaches to delimiting the ENHG period (cf. "External Signs" above). To be sure, ENHG is a composite of competing dialects as compared to prescribed Standard Modern German; the extrapolation to dialect-general or supra-dialectal features is especially recalcitrant, thus feeding the appeal to the insights of universal and natural grammar. It would seem that a *natural pragmatics* ought also to be explored, both language-dependent and language-independent, which might, for example, consider possible discourse distinctions within and across ENHG dialects. As a case in point, the East Middle German, specifically Upper Saxon ENHG ∅ plural *kunig* beside *könige* 'kings' ought be investigated for the pragmatic implications of the umlaut and/or the non-umlauted alternative. Similarly, Upper Saxon ENHG plural *tag* beside *tage* may evince language-general as well as language-specific pragmatic *effects* of clipping, contraction, ellipsis and the like in various levels of usage and text situations.

We return to a phonological *why* for the resurgent strength of ENHG -*e* plural sign. Natural Phonology, in particular syllable theory, relies on the Jespersen-Saussure *sonority scale*, which rates the phones of language from the most sonorous (*a*) to the least sonorous (*p, t, k*). How does the ENHG weakly stressed plural-*e* compare phonologically with the weakly stressed plural-*er* and -*en* suffixes? In terms of sonority assignment, it is not necessary to reconstruct the exact possible phonetic value of these weakly stressed suffixes, i.e, whether [ə, ər, ən] or [ə, ʌ, ɲ-ən] are at stake. (An ENHG [ə] is systemically and typologically assured, although graphic data show some variation of <e> especially with <i>; see Sauerbeck, Stopp, Graser *et al.* 1973: ¶¶2, 46. Penzl, 1984b: 43, notes that "für die Vokalisierung von /ər/ zu einem zentralisierten Laut, der niedriger als [ə] ist, haben wir frühnhd. noch kein Beweismaterial." In Standard NHG, schwa deletion is pragmatically constrained and in the case of -*en* also segmentally constrained; see Benware 1986: ¶6.8.)

Both sets of alternatives exhibit the same relative sonority relationships. Thus, the nasal closes the suffix syllable with less sonority than the liquid, both being less sonorous than the open suffix syllable in bare schwa. The relative sonority of [ə] compared with [ʌ1 under weak stress can be established by the syllable producing ability of [ə]; German [ʌ] never displays epenthesis. In dialect, [ʌ] can be heard in strongly stressed syllables, e.g., *hʌbʌt* 'Herbert,' while [ə] does not occur under strong stress. General phonetics and cross-linguistic evidence corroborate its unmarked sonority among weakly stressed vowels as well. Thus Heffner (1952: 109) writes: "The vowel [ə] is as nearly an unarticulated [neutral] vowel sound as is to be found in human speech," and Ladefoged (1982: 30) claims "By far the commonest unstressed vowel is [ə]." To cite but one contrasting language, English tolerates [ʌ] but not [ə] in strongly stressed syllable.

The Cə syllable which emerges from the ENHG -*e* plural is particularly felicitous in terms of syllable theory. The Cə-suffix represents the instantiation of the Jakobsonian preferred syllable structure, CV. In Natural Phonology CV can be abstracted to a level of WS (weak strong) in which strong represents not only the V but also the coda (including phantom consonants such as the possible interpretation of *ī* as VC). In distinction to all strongly stressed syllables of German, Wiese (1986: 6) maintains that "der Silbenkern, der [ə] dominiert, [besitzt] nicht VC-Struktur, sondern [besteht] nur aus einem V-element." The favorable unmarked status of the CV *e*-plural suffix is further corroborated by preferred syllable structure laws such as Vennemann's (1986: 38) "Endrandgesetz ("Ein Endrand ist um so stärker bevorzugt, (a) je kleiner die Anzahl seiner Sprachlaute ist, (b) je geringer die konsonantische Stärke seines letzten Sprachlauts ist und (c) je schärfer die konsonantische Stärke vom letzten Sprachlaut auf die Stärke des vorangehenden Nukleus zu abfällt"), and Hooper's (1976: 225) "Optimal Syllable Principle" ("The higher the strength scale value permitted in a given C position, the greater the likelihood that a C will occur in that position, and the higher the strength value for the C. Similarly, the lower the strength value permitted in a C position, the less likely that a C will occur in that position").

It is necessary to exploit the preferred CV status of the ENHG -*e* plural sign in another direction. The language-specific articulation basis of German is characterized, among other features, by relatively strong muscular tension and air pressure (cf. Rauch 1975). This is at least partly accountable for the possibility of weakly stressed CV syllables which are [ʔə] (e.g., in *Gaue* 'regions', *Rehe* 'deer' pl.) feeding the unmarked syllable preference CV. Indeed, according to Giegerich (1985: 46), syllabification generally in German is without syllable overlap and is perceived as such by the native speaker.

The *phonological basis*, and thus the prosodic system, of German certainly supports non-monosyllable forms; this is evinced by the inflection and derivation habits of German, which interdigitate with the entire grammar (cf. section above) including, of course, the *supraseg-mentals.* Simply illustrated, German supports the bisyllabic *Tage,* as opposed to, say, the English monosyllabic *days.* German is still, as was its ancient Indo-European ancestor, a *suffix language.* Indeed, Wurzel (1975: 228) analyzes the German noun stem singular in such a way that he can derive "die wichtige Generalisierung, daß alle normalen nativen Morpheme einsilbig sind." Augst (1975: 36) characterizes German nouns constrained in the selection of a plural marker neither phonologically nor by gender as "die am häufigsten gebrauchten Wörter der nhd. Sprache. Weitaus die Mehrzahl dieser Wörter ist einsilbig ..." Just as *affixation* is primary in Indo-European morphology and *ablaut* ancillary to it, suffixation retains primacy over vowel alternation/modification in the inflectional number morphology of German throughout its history. (See further Rauch 1972. From this viewpoint observe the words of Werner [1969: 123]: "Aus der Isolierung der Plural-Zeichen ergibt sich, daß die Singular-Formen, was den Numerus angeht, unbezeichnet sind [*tag*]; ... Vom Indogermanischen bis zum Althochdeutschen [Mittelhochdeutschen] hatte der N. [Sg./Pl.] ein *Suffix,* das durch andere Kas/Num-*Suffixe* ausgetauscht werden konnte ... Im Neuhochdeutschen stellt der N. Sg. eine Grundform [*Tag*] dar ..., an welche die *Suffixe* angehängt werden ...").

Neither umlaut nor vowel length plays the decisive distinguishing role in Standard High German noun number. With relatively few exceptions, umlaut acts as a redundant feature in NHG noun pluralization. Although still productive in ENHG as a plural sign on monosyllable without suffix, e.g., *Tåg, Bånck* 'bench,' it is germane to dialects which favor *e*-apocope, viz., the Upper German dialects. (The Upper German resorting to a plural umlaut marker is a strong endorsement of the *iconic* principle of singular   plural morphological marker, since umlaut is genetically a habit of the more northern dialects.) The German system-favoring suffixation can be another factor, then, in helping to explain why neither the ϕ plural (which is least iconic) nor the umlaut-plural is individually exploited to the extent that the *-e* plural sign is in ENHG. We reiterate, the suffixation is *suprasegmentally system-congruent.* Parallel apocope-like phenomena, such as ENHG contracted forms of verbs like *haben* 'have', *stehen* 'stand', *gehen* 'go', are also familiar to *-e* apocope favoring dialects. Thus, Giessmann (1981: 34) shows the dialect groups, West Middle German, East Middle German, and North Middle German (as opposed to East Upper German and West Upper German) to overwhelmingly favor bisyllabic *stehen* and *gehen* by the seventeenth century. Certainly, the various speculations attempting to predict the future path of the NHG plural marker need to recognize the articulatory basis of German as a factor to be reckoned with, in particular relative to the native monosyllabic morphology. The parsimony of language, i.e., linguistic *iconism*, aims for one plural marker; it must, however, also satisfy the often theoretically neglected suprasegmental structure of German at the given time in history.

New Growth

The *-e* morpheme dominance of the masculine and neuter (*-en* the feminine) plural in NHG (Augst 1975: 38) is no reason to reconstruct the restored ENHG *-e* plural sign as an internal linguistic hallmark sign delimiting the ENHG language period; the NHG situation is a result, not a cause. ENHG differs from both MHG and NHG in that the plural marker is by far less constrained; this is indeed the source of the *-e* plural phenomenon. As shown in the above section, the language-specific naturalness of ENHG, its articulatory basis, segmental and suprasegmental phonology, morphology, syntax, semantics, aided by principles from universal grammar, yield teleological evidence for the emergence of the ENHG *-e* plural.

Linguistic naturalness finds a strong basis in the phenomenological category of Peirce most commonly called *iconism*, but deriving, in fact, from Peircean *Firstness*. From *Firstness* obtains the factual similarity between the sign and its object which is the dynamic of iconicity as in Mayerthaler's (1987: 48, 52) "principle of iconicity." However, *Firstness* is no less represented in Mayerthaler's other system-independent morphological markedness principles of "uniformity" i.e., *invariance/isomorphism* (cf. section above) and "transparency;" in essence both of these work iconically and should be understood as such. Linguists tend to seize upon Peircean iconicity without fully exploiting his paradigm. In particular, Peirce's *Secondness* and *Thirdness*, which have correlations in the *index* and the *symbol,* respectively, are unfortunately by and large ignored or perhaps overlooked (cf., e.g., "Secondness Driving Physiological Fact," Chapter 14; "Mutual Scientific Influence," Chapter 16 above). While *Firstness* phenomena represent mere *possibility*, *Secondness* involves *compulsion* and *Thirdness convention*. None of these categories exists in isolation in a semiotic system; they are, nevertheless, isolable by their predominance in a particular linguistic sign.

Within this framework the ENHG *-e* sign which undergoes widespread apocope in consonance with the Germanic drift to end-syllable weakening displays Firstness. Although the apocope is system-congruent with the stress accent, it is the stress accent which coerces the *-e* loss and accordingly evinces the factual contiguity of *Secondness*. The reinstatement of the so-called apocopated-*e* in the seventeenth century is certainly a matter of *Firstness* and of *Secondness*, as argued by means of the naturalness rules in the section above. Yet, its return is so astounding because the *-e* plural is not the "apocopated *-e*" at all; the phonological end-syllable weakening has, in fact, not reversed itself. The phonology of the *-e* apocope is subverted in that the seventeenth-century *-e* noun element becomes conventionalized as a plural sign, if not *the* plural sign. (It is to be noted that the masculine/neuter dative singular -*e,* noted in the "Tracing a Hallmark Sign" section above, being redundant, makes no comparable comeback.) The restructured ENHG -*e* plural sign thus embodies particularly the *imputed contiguity* of Peircean *Thirdness*, i.e., convention or law. As such the ENHG -*e* as a plural suffix represents a non-degenerate, ultimate sign, viz., a *symbol.* Consider for this purpose now Peirce's (4: 447) apt observation of symbol:

> The being of a symbol consists in the real fact that something surely will be experienced if certain conditions be satisfied. Namely, it will influence the thought and conduct of its interpreters.

The investigation of the ENHG -*e* plural desinence demonstrates that it is indeed possible to adduce internal linguistic features for the delimitation of the ENHG language period, and it encourages the investigation of further linguistic features to corroborate or deny the establishment of a seventeenth-century closure for ENHG. The -*e* plural evidence under the scrutiny of particular and universal grammar, as well as universal semiotic theory, certainly appears convincing, perhaps even incontrovertible.

18

Interlingual Translation of Signs

While data in Chapter 12 centered in graphology, i.e., spelling, in Chapter 13 and 14 in phonology, in Chapter 15 in phonology as well as morphology, in Chapter 16 and 17 in morphology, this chapter (18) offers data primarily for its syntactic and semantic insights. The reader will have noticed that these various principal components of the grammar of a language readily interdigitate, i.e., influence one another, so that any component may play a role in another component. The two sets of data in Chapter 18 configurate with Saussurean concepts, in particular, that of the synchrony: diachrony axes and that of the chessboard (cf. "Saussure and Synchrony," "Physics' Law and Biology's Growth," Chapter 2 above). The two sets, moreover, demonstrate a broader and a narrower application of Peirce's (4: 127; italics mine) elegant definition of *meaning* as "the *translation* of a sign into another system of signs."

Interlanguage and Historical Text

When we approach a historical language, do we actually hope to achieve any degree of language competence as befits a second-language learner in an era in which second-language learning is a commonplace? Or do we regard a *historical language* more as a historical artifact, perhaps analogous to an antique chair which is to be looked at, discussed, but not to be sat upon, i.e, used? Every teacher and/or student must have some philosophy of language learning in the reading of an older text. Do we actually stand to gain anything by admitting the strategies of the second-language learner into our reading (teaching/learning) experience? Necessarily, these strategies share features with strategies of the first-language learner, as well as with universals of all language learning. If, in fact, the learning of a historical language represents genuine language learning, then it is not up to us to admit or not to admit strategies, since universal strategies of language learning inhere in the human *cognitive ability*. Little wonder then, that our instincts about this basic semiotic function, i.e, the "uncritical" reading of a text, lead us to perceive it somewhat as a given, a natural endowment.

If we think, for example, in terms of such historical Germanic languages as Gothic of the fourth to sixth century or Old Saxon of the ninth to tenth century, what might the learning of these languages have in common with the learning of Modern German or English as a second language? One of the key concepts of second-language learning is that of *interlanguage*. Selinker's 1969 (1979: 60) classic introduction of this concept in his IRAL article of the same name reads:

> Since we can observe that these two sets of utterances (that of the target language and that of the source language) are not identical, then in the making of constructs relevant to a theory of second-language learning, one would be completely justified in hypothesizing, perhaps even compelled to hypothesize, the existence of a separate linguistic system based on the observable output which results from a learner's attempted production of a T(arget) L(anguage) norm. This linguistic system we will call 'interlanguage' (IL).

Quite succinctly, Tarone (1984: 11) clarifies *interlanguage* as "the linguistic system which underlies a learner's attempted utterances in the T(arget) L(anguage)." Our immediate reaction to the notion of interlanguage in relation to the learning of a historical text is that it is incongruous; inappropriate because, in spite of scattered, mostly tongue-in-cheek attempts to write, speak, or even to converse in a historical language, the language learner of Gothic, for example, is projected as a passive second-language learner, i.e, a translator of sorts. Still, interlanguage studies distinguish between *language learning* and *language acquisition*, the former of which results in cognizing the structure of the target language, while the latter results in communicating by means of the cognized structure of the second language. This is not altogether foreign to the language *competence* versus *performance* controversy. And it is in close proximity to the German distinction between *übersetzen* and *dolmetschen*, implying perhaps the difference between what is understood by English *translation* versus *rendition* or *interpretation*. respectively.

Accordingly, we may want to grant then, that the reading of a historical text is literally second-language learning rather than second-language acquisition (henceforth we maintain this distinction), and we may wish to consider it analogous to that learning which the student engages in when s/he satisfies the higher degree language requirements, such as the translation of a scholarly text in a modern European language, e.g., Spanish, French, or even the translation of a Latin text such as the *Aeneid* or *Cicero*. If this is the case, that is, if we view the reading of a historical text as an exercise in translation, then our discussion is reduced to a comparison between *translation theory* and *interlanguage theory*. To be sure, given the following set of data, we could not identify with absolute certainty whether the data belong to the testing of advanced learners acquiring a second language or to the testing of learners translating a second or foreign language. The data, from Hartmann (1980: 54), are the first line of a Beatles' song functioning as the source language:

(1) You don't realize how much I need you.

The German target data read:

(1a) Du tust nicht realisieren, wieviel ich brauche dich.
(1b) Du weißt nicht, wie sehr ich dich brauche.
(1c) Ahnst du nicht, wie sehr ich an dir hänge?

We find, particularly in informant (1a)'s rendition, strategies familiar to interlanguage, for example, transfer from English linear syntax, thus non-transposition of subordinated verb, as well as phonological word *interference*; thus *tust nicht realisieren* in the target language— German, in this instance. We notice that informant (1c) not only decodes from the source language but also encodes into the target language by expressing the Beatles' line in the situationally equivalent idiom of German. In the case of a student translating a foreign text to satisfy a language requirement, as well as in the case of the learner of Gothic or Old Saxon, the roles of the target language and the source language are reversed from those of the language acquirer. That is, the source language in language acquisition is a student's first language, while the source language in language learning is a student's second language; the interlanguage in both are the target languages, but in acquisition it is the second language, while in learning, it is the first. Both require decoding and encoding, however, with the reversal of first and second languages.

Perhaps this fact, this reversal, is enough to disallow the term *interlanguage* in the case of the language learner, he who renders out of a second language. Yet the data of the language learner do indeed show interference and transfer, reflective of a universal of interlanguage, viz. that the categories of interlanguage are assumed to be the same as the categories of the source language (transfer hypothesis). Empirical evidence from classroom testing in the learning of Gothic, for example, demonstrates language *interference* from English as well as from Gothic. Consider the simple sentence of four Gothic words from Luke 2, 12 (Wright 1958):

> (2) Jah þata izwiz táikns.
> literally   And that to you sign.

meaning "And this is a sign to you."

Four of eight informants write the hypothesized *And this is a sign to you*. The remaining four write:

> (2a) And this/these are signs for you.
> (2b) And this your sign.
> (2c) And that sign is for you.
> (2d) Und das sei Euch das Zeichen.
> literally   (2d) And that be to you the sign.

Informant (2a) reverse-transferred English morphology to Gothic, confusing Gothic *s* of *táikns* with the English plural *s* morpheme. Informant (2b) literally yields the Gothic rhetorical convention of *schesis onamaton* (ellipsis of the copula), but this informant yields the Gothic dative *izwis* as a possessive genitive 'your' (Gothic *izwara*). Informant (2c), reading *And that sign is for you*, overgeneralizes the possible, i.e., allowable, disjunction of noun and modifier in Gothic by rendering *þata* as a demonstrative adjective with *sign* as subject, rather than as a demonstrative pronoun with *sign* as predicate nominative. In addition, informant (2c) writes *that sign*, which misleadingly reads as anaphoric, backward, in the text, or emphatic forward in the text. Similarly, informant (2d), writing in German, uses the definite article *das Zeichen* instead of *ein Zeichen* (for Gothic zero-article plus noun *táikns*) perhaps for cataphoric purposes or emphasis; he further renders Gothic *þata* by the remote demonstrative, German *das* 'that,' perhaps through reverse *phonological transfer*.

We observe that *interference* from transfer of the first language (the target language in the case of a translation) as well as overgeneralization from the second language (the source language in the case of translation) take place. Certainly, these strategies from second-language acquisition applied to the rich Gothic-English/German data yield provocative interlanguage-like insights, if not legitimate interlanguage insights. Pending further study of the juxtaposition of this method from contemporary language applied to the "uncritical" reading of a historical text, we may wish to speak of *historical interlanguage,* instead of interlanguage.

Cognizing the Text

We now turn to how the reader of a historical text might approach the *semiotic processing* of that text, yielding at the minimum an "uncritical" reading. The standard grammars of historical languages, e.g., *Wright's Grammar of the Gothic Language* or Holthausen's *Altsächsisches Elementarbuch*, feature a compendious phonology and morphology, both inflectional and derivational, and some brief remarks concerning non-linear syntax. All of these grammatical components are presented primarily with a view toward *linguistic genetics*, i.e., their Germanic and Indo-European relationships. An attempt is nevertheless made, for example, by Wright, to discuss the phonemic inventory of Gothic synchronically. We shall see, however, that in the approach to the reading of a historical text, the semantic infrastructure takes precedence, whether we find it by means of the lexicon, the syntax (linear and non-linear), the morphology, and/or the phonology.

The primary data for Old Saxon (cf. Chapter 12; "Drawl in a Dead Language," Chapter 13 above) is the *Heliand*, a ninth/tenth century narrative epic with 5983 alliterative lines extant; and the *Genesis*, a ninth-century narrative epic with 337 alliterative lines extant (cf. Behaghel, 9th edition 1984). Accordingly, the reader has at his/her disposal a substantial coherent text, whose macrostructure s/he cognizes through successive *semantic* and *pragmatic* decisions. The reader thereby discovers the *narrative propositional* and *modal* content of the macrotext. S/he analyzes the interrelatedness of *cognitive constituents* such as topicalization, reference, and sequence. Finally, the reader concentrates on individual sentences and their immediate connectedness, i.e., the microtext. Again, s/he engages in a series of cognitive decisions ultimately focusing on the syntactic, morphological, and phonological components of the grammar; again s/he is processing propositional or inferential content. While the discourse of the macrostructure entails mainly *text linguistics*, the discourse of the microstructure entails largely *sentence linguistics*.

Basic to all reading is the *word*, the linguistic entity which plays a major role in expressing propositional content of both the macro- and microstructure. The reader of a second language, literally gasping and grasping for all the meaning s/he can get, has immediate although partial access to the words of the language through its lexicon. An Old Saxon word is listed in the lexicon in its fundamental identifying form, together with its grammatical specifications, selection restrictions, and glosses. Consider, for example, the *Heliand* sentence (Behaghel 1984: 1.119):

(3) Ic is engil bium.

consisting of the relation 'am his angel' and the argument ''I.'' Whereas a word such as *engil* occurring syntagmatically, that is, in a narrative chain, is homophonous paradigmatically, that is, with its fundamental identifying form, in the lexicon, which is also *engil*, the word *bium*, likewise of the above sentence, requires decisions on the part of the reader whereby s/he comes to associate it with its fundamental identifying form *wesan* in the lexicon; as an anomaly it is relegated to the reader's memory.

Consider now the *Heliand* sentence (Behaghel 1984: 1.2856):

(4) Gaf it is iungaron ford.
    'He gave it to his disciples.'

Since the sign of the unmarked word order in the *Heliand* is verb-first, the reader may early on consider *gaf* as a possible verb form. He observes that the vowel a of the root can occur in sets 3, 4, 5, 6, or 7 of the traditional Germanic seven verb ablaut series. This can be done, however, without recourse to *linguistic genetics*, that is, Germanic and/or Indo-European. It can simply be seen as a synchronic vowel alternation. The reader may further narrow his choices in the identification of *gaf* by observing the root shape. i.e., by noticing that the root *a* is not followed by a resonant, thereby eliminating ablaut sets 3 and 4 as possibilities in deciding the fundamental identifying form of the verb for the purpose of ascertaining its *lexical meaning*. Other accompanying consonant characteristics can also be helpful in deciding the fundamental identifying form of *gaf*. The reader may opt for a fundamental form **gafan*, which s/he will observe is not in the Old Saxon lexicon. Since the existent *gaf* is a word without suffix, the reader can now have recourse to a synchronic consonantal rule of final consonant devoicing which suggests to him/her a fundamental identifying form with vowel alternation *e*, thus *geƀan*. To be sure, *geƀan* is listed in the *Heliand* lexicon as belonging to ablaut set 5 and with the meaning 'give.' We notice that the reader up to this point makes decisions as though s/he were an Old Saxon, rather than an etymologist, an Indo-European.

Let us now consider a final third *Heliand* sentence (Behaghel 1984: 1.3263):

(5) Hwat quiðis thu umbi goðon?
     'Why are you speaking about a Good One?'

Again the reader of the *Heliand* text sets out to identify the fundamental identifying form of the words signaling the relation and arguments of the *proposition*. By a series of decisions concerning the root vowel and the suffix for verb identification, the reader will again conclude that *quiðis* of sentence (5) is listed in the lexicon under the fundamental identifying form *queðan* with the meaning 'speak.' The difference in root vowel *e* and *i* need not be memorized, since the reader expects or can predict this difference in the synchronic reflexes of a *genetic phonological rule*, whereby the mid vowel of the root *e* is raised to *i* before a high vowel *i, u*, or a j of the suffix, or before an intervening nasal consonant. Recourse to prehistory in this rule eases the burden on the memory of the reader, since it greatly maximizes the application of the rule, which is no longer productive and which can be observed by subsequent changes such as the loss of the suffixal conditioner, thus *quiðes* or *quiðas* (cf. Chapter 12 above).

Thus far in discussing the reader's approach to the *Heliand* text, we notice that first and foremost s/he has been intent on extrapolating lexical meaning for the three syntagmatic verbs of sentences (3), (4), and (5) above. Although Old Saxon is primarily a *suffix language*, the suffix morphology in the reader's initial search for meaning has universally low level priority. (Witness purely lexical juxtapositions in the syntagms of the early learning stages of modern language.) The reader is, however, groping for the functional, pragmatic, or *discourse* meaning of the verb in the three *Heliand* sentences. S/he observes that *quidis* of sentence (5) follows an *hw*-word, which is the unmarked syntagm for an interrogative sentence. According to its linear syntax, verb-object (VO), *gaf* of sentence (4) can have either declarative or interrogative function; its past tense meaning precludes a possible imperative meaning. The decision as to the functional meaning of sentence (4) can only be made by recourse to its setting in its greater *discourse* (Behaghel 1984: 11. 2852–2857):

> That folc stillo bēd,
> sat gesiđi mikil; undar thiu he thurh is selbes craft,
> manno drohtin, thene meti wīhide,
> hēlag hebencuning, endi mid is handun brak,
> *gaf it is jungarun forđ*, endi it sie
> > undar themu gumskepie hēt
> dragan endi dēlien.

> The people waited quietly,
> a great crowd was sitting; meanwhile he through
> his own power, the Lord of men, blessed
> the food, the holy King of heaven, and
> with his hands he broke (it), *He gave it*
> *to his disciples*, and he ordered that they
> bring it and divide it among the
> multitude.

Sentence (4) clearly does not convey interrogative meaning; it is one of a series of narrative statements. As a declarative sentence it is to be compared, then, with sentence (3) where the finite verb *bium* 'am' linearly follows its subject. Subject-verb (SV) is marked position for any function in the *Heliand* text. To ascertain the positional meaning of *bium*, sentence (3), too, must be observed in its wider discourse (Behaghel 1984: 11. 116–122):

> "Thīna dādi sind," quađ he,
> "waldanda werđe endi thīn word sō self,

thīn thionost is im an thanke, that thu sulica
                              githāht habes
an is ēnes craft. *Ic is engil bium,*
Gabriel bium ic hētan, the gio for goda standu, and-
ward for them alowaldon, ne sī that he me
                              an is ārundi hwarod
sendean willea."

              "Your deeds are," said he,
"pleasing to the Lord, and your words as well,
your service is appreciated by him, since you
have such faith in his power alone. *I am
His angel.* Gabriel am I called, who ever
stands before God, present before the
Almighty, unless he might want to send
me somewhere on his errand."

Again the greater discourse reveals the declarative meaning of the sentence; it is one of a series of uttered assertions.

The next task for the reader is to decide why declarative meaning is
conveyed by differential *linear syntax* in sentences (3)and (4). Both
sentences are overtly constative, i.e., they describe an event or state of
affairs. Sentence (3), however, is less implicitly performative than is
sentence (4), since it is a direct quotation indicative of performing the
act of speaking, explicitly introduced in the wider narrative speech
situation of sentence (3) by *quað he* 'said he.' In contrast, sentence (4)
can be considered implicitly performative by virtue of the *Heliand*
author's act of recounting events to his readers, which he does
throughout his text. The *quað he* syntagm associated with sentence (3)
is then another *speech act* beyond or within that of the author's narration. To be sure, many other discourse features such as 1 person
singular and present tense of sentence (3) contrasting with 3 person
singular and preterite tense of sentence (4) contribute to the different
text meaning of two declarative sentences. At issue here, however, is
why declarative sentences (3) and (4) employ SV and VO word order,
respectively, and how their linear syntax interdigitates with the
constative: performative speech act difference observed above.

Direct quotations, according to Ries (1880: 31) occur more frequently in the unmarked declarative order verb-subject-object (with an
optional preceding element, thus (X)VSO), than in the marked orders.

The SV order with the intervening predicate noun *engil* of sentence (3), placing *bium* last in the sentence, accordingly is striking by its marked order. The linear dynamic of the self-introduction, self-identification of Gabriel to Zacharias certainly conveys a meaning of directness, of straightforwardness. The components of the comment 'am his angel' are inverted so that the position of *engil* before *bium* lends definiteness to the predicate noun. Whether metrical considerations, namely that *engil* houses the key alliteration of the entire line, influenced the position of *bium*, or whether the desired pragmatic meaning of the sentence is accountable for the placement of *engil* into the principal stress position of the *linear syntax* can only be answered by the *Heliand* author. Either or both strategies certainly affect the textual meaning of sentence (3) and accordingly aid in the fine-tuning of the meaning of the syntagmatic *bium*.

Finally, the question arises as to what the textual meanings of the *Heliand* unmarked VSO linear order are, as represented in sentence (4) *Gaf is iungaron ford.* One of the most common functions of the strategy of VO linear order in the *Heliand* is concatenation or continuation in a narrative sequence. Sentence (4) expresses one of a series of actions enumerated in the particular narrative scenario of which it is a part. The semantic linkage of sentence (4) with the immediately preceding sentence is strengthened by virtue of the position of *gaf* directly contiguous to the preceding sentence *endi mid is handun brak.* The concatenation meaning of this pragmatic strategy follows Behaghel's two universal linguistic generalizations, which hold that semantically related linguistic units are contiguous or adjacent in their linear syntax (Behaghel Rule 1), and that old information precedes new information in a sentence (Behaghel Rule 2; Behaghel 1932: 4). The meaning of old information in *Gaf* of sentence (4) refers to the fact that the verb represents an action which is part of a series of actions before it and that it is consequent to those actions, even if the actions in themselves are new. *Gaf* in concatenative or conjunctive first position links sentence (4) to the preceding sentence, as the conjunction *endi* 'and' of that preceding sentence containing the verb *brak* 'broke' functions to link it with the preceding sentence containing the verb *wīhide* 'blessed.' The action subsequent to *wīhide, brak,* and *gaf,* which is *hēt* 'ordered,' is linked to *gaf* by another occurrence of the conjunction *endi.* That *gaf* is an alliterating word does not necessarily require its first position in the halfline in which it occurs; accordingly, pragmatic rather than metrical constraints account for the

VO linear order of sentence (4). This common concatenative function, which thus enhances the textual meaning of *gaf,* interdigitates, however, with several other pragmatic strategies functional in the *Heliand* text (cf. Rauch 1992c).

Saussure's Axes

Thus we see that the reader's decisions in grasping at the "uncritical" meaning of the micro- and macrotext of this historical language (the *Heliand* text) have much in common with the cognitive processes of second-language learners of contemporary languages. The reader of the Old Saxon text approaches the data as belonging to one fixed time frame in history, i.e, ninth/tenth century. S/he assumes s/he is learning a certain language of a certain time; this is the implication of the term *synchronic*. The reader, accordingly, does not need to view the data in terms of their linguistic ancestry nor their linguistic descendants any more than does the second-language learner of, for example, Modern English. Doing so, however, is what is meant by the term *diachronic*. In point of fact, the reader of a historical text deals with a *diachronic synchrony*, since the concept of a time frame in which language data are static is a fiction. Synchronic variation entails diachrony, i.e., process or change at least from one linguistic moment to the next. The term diachronic, then, is appropriate to any meaningful data change or variation regardless of whether it is within the Old Saxon time frame, prior to it, or subsequent to it. Accordingly, the term diachronic as equated solely with an ancestor stage of Old Saxon is dysfunctional; the appropriate term is *genetic*. Reference to genetic rule in the reading of a historical text merely enhances explanatory power; it is a convenience, not a necessity, in easing the memory burden for the language learner. Obviously, then, the positing of an interlanguage in the "uncritical" reading of a historical text subverts the Saussurean diachronic: synchronic axes, as well it should.

Saussure's Chessboard

As reiterated time and again in preceding chapters, most recently Chapter 17 (cf. "Competing Signs"), linguistic method is dominated by the time-proven, powerful working principle of *biuniqueness* or *isomorphism* whereby we aim to disambiguate and identify unequivocally any linguistic entity. Basically, it requires that one form have one meaning. This principle derives from the Humboldt-Saussure concept of system as representing a relational network of similarities and differences; semiotically it is understood as *iconism*. A principle such as this is rarely found operative in linguistic realia or data; it is a working hypothesis.

The isomorphic principle would appear quite odious to literary Deconstructionists, who, while building on the Saussurean paradigm, find that the flaw in Saussure which subverts his thinking is that the concept of *difference* is not sufficiently exploited. Thus Derrida's lack of a "center," "infinite number of sign substitutions" (1978: 280), Barthes' "innumerable centers" (1977: 146), and Foucault's "variable and relative [...] unity" (1972: 23) would require the differences and similarities which face off on the Saussurean chessboard to be quasi-infinite. (Cf. "Deconstruction," Chapter 1 above) Saussure (1959: 88), however, can in fact comply; we read in his *Course in General Linguistics* (emphasis mine):

A state of the set of chessmen corresponds closely to a state of language. The respective value of the pieces depends on their position on the chessboard just as each linguistic term derives its value from its opposition to all other terms. *The system is always momentary;* it varies from one position to the next. It is also true that values depend above all else on an unchangeable conviction, the set of rules that exists before a game begins and persists after each move. Rules that are agreed upon once and for all exist in language too; they are the constraint principles of semiology ... to pass from one state of equilibrium to the next ... from one synchrony to the next, only one chesspiece has to be moved; there is no general rummage.

Toward Isomorphism

The richness of the interdigitation of linguistic method and semiotic method invites the investigation of codes other than language (cf. "Object Semiotic," Chapter 5 above). Such a code is the *medical code*, which is, however, as universal as language itself. Within the medical code, the *language-like* structure of the DNA genetic molecule with its four information-bearing nitrogen features or bases (adenine, thymine, guanine, cytosine), tactically linked to each other by given rules of similarities and differences into a hereditary statement or

double helix, is aesthetically a most attractive code to contemplate—
for good reason it is termed a code, the genetic code. However, as linguists we deal with verbal scenarios between doctor and patient; so,
too, do psychiatrists, as well as anthropologists and hard scientists,
biologists, chemists, physicists (cf. "Medicine," Chapter 9 above).

Integral to the verbal medical scenario is the symptom, defined by
Sebeok 1994: 24) as "a compulsive, automatic, non-arbitrary sign,
such that the signifier [is] coupled with the signified in the manner of
a natural link." Just as a linguistic sign, a medical symptom has *form*,
e.g., heat in the case of fever, but also in the case of a burn, and a
medical symptom has *content* which has both *sense* and *reference* and
may be ambiguous or polysemous (cf. "Symptom," "Meaning,"
Chapter 9 above). Galen already recognized that a symptom has variant reference: its locus does not necessarily signal that the particular
part of the body is the diseased part. The analogue to the Saussurean
chessboard (cf. section above) is clear: a move in one part of the system effects a move in another part (near or remote) of the system, thus
the possible *non-isomorphic, non-biunique, non-iconic* (cf. "Language
Grows," Introduction above) fit between the form and the meaning is
thereby demonstrated.

Let us consider, e.g., the word "fever." When we hear it in the collocation "Ford fever" on the TV commercial "Ford fever is gonna
make a believer out of you" or read it in TIME magazine (August 31,
1987) as "franchising fever," we are fairly certain of the sense of the
word, namely, something conveying enthusiasm. If we hear "fever" in
the collocation "Mary's fever," the meaning "enthusiasm"may be denoted, but also the medical symptom. If medical "fever" is denoted, its
semantic extension is polysemous, that is, it has multiple references,
e.g., pneumonia, gangrene, and other possible diseases.

With a view to the semantics of a symptom, consider now the late
eighth-century Old High German medical prescription known as the
Recipe (Prescription) from Basel I (reprinted from Barber 1951: 15;
English translation mine):

1   Murra, seuina, uuiroh daz rota, peffur, uuiroh daz uuizza,
     uueramota, antar, suebal, fenuhal, pipoz, uuegabreita,
     uuegarih, heimuurz, zua flasgun uuines, deo uurzi ana zi
     ribanne : eogiuuelihha suntringun. enti danne geoze zi
5   samane enti laze drio naht gigesen enti danne trincen einan

stauf in morgan, danne in iz fahe; andran in naht, danne he en
petti gange. feorzuc nahto uuarte he e tages getanes, daz he
ni protes ni lides ni neouuihtes des e tages gitan si ni des
uuazares nenpize des man des tages gisohe, ni in demo ni
10   duuahe ni in demo ni pado, ni cullantres ni inpiize ni der eies
des in demo tage gelegit si. ni eino ni si, ni in tag ni in naht,
eino ni slaffe, ni neouuiht ni uuirce nipuz de gisehe de imo
daz tranc gebe enti simplum piuuartan habe. erist do man es
eina flasgun, unzin dera giuuere: ipu iz noh danne fahe, danne
15   diu nah gitruncan si, danne gigare man de antra flasgun folla.

1   Sweet cicely, juniper, red incense, pepper, white incense,
wormwood, horehound, sulfur, fennel, mugwort, plantain,
plantain, homewort, two bottles wine, the roots to
rub on each separately. And then pour together
5   and let ferment three nights and then drink one
cup in the morning, when it seize him; another (cup) at night
when he to bed goes. Forty nights let him refrain from that
made earlier on that day, that neither of bread nor of wine nor
of anything that be made on that day, nor
10   wash himself, nor bathe, nor of coriander partake, nor of egg,
which on that day be laid. Alone let him be, neither day nor
night, alone not sleep, nor anything let him do except it he
see, who him the drink give and always have a watcher. First
let one do one bottle as long as he prepare one: if it then still
seize him, then
15   (when) that (bottle) be nearly drunk, then let one prepare a
second bottle full.

This prescription is quite precise in specifying, e.g., some thirteen drugs (11.1–3); two bottles of wine (1.3); the mixture is to ferment for three nights (1.5); the patient is to drink one cup in the morning and one at night (1.6). Further, it specifies that the patient should not be left alone, neither by day nor by night and should be constantly watched by the person who administered the drugs (11.11 and 13).

The symptom to which this medical prescription is to react is not identified. It is referred to as "it," thus, (1.6) "when *it* seize him" and (1.14) "if *it* then still seize him." The degree of precision exhibited otherwise in this medical prescription leads readily to the inference that the symptom referred to is likely polysemous. Indeed, Kögel (in Bostock 1955: 104) suggests it is a fever, and Steinmeyer, responding to the prescribed constant surveillance, suggests epilepsy. Grienberger (1920: 409) opts for typhoid fever with accompanying hallucinations. Be that as it may, the *Recipe from Basel I* shows that, contrary to both non-specialized codes and other technical codes, semantic disambiguation of the medical symptom is at times achieved through negotiation between doctor and patient or patient representative, that is, through variable reference, rather than through convention, that is, through constant reference, thus leading to *isomorphism* in the medical communicative act (cf. "Medicine and Anthropology," Chapter 9 above).

19

Language Change/Growth Begins

Just as there are typological universals of language structure, so also we recognize universals of language change/growth. To a large extent this recognition proceeds from the typological universals themselves. The observation that *variation* in linguistic *synchrony* and *change* in linguistic *diachrony* are one and the same is an automatic corollary. The corollary is supported by the *uniformitarian principle*, which holds that we can infer historical operations in language by observing present operations. The opposite is, of course, also true, although it is more uncertain and risk-taking; that is, that we can predict present, in-progress linguistic operations via extrapolations from past linguistic operations. Just as future linguistic change/growth is not within our experience, so too, past linguistic change/growth is not within our experience, and its reconstruction is likewise risk-taking. The point is, that when we as linguists speak of language change in process, we do not necessarily refer to current change from the point of view of our experience; we speak also of past or future change from the point of view of our experience, but in all cases we observe the change under development, that is, in the process of becoming. In effect, this focus toward any change in time subverts the Saussurean synchrony: diachrony axes; a given language change is thus observed as ongoing regardless of the relative position of the linguist in time (cf. "Saussure's Axes," Chapter 18 above). Language change in progress obviously speaks, then, in particular to so-called intermediate or, indeed, initial stage or stages in language change, whether the change is current, historical, or yet to take place. Technically, the last or final stage of a language change would still concern change in progress, leading to emicization, *restructuring,* and/or external conditions closing the change.

Change in progress, thus understood as a universal, will allow in this chapter (19) the introduction of further data immediately preceding the modern linguistic era, namely evidence from Early New High German (cf. Chapter 17 above). In the myriad parameters entailed in language change/growth, the etiological question is always paramount. Within that question, linguists pursue *why* and *how* the change ever started (cf. Chapter 14 above). There is consensus that language *variation* originates in the individual, while its *actuation* is societal. For example, columnist Bob Greene's initial naming in print of the word *yuppie* in analogy to Jerry Rubin's word *yippie* represents a case of societal actuation, through the role of the media. However, what is the role of the individual at Rubin's networking party for young businessmen and businesswomen, whom Greene overheard first mention the word *yuppie*?

Chapter 19 addresses the nature of such an act of language creation; in particular, it seeks to recover the initial stage in the language change and within this stage the putative ingredient of *privacy*, which has not been exploited in language-change theory. The study of such an initial stage for both a present and past language change is obviously past in the experience of the linguist, but it is quasi-timeless under his/her linguistic scrutiny. We can readily empathize or experience vicariously similar acts of creation in the current explosion of neologisms such as *Irangate, Contragate, Travelgate, Iranscam, NS-scam* (National Security Scam), *mompreneur* (stay-at-home mother entrepreneur), and the like.

Two Intralingual Naive Texts

The suitability of Early New High German data for the demonstration of initial stages or change in progress is obvious from the cultural/historical setting of the language of fifteenth-century Germany (cf. Chapter 17 above). Specifically, the invention of printing in the middle of the century represents an opportunity to reformulate an orthography *de novo*. Secondly, even though printing tends to become conventionalized, very early evidence would show a minimum of standardization, if any. The challenge of Early New High German is precisely the linguistic naiveté of its data.

Observe, for example, an extract from two early diplomatic renditions of Johannes Tepl's *Ackermann aus Böhmen* 'Plowman from Bohemia' (reprinted from Penzl 1984: 68–9; translation and emphases mine). The contrasts between the two texts are in part a measure of the naiveté (compare the linguistically sought after naive speaker) of each particular text. So, for example, the presence of the modal particle *neur* (item 215) of the Bamberg text, which does not occur in the corresponding Esslingen clause, or the linear order of the phrase *Pesserūg kondt mir vō euch* (169–173) of the Bamberg text compared with *Beserung von uch kúnde mir* in the Esslingen text. These are not dialect characteristics; they speak rather to the ingenuousness of each given text. Certainly, a great many of the contrasts between the respective texts attest to dialect identification; so, for example, the hallmark New High German diphthongization, which shows up clearly in the Bamberg text, thus, *zeit* (item 126), *euch* (item 173), and which reflects the East Franconian dialect of the Bamberg area. That it is not a contrastive matter of time in sound change relative to the non-diphthongizing Swabian Esslingen text is obvious, since the latter postdates the Bamberg text by thirteen years.

Bamberg (1461)

5   10
Nach schaden volgt spottē das enpfindē wol die betrubten. Also

15
geschicht vō euch mir beschedigten manne · Liebes entspent leides

20   25   30
gewent habt ir mich als lang got wil muß ich es vō euch leidē · wy

35   40   45
stupf ich pin · wie wenig ich han · vnd nicht gesezt pin zu synnreichē

50   55
hohē meistern · Dānoch weiß ich wol das ir meiner erē rauber

60   65
meiner freudē diep · meiner gut lebtag steler · meiner wundē

70   75
verichter · vn̄ alles des das mir wūsames lebe gelubt vnd gemachet hat

80   85   90
ein zu storer seit · wes sol ich mich nu freuen. wo sol ich trost suchē ·

95   100   105
wo hin sol ich zu flucht habē · wo sol ich heilstet vindē · wo sol ich

110   115   120
treuen rat holen · Hin ist hin · Alle freud ist mir vn̄d meinē kindē ee

125   130   135
der rechten zeit verschwundē zu fru ist sie vns entwischt · Allzu schir
140   145
habt ir sie vns enzucket die treuē die geheurn · wan ich mich zu
150   155
wittwar vnd meine kinder zu waysen so vngenediclich habt gemachet ·
160   165
Elend alley vn̄ leides wol beleib ich von euch vnergezet · Pesserūg
170   175   180
kondt mir vō euch nach grosser missetat noch nye widerfarē · wie ist
185   190
dē her todt · aller leut ebrecher an euch ka nymāt ichts gutes verdienē·
195   200   205
Nach vntat wollet ir nymāts genug thū vbels wolt ir nymats ergezen ·
210   215
Ich pruff das parmherzikeit nicht pei euch wonet · neur fluchēs seit ir
220   225   230
gewāt gnadēloß seit ir an allen orte · solch gutet die ir beweisset an
235   240   245
dē leutē · Solch gnad so die leut vō euch entpfahē · Solchen lon als ir
250   255
den leutē gebt · Solch eud als ir dē leuten thut · schickt euch der · der
260   265
des todes vnd lebēs gewaltig ist · Furst himlischer geschopf ergeze
270   275
mich vngeheur ūlust · michels schadēs · vnseliges trubsals · vnd
280   285
iemerlichs waffētumß · do pei gerich mich an de erzschalck dem tode
292
got aller vnthat gerecher.

Esslingen (1474)

anch schaden spotten volget dies entpfindent die betrúpten als beschit
mir von uch mir bescheidigen māne liebes entspent vn leides gewent
habend ir mich als lang gott wil můß ich es tulden wie stunpf ich bin
wie wenig ich hā zů siriches meisters wißheit gezucket dennocht weis
ich wol dz ir miner erērouber miner freidē diep miner gůttē lebtagen
steler miner wunnē vernichter vnd alles des so mir lustsā lebē gemacht

vñ geliebet hat zerstörr sind wes sol ich mich mů frowē wa sol ich
trost suchen war sol ich zů flucht habē wa sol ich heil stet findē wa sol
ich getruwen ratt reichen hin ist da hin alle min freid ist mir ee die zit
verschwunden zu fru ist si mir entwichen zu schier habent ir si mir
entzucket die getruwe die gehure wann ir mich enig zů wittwer vnd
mine kind zů weissen so vngeneglich hand gemacht ellēd allein vnd
leides vol blib ich von uch vnergetz Beserung von uch kúnde mir nach
grosser missetat noch nie widerfarē wie ist dem herre dot aller eren
brecher an uch kan niemā nútz gůttes verdienen noch finden niemand
wöllend ir genůg thůn nach ergetzen ich prúffe barmhertzikeit wonet
nit by uch flůchens sind ir gewone genadloß sind ir an allen orten
söllich gůtt dette die ir bewisent an den lútten sölliche genade so die
lútee von uch entpfahent söllichen lon so ir den lútē geben sölliche
ende so ir den lůtten thůnd schicke vnd sende uch der der dodes vnd
lebens gewaltig ist fůrst hymelischer masseneien ergetzt mich
vngehúres verlustes michels schadens vnsegliches trúbsales vnd
iemerliches waffenkumers da by riche mich an dē ertzschalck dem dot
gott aller vndatte recher

5
After injury follows scorn, that experience certainly the downcast.
10   15
Thus (it) happens by you to me, injured man. Of love deprived, to
20   25   30
pain accustomed have you me; as long as God will must I it from you
35   40   45
endure; how apathetic I am; how little I have; and not attuned am I to
50   55
ingenious elevated masters. Nevertheless, know I well that you (are)
60
the robber of my honors. the thief of my joys, of all the good days of
65   70
my life the stealer, of my <u>wounds</u> the annihilator, and of all that which
75   80
me a winsome life has pledged and made, a destroyer (you) are. Why
85   90   95
should I be happy? Where shall I solace seek? Where can I take
100   105   110
refuge? Where can I asylum find? From where shall I receive trusted

¹¹⁵   ¹²⁰
advice? What is lost is lost. All joy has for me and my children before

115   120
advice? What is lost is lost. All joy has for me and my children before

125   130   135
the right time vanished; too early has she slipped away. All too soon

140   145
have you her from us plucked, the faithful one, the wife, for I me to a

150   155
widower and my children to orphans so ungraciously have made.

160   165
Distressed alone and of sorrow <u>certainly</u> remain I by you

170   175
uncompensated. Betterment could to me from you after great misdeed

180   185
never happen. How is (it) for the lord Death, of all people the

190   195
adulterer, from you can no one anything good earn. After misdeeds

200   205
wish you to no one to make amends. For evil wish you no one to

210   215
compensate. I recognize that compassion not with you dwells. Only

220   225
to malediction are you accustomed, ungracious are you everywhere;

230   235
such good deed which you show the people. Such grace which the

240   245
people from you receive. Such reward which you the people give.

250   255   260
Such an end as you the people do (give), sends to you he who of (the)

265   270
death and life the power has. Lord, heavenly creature, compensate me

275
for my huge loss, enormous injury, wretched misery and pitiable

280   285
lamentation; thereby avenge me against the arch scoundrel, (the)

292
Death, (oh) God of all misdeeds (the) avenger.

The two *Ackermann* texts should therefore be gleaned primarily individually for evidence of *change in progress*. The Bamberg text consistently attests to the New High German monophthongization of *uo* to *ū*, for example, *gutes* (item 193), *fluchēs* (item 216). The monophthongization of the front diphthong *ie* to *ī* shows some graphic variation, thus, the pairs *wy: wie* (items 34; 38), *nye: nymat* (items 178: 191) along with *die* (item 8), *verdienē* (item 194) and *schir* (item 135). That this variation is not indicative of sound change in progress (monophthongization), but that it is rather purely orthographic is obvious from the already mentioned consistent monophthongal spelling of its parallel back monophthong *ū*, and from the fact that New High German employs the digraph spelling to represent the high front monophthong. Interestingly, however, both texts show some confusion of intervocalic *s* from Germanic **s* with intervocalic *ss* from Germanic **t*. From Germanic **s* the Bamberg text has the expected *waysen* (item 154), but unexpected *beweisset* (item 230); from Germanic **t* it has expected *Pesserūg* (item 169) and expected *grosser* (item 175). The Esslingen text has, however, beside expected *biwisent*, unexpected *weissen*, and beside expected *grosser*, unexpected *Beserung*, indicating a *linguistic merger* in progress of at least one feature distinguishing the two *s*'es (cf. "Internal Signs," Chapter 18 above).

Three Printing Errors

Although this *Ackermann* evidence for *s* speaks to language change in progress, without detailed analysis of all occurrences in the *Ackermann* text we can make no judgment as to the relative stage of the change. As stated in the beginning, we seek to uncover an initial stage in a change with a focus on "privacy" in that stage. One of the many possible factors feeding into language change is *speech errors*, which appear abrupt, instantaneous, unorchestrated. Through reinforcement by repetition, speech error can actually result in language change. Thus Osthoff (1897: 36–7), referring to morphological change via analogy, observed: "... die allermeisten unserer jetzt schriftgemäss gewordenen Formen (waren) anfänglich auch nichts anderes ..., als ebensolche Sprachfehler ..."—words certainly consonant with Nietzsche's observation (1874: 300) that "A figure which finds no followers becomes an error. An error sanctioned by any *usus* becomes a figure." We hasten to say, however, that a *hapax legomenon* is not sanctioned by use; indeed, its nature is its unique occurrence. It is not considered a speech error; but it is certainly not considered language change either.

The spontaneity and apparent unintentionality of speech errors, regardless of their fate, present us with possible early stage data of language change in progress; such unintentional data which are of a phenomenological nature of "mere may-be," "mere possibility" belong to the Peircean semiotic category termed *Firstness* (1: 304, 537; cf. also "What is Semiotics?" Introduction above). The naiveté of the diplomatic renditions of the *Ackermann* texts contributes a number of speech and/or printing errors, which upon comparison of the Bamberg with the Esslingen text show them to be peculiar to the individual text; one would, then, not consider them writing errors on the part of the author, Johannes von Tepl. Nevertheless, they are not merely speech errors; they are permanent evidence by being etched in writing, that is, in print. Since they are peculiar to the individual text, we know that they did not result in language change. They do, however, offer the potential of early stage data even though they did not succeed in permanent change. We repeat, their permanence to this day is secured by writing/printing; they are, accordingly, fossil evidence.

The Bamberg text yields more errors than the Esslingen text; three of these are not entirely convincing as mere mechanical errors, that is, slips of the hand or fingers in setting the type. These are *wundē* (item 67), *ich* (item 146), and *wol* (item 163), all three perfectly grammatical Early New High German words in paradigm, that is, as lexicon. These words actually exist; they are natural to the lexicon, but they are unexpected in the given syntagm. If the printer did not mechanically set these words by mistake (we noted earlier the individuality on the part of the printer, namely, the peculiar syntax, item 169–173 *Pesserūg kondt mir vō euch* and the peculiar word insertion *neur*, item 215, compared with the Esslingen text), then something in the syntagm betrays a naturalness for the use of these three words, so-called "errors."

Item 146, *ich*, appears to be possibly phonologically induced by the contiguous *mich* (item 147). This *iconism* would represent a very natural regressive assimilation. (When interviewed on TV, Tyne Daly engaged in a similar type of iconism by referring unintentionally to "Lagney and Cacy.") Moreover, with *ich* the printer replaced a pronoun, *ir*, with a pronoun. It is, however, *syntactically incongruous* in the syntagm. The printer also replaced a noun with a noun in the case of *wundē* (item 67). Phonological iconism in the case of *wundē* is, of course, from *wunnē* itself; iconism with regard to the -*d*-, however, seems remote, and possible epenthetic -*d* insertion contiguous to *n*- is far-fetched. In the case of *wol* (item 163), the printer replaced an adjective with an adverb/particle. While the graph *v-* varies freely with the graph *f-* in initial position (see, for example, *vindē,* item 106, and *freud,* item 117), neither *f-* nor *v-* vary with initial graph *w-*. The phonetic confusion of Early New High German *w-* with the Pre-Early New High German *v-* can then hardly be accountable for the printing "error" *wol.* Further, the unaccompanied genitive *leides* (item 162), with *wol* as adverb/particle, bespeaks syntactic incongruity. This is not to deny the iconicity of *wol* with *vol,* however.

Although there is no doubt about the *phonetic iconicity* of *wundē* with *wunnē, wol* with *vol,* and *ich* with *mich,* a pragmatic or discourse iconicity may further play a role in these three so-called printing "errors." If, in the course of setting the print, the printer has been mentally engaged in the dialogue between Death and the Plowman, the increasing pathos which swells to what Stolt (1974: 22) characterizes as "'die erschütternde Verlassenheit in den rhetorischen Fragen: "Wes sol ich mich nu frewen? Wo sol ich trost suchen? Wohin sol ich zuflucht haben? Wo sol ich heilstet finden? Wo sol ich getrewen rat holen?" (items 84 through 112) may actually evoke empathy on the part of the printer. Certainly, the unrelenting succession of *ich*'s could help engender the erroneously printed *ich.* Further the negative crescendo of the Plowman's lament could suggest to the printer *wunden* 'wounds' instead of *wonnen* 'joys' in spite of its *semantic incongruity* with *vernichter* (item 68). Finally, because of his vicarious experience, the printer may reinterpret item 163, *voll* 'full' as a modal particle meaning 'certainly' and modifying the *bleiben* clause rather than the epithetic *leides,* which then becomes *grammatically incongruent.* Such disjunction could serve, however, to serendipitously heighten the emotional content of the dialogue.

Abduction = Essential Preliminary Trigger

The above noted similarities in the *Plowman* texts which suggest themselves between form and form, form and meaning, form and sound, and form and syntax in the three so-called printing "errors," display, beside *possibility,* another characteristic of Peircean *Firstness,* viz. the identified iconicity. Iconicity entails the very rudimentary dynamics of the laws of association or *analogy.* Such analogies or inferences are of the basic type of reasoning known as abduction, which in itself is a *Firstness* phenomenon as well. An *abduction* is that kind of subconscious illation whereby a possible, not necessarily infallible, minor premise is derived from the major premise and from the conclusion. The first premise itself is a *perceptual judgment*, viz. the formation of a mental proposition concerned with sense experience. Peirce (5: 54) defines this innate manner of interpreting an experience or a perceived object as "a judgment asserting in propositional form what a character of a percept, directly present to the mind is." He thus provides his contemporary Hermann Paul (1880: 25) with the dynamics behind the "psychischer Organismus" of the individual, the speaker-hearer, in whom language change originates. Weinreich, Labov, and Herzog (1968: 107–8) report: "On the intra-individual, spontaneous mechanism Paul has little else to say; he refers just once more to the role of an individual's personal peculiarities and the peculiar stimulations ... of his own mental and bodily make-up ..." Indeed, the first or instinctive impulse triggering language change in progress is definitely in the individual; it is *private*. However, if several individuals were presented separately with an analogical pair, e.g., in the conditions leading to the above mentioned speech error of "Lagney and Cacy," the chances are excellent that most of the individuals would separately abduce a closely similar, if not the identical speech error. The situation is the same in the case of the *Plowman* "errors." Given the same frame of mind and emotions in which the printer found himself, comparable so-called printing "errors" may be produced by other printers as well. A fundamental abduction (cf. "Abductive Processing of Features." Chapter 6 above) such as the following is indicative of the laws of association operative in these "errors":

Major premise: Contiguous sounds (whether in paradigm or in syntagm) are alike.
Conclusion: *Mich* and *ich* are alike.
Minor premise: Therefore, *mich* and *ich* are contiguous sounds.

From this point of view, then, language change in progress, even in its earliest stage, is not entirely private, since linguistic ontogeny and phylogeny intersect.

We witness so-called speech/printing errors of the *Plowman* text as partial microcosms of language change or at least as evincing many of the parameters of language change/growth. In particular, we have observed an underlying, basic, early mechanism responsible for their production—*Firstness*; that it functions in phonetic iconism of the three "errors" is hardly contestable. Admittedly, the final stages and the actuation of a language change are lacking to speech/printing errors; in this fashion these errors resemble *hapax legomenon* material. Speech/printing errors are thus quasi-stillborn language phenomena. This characteristic is, however, precisely that which allows the linguist access to relatively facile scrutiny of the initial stage processes of language change. At their earliest, all three of the Bamberg *Plowman* printing errors can be reconstructed as spontaneous, unintentional association creations (*Firstness* phenomena) emanating from the instinctive process of abduction (a *Firstness* phenomenon) residing in the private individual, but with common or nearly common results among individuals with similar or the same attendant conditions. Clearly, it is abduction which plays a fundamental role in every language change in progress; it is the essential preliminary trigger, that is, it paves the way for the search for particular cause in any language change (cf. "Linguistic Analogy and Semiotic Abduction," Chapter 2 above). It remains to be seen whether any number of *Firsts*, e.g.,"Ungumped" in the TIME magazine (8/29/94) sentence: "For the as yet *ungumped*, here is a jaundiced synopsis," with reference to Forrest Gump, is stillborn. On the other hand, the phonologically iconic *yadda-yadda* has taken root, i.e., is conventionalized (*Webster's College Dictionary* 1997), and thus a *Third*.

20

The Lie

It is appropriate that the final data evidence in this volume speaks to mendacity or signs yielding false information. For that matter, all signs are disingenuous insofar as they are a representation of an object, i.e., *aliquid stat pro aliquo*. Certainly Eco subsumes this broader interpretation when he (1975: 120) writes that "the fundamental characteristic of the sign is that I can use it to *lie*." Outright focus on prevarication data necessarily requires yet one more revisiting of a primary *leitmotiv* of this volume, viz., the semiotic-linguistic understanding of language.

Defining Language — 3

The philosopher Peter Caws (1969: 1380) observes that "truth ... is a comparative latecomer on the linguistic scene, and it is certainly a mistake to suppose that language was invented for the purpose of telling it," while the linguist Edgar Sturtevant (1947: 48) writes: "language must have been invented for the purpose of lying." Such cross-disciplinary testimony to the fundamental nature of mendacity, although available, somehow resists being brought into the spotlight of linguistic research. Interestingly, by concealing or relegating the *lie*, or degrees and variations of it largely to an unspoken assumption in language research as a whole, we unwittingly enact the phenomenon itself. We assume, rather, that the "neutral gear" of language as research data is *veracity*. But, in fact, as Lyons (1977: 83) points out: "Many authors consider that prevarication is the property which, with reflexivity (the ability to make a statement about oneself), most clearly distinguishes language as a semiotic system from all other signaling-systems." This raises again the ever nagging problem of attempting to define language in whatever linguistic research we are involved (cf. "Defining Language—1," Chapter 3; "Object Language," Chapter 5; "Defining Language—2," Chapter 6 above). The problem allows no solution; it simply tolerates a working hypothesis (cf. "Illation and the Signifying Animal," Chapter 6 above). We ask ourselves why Hockett (1963: 6–14) proposed as one of his sixteen so-called design features of language "prevarication", rather than "truth", that is, is *prevarication* the unmarked member of the pair truth: falsity as an ingredient in language. Immediately, a host of attendant questions arise. Some of these are implicated in asking why Hockett, in his earlier (1958: 354–355) discussion of the *design features of language*, subsumed prevarication under the design feature "displacement," which holds that language can signify the non-present, indeed, the non-existent. Fascinatingly, Lyons, in his (1981: 18) *Language and Linguistics*, states without realizing the full consequences that "Perhaps the most striking characteristic of language by comparison with other codes or communication-systems is its flexibility and versatility." Although Lyons (1981: 19) singles out the design features "arbitrariness, duality, discreteness, and productivity" as indicative of flexibility and versatility, he explains the latter, striking characteristics by writing: "We can make reference to the past, present and future— *even to things that need not exist and could not exist*" (emphasis mine). This is, without doubt, the feature *displacement*, even though Lyons does not say so. Whether we rely on Hockett's 1958 displacement, the conviction of many authors that prevarication is fundamental (Lyons 1977, above), or Lyons' (1981) consequential reference to flexibility and versatility, the arguments appear strong for an unmarked feature of *mendacity* in language. In view of this, the opening statements of Eco, Caws, and Sturtevant hardly impress as spectacular, humorous, or entertaining. They are simply statements of fact, even though we may be reluctant to admit it. (See, however, Sternberger in Weinrich 1974: 80.)

Before leaving the question of the *lie* as an essential ingredient in language, let us consider briefly two intimately related questions, namely, whether *animals* possess language and whether they are capable of lying, insofar as the answers to these questions may shed light on human prevarication. As can well be imagined, Lyons wrestles with these questions in his attempt to define language. A key factor in this discussion is communicator *intention*. For Lyons 1977: 32, emphases mine) the principal communicative system of humans is language, where communication is "the *intentional* transmission of information by means of some established signaling-system, ... the *intentional* transmission of factual, or propositional, information." In answer to his own question (1977: 83–84): "Does the behaviour of a bird which shows injury and tempts a predator to pursue it away from the nest justify the use of the term 'prevarication?'" Lyons says patently "no," writing: "... In the study of animal signaling we are obliged to give an external account of the phenomena ... In the study of human signaling, on the other hand, it would be stultifying to impose upon oneself such gratuitous and unnecessary restrictions and to eschew, on principle, any appeal to beliefs and intentions." Lyons adds: "Freedom from stimulus-control is presumably a precondition of mendacity and deception in the strict sense of these terms: and it is therefore a precondition of prevarication." By 1981 Lyons broadens his definition of communication to "not necessarily implying the intention to inform" (17), so that "one can talk about animal communication without begging some controversial philosophical questions." Lyons accordingly (1981: 144) distinguishes *human* from *animal communication* by attributing "descriptive meaning" exclusively to the former, but "social expressive meaning" to both the former and the latter. Ultimately, however, Lyons coopts the answer, maintaining that the researcher's attitude toward a definition of language (and, *ceteris paribus, prevarication*) is influenced by his/her profession. So (24): "the linguist, the psychologist and the philosopher may tend to emphasize (striking differences ... between language and non-language) ...; the ethologist, the zoologist and the semiotician would probably stress ... (the no less striking similarities ... between language and non-language.)"

Without addressing Lyons' stimulating conviction that our profession influences our thought, let us focus for a moment on the question of *intention*. Jonathan Bennett (1976), albeit a philosopher, and following Grice, holds that *meaning* is a type of *intention* and accordingly, he reserves meaning for *intending* beings, i.e., humans. Bennett (1976: 206), however, achieves a synthesis between "intention-dependent evidence" (human communication) and "display-dependent evidence" (non-human communication). For Bennett the basic function of both human and non-human signifying is to communicate, and according to Bennett, the control which *intention* effects in human communication is effected in non-human communication by *natural selection*. He writes (1976: 205): "individual intention is significantly like biological function." Witness also the proclamation of Peirce, albeit philosopher, semiotist, mathematician, scientist, indeed polyhistor, that (2: 754): "... all human knowledge, up to the highest flights of science, is but the development of our inborn animal instincts" (cf. "Illation and the Signifying Animal," Chapter 6 above). Finally, compare Dwight Bolinger's daring approach to his conviction that "Truth is a Linguistic Question" (1973: 542, 545; second emphasis mine) stating: "I am trying to paint the lie as black as I can by not requiring that it be intentional ... I suspect that some syntactic lies are beyond our control. When a child is caught red-handed and says *I didn't do it*, it may be an instinctive reaction of self-defense." Indeed, Bennett's, Peirce's, and Bolinger's convictions prompt us to link *mendacity* in humans with *instinct,* which, in turn, relates to the animal world. In short, while veracious language is generally defined anthropomorphically, mendacious language here finds explanation zoologically.

Detecting the Lie

If mendacity is, in fact, an unmarked design feature of language, we are astounded not to find a booming general bibliography on the lie. This points to the fact that the field of the lie is at once so vast and so subliminal that it is quite elusive and difficult to harness—perhaps an indicator of the lie's commonality. Sebeok (1976: 144) gives an indication of the universe of the lie, pointing out:

> the crucial dependence of the lie on double deictic anchorage, namely, the question how, precisely, a false utterance is integrated both in its linguistic context and extralinguistic cotext; the subtle distinctions between lying and ambiguity, figures of speech, delusions, errors, fiction, especially drama, the notion of playing, the performance of ritual, the formulation of hypotheses, the wielding of models; and, furthermore, the developmental, or ontogenetic dimension of all of the aforementioned.

Ubiquitous though the lie is, it is infrequently approached with lessened taboo. It is somewhat expected in the media, in the courts, in politics in general, and as an object of study in a few disciplines. So, for example, Roger Rosenblatt in a *Time* (1984: 88) essay disputes the claim of Alastair Reid of *The New Yorker* that "A reporter might take liberties with the factual circumstances to make the larger truth clear."

Recall the aura of prevarication enveloping the Watergate crisis and consider now the 1996 election fund raising investigations in the United States. Recall, as well, one of the defendants in the sensational Massachusetts Barroom Rape Trial in 1984, saying under oath: "I don't know exactly; I swear to God, I want to tell the truth," a statement which encapsulates the position of truth/prevarication in such a court case. A headline in the *San Francisco Chronicle* (9/10/97: E 10) reads as a telling symbol: "Everyday Ethics; Everyday Lies." The lie, or rather the truth, is the focal point of study in the field of philosophy, and it is widely pursued in psychology. Linguistics borrows insights from philosophy, in particular *speech act theory*, in an effort to understand the lie. With the help of psychological research, linguistics can begin to deal with the communicative competence of both the *Machiavellian speaker* and the *lie-detecting listener*. Unfortunately, much of the *modus operandi* of the lie in communication is known, via psychology, only for the *non-verbal* channel. This is not surprising, since the verbal expression of prevarication by definition eludes detection. A Vedic papyrus of 900 B.C. defined a liar as follows: "He does not answer questions, or they are evasive answers; he speaks nonsense, rubs the great toe along the ground, and shivers; his face is discolored, he rubs the roots of the hair with his fingers" (quoted in Trovillo 1939: 849). Almost three millennia later Freud (1905: 94) writes of the liar: "If his lips are silent, he chatters with his fingertips; betrayal oozes out of him at every pore." Purely linguistic data are not readily identified in the composition of the lie; in fact, lack of verbal data or *silence* may be one of the first cues to deception. However, the paralinguistic *tone of voice* plays a large role in detecting leakage of a lie; moreover, psychologists find that it is less controllable on the part of the liar than *facial expression* (Zuckerman, DePaulo, Rosenthal 1981: 6). As linguists we are challenged, then, to seek clues in the segmental data of a prevaricator and, if mendacity is a common mode in language, we are challenged to seek it in quotidian language, or, let us say, in the everyday verbal encounter. This would exclude such expected loci of prevarication as those mentioned above and related scenarios, such as card games and the like (cf. Hankiss 1980, Hayano 1980). In the next section of this chapter we propose, then, to consider two texts in German of everyday verbal encounters, not only to identify some of the generic or universal elements of the lie discussed above, but also to gain an insight into how the German language provides linguistically for the possibility of prevarication.

Two Telephone Scenarios

We choose data which are not directly identified with outright or bla-
tant prevarication; they fall rather into the realm of light deviousness,
pretension, put-on, fakery, talking-past-one-another in an ordinary
telephone conversation. In fact, the *mendacious mode* generally goes
undetected, overtly at least, in these types of verbal encounters. The
data are taken from *Texte gesprochener deutscher Standardsprache
III* of the Freiburg Institut für deutsche Sprache, edited by Fuchs and
Schank. We will discuss data from portions of the verbal interactions
entitled I. "Verabredung zu einem Besuch" 'Arranging a Visit' (60–
69), and II. "Moralische Bedenken gegen Wohnungsbesichtigung bei
unverheiratetem Freund" 'Moral scruples concerning apartment inspection at unmarried friend's place'(141–149). We will strip the texts
largely of non-verbal and paralinguistic clues, so that we might sort
out purely *linguistic prevarication* strategies. Scenario I includes the
following discourse (translation mine):

```
 1   B   Morgen, A.
     A │ Hallo.│
     B │ Hallo.│ ich wollt dich einmal aufwecken.
     A   Das ist aber gut. Ich bin schon längst aufgeweckt, B.
 5   B   Äh von wem?
     A   Ja, also von selbst. │ Nicht? Ich werde │
     B                        │ ach so, also.    │
     A   ja, selbst wach,│ ne? │
     B                   │ Ah, │  du wirst von selb, ich hab
10       gedacht, haha, ah ja, stimmt, na, aber aufgeweckt warst du ja
         schon immer, nich? und da
     A   Ja,│ doch, B.              │
     B      │ is das natürlich │ keine Schwierigkeit, │ nich?  │
     A                                                │ Ja, ja.│
15       Ja, seit wann bist du denn wieder im │ Lande?        │
     B                                        │ Äh, seit│gestern abend.
     A   Du kli … du klingst also sehr verschlafen.
     B   Nein, ich hab ein bißchen Schnupfen.
     A   Aha.
20   B   Ich bin dadurch, bin ich immer um äh acht aufgestanden,
         nicht?
     A   │ Mhm. │
```

B | Und da | drum bin | ich auch schon so früh wach. |
A | Und dann kriegst |
25   dann kriegst du n Schnupfen
        wenn du um acht aufstehst, ja?
B   Ja, auch noch etwas fett bin ich geworden,
        das heißt, noch fetter, nicht | wahr? Abe |
A | Ja, also ich auch |
30 B | mhm. |
        das macht über Weihnachten. Aber das das das das macht
        nichts mir einmal nicht. Ich brauch äh doch Unterlagen für
        Kundfahrten, nicht?

The conversation between A and B continues; they make plans to
meet later in the day at the home of A. Before concluding this conversation, they arrange coffee provisions as follows:

B   Bereit einen Kaffee, nicht? | und |
35 A | Öh | dann bring mal n bißchen
        Pulver mit. Ich hab nämlich zu wenig Pulver.
B   Ach so. Ja, | wir |
A | Ja. |
B   brauchen keinen, aber wenn s gern bring ich mit.
40   Willst du | einen? |
A | Ja, | ja, ja, doch, doch.
B   Doch dann | äh gemahlenen. |
A | Tee hab ich auch | ja, ja, ja, ja, daß ich filtern kann, ne?
B   Ah, | gut.
A | Ich hab nämlich | vergessen zu … einzukaufen. Also, ich
45 A
        hätt äh gerade noch, na, ich weiß gar nich, ob es für zwei
        Tassen … reicht, also ich hab das noch nicht abgeschätzt.
B   Nee, nee, ich bring schon mit
        bring schon mit
50   na das ist | kein Problem. |
A | Das wäre | gut, ne?
B   Ja, | selbstverständich. |
A | Ja. |
B   Gut, also | bis
55 A | Gut, | B, ja, und werd
        richtig wach, nicht? und | kurier |
B | Ja. |

A   deinen Schnupfen.
B   Das kommt schon.
60 A   Gut | good-bye, wiederhören. |
B | Also. |
A   Bis dann.

1 B   Morning, A.
A   Hello.
B   Hello. I wanted to wake you.
A   That's a good one. I was already awakened a long time ago,
     B.
5 B   Eh, by whom?
A   Yes, by myself. right? I was
B   Oh, so, well.
A   Yes, myself awake, right?
B   Ah, you are by yourself. I
10   thought, ha-ha, yes, right, well, but awakened were you
     already always, right? and then
A   Yes, surely, B.
B   that is naturally no difficulty, right?
A   Yes, yes.
15   Yes, how long have you been back in the country?
                    Eh, since last evening.
A   You sou … you sound very sleepy.
B   No, I have a bit of the sniffles.
A   Aha.
20 B   I have always, I have always gotten up around eh eight,
     right?
A   Mhm.
B   And that's why I am already awake so early.
A   And then you get
25   then you you catch a cold
     when you get up at eight, yes?
B   Yes, also I've gotten somewhat fat,
                    that is, still fatter, right? But
A   Yes, me too.
30   Mhm.
B   That happens around Christmas. But that that that that doesn't
     matter to me. I need eh provisions for
     business, right?

B Prepare coffee, right? and
35 A   Eh, then bring a little
(coffee) powder along. I have, of course, too little powder.
B Ah, so. Yes, we
A   Yes.
B need none, but if (you) want some I'll bring (it) along.
40   Do you want some?
A   Yes, yes, yes, sure, sure.
B But then eh ground (coffee).
A   Tea I also have, yes, yes, yes, yes, so that I can
(make) filtered coffee, right?
B Ah, good.
45 A   I have, of course, forgotten to go shopping. So,I
would have eh just yet, well, I don't even know if it is enough
for two cups ..., but I haven't yet estimated that.
B No, no, I'll bring some along.
50   Well, that is no problem.
A   That would be good, right?
B Yes, of course.
A   Yes.
B Good, so until
55 A   Good, B, yes. and
wake up all the way, right? and get rid of
B Yes.
A your sniffles.
B It's getting there.
60 A Good, good-bye, until we speak again.
B   Ok.
A Until then.

At first glance this conversation between A and B impresses as
completely normal and truthful. It is in fact normal and by convention
accepted, if not also perceived, as truthful. Witness that in this exchange preliminary to the actual exchange, namely the arrangement of
a visit, the focal point in the case of both speakers is time of awakening. Is Speaker A completely truthful in his answer "Ich bin schon
längst aufgeweckt" (l. 4) 'I was already awakened long ago," and in
his expanded answer "Ja, also von selbst, nich?, ich werde ja selbst
wach, ne?" (l. 6–8) 'Yes, by myself. right? I wake up by myself,
right?' Certainly B's responses to A show him to be skeptical of A's

answers, in particular of his claim that he wakes himself. Leaving aside what A's *extralinguistic knowledge* of B might be, can we find in A's language any clues to mendacity, slight though they may be? "Aufgeweckt" (l. 4) 'awakened' in A's first answer violates Grice's Conversational *Maxim of Quantity*, which reads: "Make your contribution as informative as is required for the current purposes of exchange; do not make your contribution more informative than is required" (1975: 45). A may simply have repeated the transitive verb of B which was echoing in his ear, anxious to deny B's suspicion that he (B) had awakened A. A's denial is heightened by the phrase, mildly expressive of outrage, "Das ist aber gut" (l. 4) 'That's a good one.' A's first failed answer shifts the focus from time of awakening to being awakened, which he also denies twice: "Ja, also von selbst, nich! Ich werde ja selbst wach, ne?" (l. 6-8) 'Yes, by myself. right? I wake up by myself, right?' A's reiteration of "selbs wach" including finally his repeated, *quasi-silent* monosyllabic "Ja" (l. 15) 'Yes' and change of subject "seit wann bist du denn wieder im Land?" (l. 15) 'how long have you been back in the country?' serve as possible leaks to evasiveness and less than sincere answers. Thereby, Grice's Conversational *Maxim of Quality* is violated: "Do not say what you believe to be false; do not say that for which you lack adequate evidence" (1975: 46).

Let us consider B's awakening. A charges: "Du kli, du klingst aber sehr verschlafen" (l. 17) 'You sou...you sound very sleepy.' B answers in a manner that seems to violate the third of Grice's four Conversational Maxims, the *Maxim of Relevance*: "Be relevant" (1975: 46). B says: "Nein, ich hab ein bißchen Schnupfen" (l. 18) 'No, I have a bit of the sniffles.' B further defends himself two more times saying: "Ich bin dadurch, bin ich so immer um äh acht aufgestanden, nicht" l. 20–21) 'I have always, I have always gotten up around eh eight, right?' and "Und da drum bin ich auch schon so früh wach" (l. 23) 'And that's why I am already awake so early,' implying that his sniffles caused him to be awake early, which A obviously does not believe. In denying their waking habits, both A and B tend to reiterate their defenses. They are, accordingly, not "brief", as is recommended in Grice's fourth Conversational Maxim, the *Maxim of Manner*. In addition, the Maxim of Manner, which exhorts that the speaker be perspicuous, encourages further that the speaker "avoid obscurity, ambiguity," and that he, "be orderly" (1975: 46). Neither A's nor B's answers were devoid of obscurity, and both changed the subject without the observer's gaining certainty as to the truth of their answers; in fact repetition, indirect answers, and change of subject constitute strong clues to *mendacity* in both language situations. B's change of subject leads into another topic for defensiveness, namely weight gain: "Ja, auch noch etwas fett bin ich geworden, das heißt noch fetter, nicht wahr! Abe das macht über Weihnachten. Aber das das das das macht nichts mir einmal nicht. Ich brauch äh doch Unterlagen fur Kund-fahrten, nicht?" (l. 27–28, 31–33) 'Yes, also I've gotten somewhat fat, that is, still fatter, right? But that happens around Christmas. But that that that that doesn't matter to me. I need eh provisions for business trips, right?' B's rationalization, "über Weihnachten," does not at all convince that he is indifferent to his weight problem. Again we find a clue to his misleading statement in its situation: "das das das das macht nichts mir einmal nicht."

Finally, in studying the coffee arrangements in this verbal interaction, are there any language strategies which reveal whether A does in fact have too little coffee, that is, is his statement true? Again, the conversation violates at least the Conversational Maxim of Manner. A moves from outright denial "Ich hab nämlich zu wenig Pulver" (l. 36) 'I have, of course, too little powder' to possibility, which is immediately canceled out by doubt, saying "also, ich hätt äh gerade noch, na, ich weiß es gar nich, ob noch für zwei Tassen ... reicht, also ich hab das noch nicht abgeschätzt" (l.45–47) 'So, I would have eh just yet, well, I don't even know, if it is enough for two cups ..., but I haven't yet estimated that.' The iteration, namely, the denial, possibility, and doubt, the latter two embedded in the somewhat disjointed "Ich hab nämlich vergessen zu, einzukaufen" and "also ich hab das noch nicht abgeschätzt," certainly raise suspicion as to the veracity of A's language concerning his coffee provisions.

Scenario 2, entitled "Moralische Bedenken gegen Wohnungs-besichtigung bei unverheiratetem Freund," 'Moral scruples concerning apartment inspection at unmarried friend's place' includes the following discourse (again all non-linguistic information has been deleted; translation mine):

1 Y Guten Tag ich hätte nur eine Frage
   X Hm.
   Y und zwar habe ich da einen Fall. Mein Bekannter hat
      jetzt öh eine Wohnung bekommen
5 X Hm.

Y   und zwar öh findet das nächste Woche statt.
X | Mhm. |
Y | Nun | hat er mich gebeten auch mit hin zu kommen
    und zwar um die Wohnung zu besichtigen.
10 X   Ja.
Y   Nun äh is das eine sehr gute Freundschaft. Nun wollte
    ich mal fragen, ob ich da mit hin gehen kann und die
    Wohnung besichtigen | oder nicht. |
X | Äh. | Ich wüßte nicht warum Sie
15 X   nicht dahin gehen | können |
Y | Ja. |
X   sollten.
Y   Mein Vater meint das tut man nicht.
20 X   Was heißt? "das tut man nicht". Äh ich finde warum soll
    man es nicht tun? Also wie lange kennen Sie diesen
    jungen Mann?
Y   S is n dreiviertel Jahr.
X   Und Sie sind befreundet miteinander?
25 Y   Ja.
X   Ja? eine lockere Freundschaft?
Y   Ja.
X   Ja, und Ihr Vater meint wahrscheinlich es ist dann ein wenig
    äh zu eng die Freundschaft. S wird etwas betont, was gar
30   nicht da ist, ja?
Y   Ja.
X   Oder?
Y   Ja.

The conversation continues with A's inquiry about the girl's friend
and about the necessity for having an eye-witness opinion of his
newly rented apartment. It concludes:

X   Und beabsichtigen Sie irgendwie, bald mal zu heiraten?
35 Y   Also davon hatten wir leider noch nicht gesprochen.
X   Ja.
Y   Aber.
X   Ja.
Y   kann ja noch kommen nich?
40 X   Das kann ja noch kommen. Jedenfalls augenblicklich
    geht es tatsächlich um die Wohnung und nicht um die
    Person.
Y   Ja.
X   Ja?

Y   Also könnt ich das machen?
X   Meiner Ansicht nach ja.

1   Y   Hello. I have just one question.
    X   Hm.
    Y   And, in fact, I have a problem. My acquaintance has
         now, eh, gotten an apartment
5   X   Hm.
    Y   And, in fact, eh, that will take place next week.
    X   Mhm.
    Y   Well, he has asked me also to go there
         and, in fact, for the purpose of looking at the apartment.
10 X   Yes.
    Y   Well, eh, that is a very good friendship. Well, I wanted
         to ask, if I can go along and view the apartment
         or not.
    X   Eh. I wouldn't know why you
15   cannot go there.
    Y   Yes.
    X   should.
    Y   My father thinks that isn't done.
20 X   What do you mean "that isn't done." Eh, I think why
         shouldn't one do it? Well, how long have you known
         this young man?
    Y   It's three-quarters of a year.
    X   And you are friends?
25 Y   Yes.
    X   Yes, a rather loose friendship?
    Y   Yes.
    X   Yes, and your father probably thinks then it is a bit
         eh, too close, the friendship. Something is emphasized,
30   which doesn't even exist, right?
    Y   Yes.
    X   Or?
    Y   Yes.
    X   And do you anticipate somehow to marry soon?
35 Y   Well, we had not yet spoken about that.
    X   Yes.
    Y   But.
    X   Yes.
    Y   Can still occur, right?
40 X   That can still occur. In any case, right now it concerns
         actually the apartment and not the person.

Y   Yes.
X   Yes?
Y   So, could I do that?
45 X   In my opinion, yes.

Let us briefly observe the degree of level of veracity of X and Y toward one another. Speaker X extends a type of discourse "sweetener" to Speaker Y, saying early in the interchange: Ich wüßte nicht warum sie nicht dahin gehen können" (l. 14-16) 'I wouldn't know why you cannot go there.' This statement is ambiguous in the message it sends. If Y takes X's statement to be true, it has the effect of X's siding with Y early in the conversation, X engaging the confidence of Y to offer further information. Immediately, X modifies the statement with "sollten" (l. 18) 'should,' thereby leaking the information that he does, in fact, know why Y should not go there. Further, X's use of the subjunctive "wüßte," rather than the indicative, to express a socially acceptable *lie*, adds heightened acceptability to the deception. Obviously, the sweetener is a carrot dangled to get information, because X does know general reasons why such an apartment visit would not be considered appropriate, even though X may not know the particular reasons in the case of Y.

Y introduces her problem by referring to "Mein Bekannter" (l. 3) 'my acquaintance.' She soon refers to her relationship as "eine sehr gute Freundschaft" (l. 11) 'a very good friendship,' not as "eine Bekanntschaft" 'an acquaintanceship.' When questioned by X: "Und Sie sind befreundet miteinander ... eine lockere Freundschaft" (l. 24, 26) 'And you are friends ... a rather loose friendship?' Y answers with a terse "Ja" (l. 25, 27) "Yes,' which may be the truth, but impresses as taciturnity or *silence*—often a clue to prevarication. Moreover, her affirmation of "eine lockere Freundschaft" is misleading with regard to her earlier statement of "eine sehr gute Freundschaft."

In the closing segment, X concludes that what is at issue is not the friend of B, but the apartment of Y's friend. This conclusion, which is contradicted by the preceding discussion of the person of Y's friend is strongly deceptive. X magnifies the lie by using the *definite article* and a *syntactic order* which create an aura of distance, namely, it denies that there is a problem or a question of propriety at issue. The proposition reads "Augenblicklich geht es tatsächlich um *die* Wohnung und nicht um *die* Person" (l. 40-41) 'right now it concerns actually the *apartment* and not the *person*,' instead of the possible

"Augenblicklich geht es nicht um Ihren *Bekannten* (*Freund*), sondern um seine *Wohnung*" 'right now it doesn't concern your *acquaintance* (*friend*), but his *apartment*.' Notice, too, that the modal particle "tatsächlich" acts as conviction in this mutual deception.

Lying in One Language Better than in Another

The ordinariness of *mendacity* in language prompts us to consider it a *mode* which overlies the indicative and the imperative modes, the subjunctive itself taking a middle position between prevarication and truth. We conclude with a final observation: The level of mendacity in Scenario 2 resides to a certain extent in the distinction between the German words "Freund" and "Bekannter," (cf. "Two Telephone Scenarios" above), a distinction which is disguised in the English word "friend." The Sapir-Whorf *linguistic relativity* hypothesis should certainly be considered in any larger study on mendacity; in other words, one should consider the question of whether one language lends itself better to lying than another. In approaching the answer to this question, regard for a moment a passage extracted from a piece of holocaust literature, *Jakob der Lügner* 'Jakob the Liar' by Jurek Becker (1969: 123; emphasis mine):

Es ging darum, ob Kowalski dem Wucherer Porfir Geld schuldet oder nicht. Der Schuldschein war Porfir *wie durch ein Wunder abhanden gekommen*, und ich mußte bloß aussagen, daß Kowalski ihm sein Geld zuruckgegeben hat.

The English translation of this passage reads (Becker 1975: 119; emphasis mine):

It was a question as to whether Kowalski owed Porfir, the money-lender, money. Porfir *had miraculously lost the IOU*, and I had to testify merely that Kowalski had given him back the money.

Although "wie durch ein Wunder," as well as "miraculously," give clues to prevarication, the English transitive "lost" is by far less *iconic* and accordingly more deceptive than the German "abhanden gekommen 'left or got out of (his) hands.' which both lexically and grammatically leaks information. The *open lie* which typifies the entire life of Jakob the Liar is accordingly not successfully conveyed in the English translation of this incident. Doubtlessly, this literary segment, as well as the ordinary telephone scenarios (cf. section above), strongly affirm the richness of a linguistic mendacious mode, which remains to be researched, both within German and crosslinguistically.

Conclusion: Facts and Human Factors

Perhaps the *lie* (cf. Chapter 20 above) is the *ultimate deconstruction*, indeed, a defining signifying feature at the end of the second millennium. Eco (1995: 344) explains the view of Romantic authors that Babel is a *felix culpa,* writing: "... natural languages are perfect in so far as they are many, for the truth is many-sided and falsity consists in reducing this plurality into a simple definite unity." To be sure, Eco's expression of diversity among natural languages with reference to truth reflects well *postmodernist thought,* albeit probably not the ethics of the lie. However, in the popular media we are presently inundated with observations concerning prevarication. While, e.g., George Will (1997: 78) writes: "All ascriptions of truth are arbitrary ... anybody has a right to postmodernism's protection against standards of accuracy." David Wise (1997: A21) notes: "You don't have to believe in little green men to see the admitted deception as yet another example of official lying that has eroded public trust in government." Fascinatingly, Meg Greenfield (1997: 76) remarks: "The lying isn't as good as it used to be. Neither is the self-deception."

The challenge posed by these and similar citations relative to the lie, i.e., the truth, knowledge thereof, language involved, and semiotics, calls for a postmodernist paradigm in two particular ways, which are Peircean as well as Saussurean: human factors and multiple approaches are at issue. With reference to *defining language,* the centerpiece of human signification (cf. especially "Defining Language"—1, —2, —3, Chapters 3, 6, 20, respectively, above), Tobin (1997: 4–5) reaches back to Saussure:

> From a Saussurian, sign-oriented, or semiotic point of view, language may be defined as a system of systems that is com-

posed of various subsystems (revolving around the notion of the linguistic sign) that are organized internally and systematically related to each other and that is used by human beings to communicate ... this definition of language implies a respect for and reliance on actual or real (as opposed to contrived or solely introspective) data culled from discourse and a commitment to deal with the human factor (i.e., the cognitive, perceptual linguistic and nonlinguistic behavior of human beings) as it is relevant to communication in different linguistic and situational contexts.

With regard to approaches, Thibault (1997: 15) writes of: "... a plurality of different, though complementary, conceptual frameworks which may be used to acquire knowledge ... Saussure's solution to this plurality of frameworks is strikingly similar to the theory of quantum mechanics."

Notice Saussure's "reliance on actual or real (as opposed to contrived or solely introspective) data"(cf. Tobin citation above). The data are, in and of themselves, inviolable, i.e., they are what they are (modernist insight), yet the "human touch in data analysis" (cf. "Hard and Soft Science," Introduction above) exposes them to interpretation. This is the case whether dealing with prehistoric *language growth* reconstructed on historical facts, e.g., the emergence of the past tense in Indo-European, which affects languages such as English (cf. "Secondness Driving Analogy," Chapter 15 above), or with current facts, e.g., the present and perhaps fleeting neologisms such as *stalkerazzi* or *donorgate* (cf. "Language Change/Growth Begins," Chapter 19 above). The junction, *Thirdness,* of linguistic method and semiotic method thus configurates with the tension between modernism and postmodernism, between absolute fact, *Secondness*, susceptible to laboratory (e.g., phonetic, chemistry) scrutiny, and human perception, *Firstness*, possibility, as to meaning/signification.

How effective is the most powerful tool instantiating the data and shared by both semiotics and linguistics, viz. *language*? Let us examine language finally once more in a multimodality setting, that is, *film*. For this demonstration we choose the 1995/96 BBC/A& E two-hundredth anniversary blockbuster edition of Jane Austen's *Pride and Prejudice*. The story line of the film, dramatized by Andrew Davies, produced by Sue Birtwistle, and starring Colin Firth as Darcy and Jennifer Ehle as Elizabeth (Lizzy) Bennett, matches the wits of a late eighteenth-century, relatively liberated twenty-two year old, mature, intelligent woman of moderate means against a fairly unapproachable man in his late twenties, who might be called Britain's most eligible and wealthy bachelor at that time.

We consider three particular frames or sequences of the rich data from the central scene galvanizing the sparring between Lizzy and Darcy: the failed, first proposal sequence, which begins with the necessary politeness exchanges (*Pride and Prejudice,* video volume 3). Darcy greets with "I hope you're feeling better," to which Lizzy replies: "Thank you. Will you not sit down?" Ten purely visual shots, lasting 48 seconds and alternating between an agitated, hesitating Darcy and a wondering, waiting Lizzy set a powerful *kinesic* stage. [data set (3)]. Finally Darcy begins: "In vain I have struggled; it will not do. My feelings will not be repressed. You must allow me to tell you how ardently I admire and love you." Upon Lizzy's rejection of his offer of marriage, Darcy suggests that flattery might have made Lizzy more receptive to his proposal. Lizzy instantly refutes this suggestion, saying (my emphasis and numbering of data under analysis):

> You are mistaken, Mr. Darcy. The mode of your declaration merely spared me any concern I might have felt in refusing you (1) *had you behaved in a more gentleman-like manner* ... I had not known you a month before (2a) *I felt you were the last man in the world whom I could ever marry.*

Returning to his own living quarters, a dismayed Darcy recalls Lizzy's sentence (2). The film (*Pride and Prejudice,* video volume 4) shows Darcy with a voice-over of Lizzy, saying (sentence 2b): "You are the last man in the world whom I could ever marry." On one level, i.e., relative to the visual spatial sequence, sentence (2b) can be said to be counterfactual; it renders *virtual mental space* rather than actual space. The voice is not congruent with the visual connector, Darcy, who accordingly, is not coreferential with "I," although Lizzy is in the head space of Darcy; the hearer equals the speaker. Such virtual mental space is a mental *point of view* phenomenon both in filmic and in cognitive grammar known as Space Grammar (allied with "Prototype Theory," cf. Chapter 1 above). Stripped of extralinguistic considerations, sentence (2b) still lacks mental equivalence with sentence (2a). The copula function connector or identity function of (2b) is in the present indicative *you are,* that of (2a) is in the past tense and/or subjunctive, *you were*, introduced by the space builder *I felt*, yielding mental space incompatible in speaker/hearer viewpoint. The point of view expressed by Darcy's virtual space (2b) is thus more real and accordingly more devastating than that expressed originally by Lizzy (2a). Note well that it is the linguistic data/facts and not the visual that map this semantic/pragmatic nuance.

Sentence (1a) occurs a second time, also as a voice-over in virtual mental space as Darcy angrily and grimly recalls Lizzy's retort in the same sequence as (2b) (*Pride and Prejudice, video volume 4*). It occurs a third time in reported speech in which a pleased (without pride) Darcy, upon acceptance by a receptive (without prejudice) Lizzy of his second proposal, self-reflectively recalls the learning challenge Lizzy had inadvertently inspired (*Pride and Prejudice*, video volume 6). To be sure, the visual frames of the thrice spoken sentence (1) differ as to locus and as to speaker. Although the words of the three occurrences are identical, if the visual data were deleted, the *suprasegmental intonation data*, i.e., language data, would provide three pragmatic meaning distinctions linguistically.

Finally, data set (3), as noted above, yields no word data and accordingly also no intonation data., only 48 seconds of linguistic *silence*, framed by Darcy's/Lizzy's initial greeting and Darcy's proposal. We say "linguistic silence" in deference to Jaworski's identification of silence in Japanese painting. Considering a stone garden of rock arranged in white sand, Jaworski (1993: 152, emphasis mine) explains:

> ... meditative emphasis is characteristic of much Japanese Zen art. On the one hand it allows framing the forms that it surrounds and thus makes them meaningful. On the other hand, because the process is reciprocal, the forms embedded in the emptiness provide it with the necessary contrast that enables the spectators to notice the *silence*.

The spectacular 48-second sound of silence of Darcy's first proposal (set 3) is punctured by a small set of dim sounds of steps and shuffling of feet, interspersed by weak bird twitter, and finally by human breathing. Absent the visual, the slight *paralinguistic* (cf. Chapter 13 above) sounds are inadequate to decode the semantics of these 48 silent seconds of the film. Accordingly, the *functional load* of the visual shots is enormous in this sequence, and, in fact, gives meaning to the 48 seconds of silence, which, for their part, reciprocally exacerbates the sight of Darcy's agitation and of Lizzy's dumbfoundedness, both wordless constructs of highly affective meaning relative to the listener/viewer. Thus, while on the one hand, the *wordless* data in set (3) demonstrate well, as Fauconnier (1994: xxxviii) says: "... the extraordinary underspecification of cognitive mental space configurations by language," on the other hand, the sentence data in sets (1) and (2) attest to the power of language via a quite modest set of language signifiers.

Reference to space being proximate, it is appropriate to conclude with a series of questions concerning outer space: What is it that we expect to see when we survey the horizon of the Mars panorama of the Ares Vallis floodplain transmitted by the Pathfinder spacecraft? Why do we avidly keep scrutinizing that horizon every time it appears on the TV screen? Are we hopefully and fearfully searching for the possible appearance of a creature, perhaps upright, emerging over the horizon? The Mars rockscape is reality, while the creature is virtual, yet the fire in the belly (cf. Chapter 1 above) is, in fact, for the latter.

Bibliography

Adelung, Johann Christoph. (1781). *Über die Geschichte der Deutschen Sprache, über Deutsche Mundarten und Deutsche Sprachlehre.* Leipzig.

Akmajian, A., R. A. Demers, and R. M. Harnish. (1979[1], 1984[2]). *Linguistics: An Introduction to Language and Communication.* Cambridge, Mass.: M.I.T. Press.

Alston, William P. (1971). Philosophical Analysis and Structural Linguistics. In Colin Lyas (ed.), *Philosophy and Linguistics,* 284–296. London: Macmillan St. Martin's Press.

Andersen, Henning. (1973). Abductive and Deductive Change. *Language* 49: 765–94.

— (1974). Towards a Typology of Change: Bifurcating Changes and Binary Relations. In J. M. Anderson and C. Jones (eds.), *Historical Linguistics II,* 17–60. Amsterdam: North Holland.

Anttila, Raimo. (1972, 1988[2]). *An Introduction to Historical and Comparative Linguistics.* New York: Macmillan.

Augst, Gerhard. (1975). *Untersuchungen zum Morpheminventar der deutschen Gegenwartssprache.* (Forschungsberichte des Instituts für deutsche Sprache 25). Tübingen.

Bal, Mieke. (1997[2]). *Narratology: Introduction to the Theory of Narrative.* Trans. C. van Boheemen. Toronto: University of Toronto Press.

Baer, Eugen. (1975). *Semiotic Approaches to Psychotherapy.* Bloomington: Research Center for Language and Semiotic Studies.

— (1979). Tom Sebeok's Thomism. *Semiotica* 28: 349–70.

— (1982). The Medical Symptom. *American Journal of Semiotics* 1: 17–34.

Banfield, Ann. (1978). Where Epistemology, Style, and Grammar Meet Literary History: The Development of Represented Speech and Thought. *New Literary History* 9: 415–54.

Barber, Charles Clyde. (1951). *An Old High German Reader*. Oxford: Basil Blackwell.

Barnes, Mervin. (1971). *Phonological and Morphological Rules in Old Saxon*. Unpubl. dissertation, University of California, Los Angeles.

Barthes, Roland. (1966). Introduction à l'analyse structurale des récits. *Communications* 8: 1–27.

— (1968). *Elements of Semiology*. Trans. A. Lavers and C. Smith. New York: Hill and Wang.

— (1971). De l'oeuvre au texte. *Revue d'Esthétique* 24: 225–32.

— (1977). *Image, Music, Text*. New York: Hill and Wang.

— (1970). *Writing Degree Zero (and) Elements of Semiology*. Trans. A. Lavers and C. Smith. Boston: Beacon Press.

Becker, Jurek. (1969). *Jakob der Lügner*. Berlin: Aufbau-Verlag.

— (1979). *Jakob the Liar*. New York: Harcourt Brace Jovanovich.

Begley, Sharon. (1983). What the Trees Really Say. *Newsweek* June 20, 72.

Behaghel, Otto. (1901). Geschichte der deutschen Sprache. In Hermann Paul (ed.), *Grundriß der germanischen Philologie*. 650–780. Straßburg: Trübner.

— (1932). *Deutsche Syntax*. vol. 4. Heidelberg: Carl Winter.

— (1984⁹). *Heliand und Genesis*. Rev. by Burkhard Taeger. Tübingen: Niemeyer.

Bennett. Jonathan. (1976). *Linguistic Behaviour*. Cambridge: Cambridge University Press.

Bentham, J. (1969). *A Bentham Reader*, M. P. Mack (ed.). New York: Pegasus.

Benveniste, Emile. (1968). Mutations of Linguistic Categories. In W. P. Lehmann and Y. Malkiel (eds.), *Directions for Historical Linguistics*, 83–94. Austin: University of Texas Press.

Benware, A. Wilbur. (1986). *Phonetics and Phonology of Modern German: An Introduction*. Washington: Georgetown University Press.

Berlin, Brent and Paul Kay. (1969). *Basic Color Terms: Their Universality and Evolution*. Berkeley: University of California Press.

Bernard, Jeff, Antonino Butttitta, and Gloria Withalm (eds.). (1989). *IASS-AIS Bulletin* (March-April), Special Issue.

Bertalanffy, Ludwig von. (1968). *General System Theory.* New York: Braziller.

Bever, T. G. and D. T. Langendoen. (1972). The Interaction of Speech Perception and Grammatical Structure in the Evolution of Language. In R. P. Stockwell and R. K. S. Macaulay (eds.), *Linguistic Change and Generative Theory*, 32–95. Bloomington: Indiana University Press.

Bharati, Agehananda. (1985). The Self in Hindu Thought and Action. In A. Marsella, G. Devos, and F. L. K. Hsu (eds.), 185–230.

Bierwish, Manfred. (1967). Some Semantic Universals of German Adjectivals. *Foundations of Language* 3: 1–36.

— (1970). Semantics. In John Lyons (ed.), *New Horizons in Linguistics*, 166–184. Harmondsworth, Middlesex: Penguin Books.

Birdwhistell, R. L. (1952). *Introduction to Kinesics.* Louisville: University of Louisville Press.

— (1970). *Kinesics and Context.* Philadelphia: University of Pennsylvania Press.

Blanshard, Charles S. (1940). *The Nature of Thought I.* New York: Macmillan.

Bloomfield, Leonard. (1933). *Language.* New York: Holt, Rinehart, Winston.

— (1939). Linguistic Aspects of Science (*International Encyclopedia of Unified Science* 1(4): 25. Chicago: University of Chicago Press.

Bolinger, Dwight. (1973). Truth Is a Linguistic Question. *Language* 49: 539–50.

Bopp, Franz. (1836). *Vocalismus oder vergleichende Kritiken über J. Grimm's deutsche Grammatik und Graff's Althochdeutschen Sprachschatz.* Berlin: Nicholaischen Buchhandlung.

Borbé, Tasso. (1983). General Preface. In Tasso Borbé (ed.), *Semiotics Unfolding: Proceedings of the Second Congress of the International Association for Semiotic Studies, Vienna, July 1979 , I,* v–viii. (Approaches to Semiotics 68). Berlin: Mouton de Gruyter.

Boretz, B. (1969). Meta-variations: Studies in the Foundations of Musical Thought, I. *Perspectives of New Music* 8: 1–74.

Bostock, J. Knight. (1955). *A Handbook on Old High German Literature.* Oxford: Clarendon Press.

Bouissac, Paul (1976). The 'Golden Legend' of Semiotics. *Semiotica* 17:371–84.

— (1977). Semiotics and Spectacles: The Circus Institution and Representations. In T.A. Sebeok (ed.), *A Profusion of Signs,* 143–52. Bloomington: Indiana University Press.

British Broadcasting Corporation, MCPS and Arts and Entertainment Television Networks. (1995/1996). *Pride and Prejudice.*

Brooke, Kenneth. (1955). *An Introduction to Early New High German.* Oxford: Basil Blackwell.

Brown, Roger Langham. (1967). *Wilhelm von Humboldt's Conception of Linguistic Relativity.* The Hague: Mouton.

Brown, Roger. (1973). Schizophrenia, Language, and Reality. *American Psychologist* 28: 395–403.

Burrell, David. (1973). *Analogy and Philosophical Language.* New Haven: Yale University Press.

Butterworth, Brian. (1978). Maxims for Studying Conversations. *Semiotica* 24: 317–39.

Carnap, R. (1942). *Introduction to Semantics and Foundation of Logic.* Cambridge: Harvard University Press.

Carroll, John B. (ed.). (1956). *Language, Thought, and Reality.* Cambridge: MA: MIT Press.

Caws, P. (1969). The Structure of Discovery. *Science* 166: 1375–80.

Chaika, Elaine. (1974). A Linguist Looks at "Schizophrenic Language." *Brain and Language* 1: 257–77.

Chambers, Frank P. (1961). *Perception, Understanding and Society.* London: Sidgwick and Jackson.

Chatman, Seymour, Umberto Eco, and J.-M. Klinkenberg (eds.). (1979). *A Semiotic Landscape: Proceedings from the First Congress of the International Association for Semiotic Studies, Milan, June 1974.* (Approaches to Semiotics 29). The Hague: Mouton.

Chinen, Allen B. (1989). Scientific, Humanistic and Practical Modes of Understanding: A Semiotic Analysis from Psychotherapy. In I. Rauch and G. F. Carr (eds.), 227–39.

Chomsky, Noam. (1957). *Syntactic Structures.* The Hague: Mouton.

— (1964). Current Issues in Linguistic Theory. In J.A. Fodor and J.J. Katz (eds.), *The Structure of Language: Readings in the Philosophy of Language,* 50–118. Englewood Cliffs: Prentice Hall.

— (1967). The General Properties of Language. In Frederic J. Darley (ed.), *Brain Mechanisms Underlying Speech and Language*. New York: Grune and Stratton.

— (1972). *Language and Mind*. Enlarged edition. New York: Harcourt Brace Jovanovich, Inc.

— (1979). Human Language and other Semiotic Systems. *Semiotica* 25: 31–44.

— (1980). *Rules and Representations*. New York: Columbia University Press.

Chu, Godwin C. (1985). The Changing Concept of Self in Contemporary China. In A. Marsella, G. Devos, and F. L. K. Hsu (eds.), 252–77.

Cohen, L. Jonathan. (1975). Spoken and Unspoken Meanings. In Thomas A. Sebeok (ed.), 19–25.

Collingwood, R. G. (1940). *An Essay on Metaphysics*. Oxford: Clarendon Press.

Corti, Maria. (1978). *An Introduction to Literary Semiotics*. Bloomington: Indiana University Press.

Courtés, Joseph. (1976). *Introduction à la sémiotique narrative et discursive*. Préface de A. J. Greimas. Paris: Hachette.

Crystal, D. (1974). Paralinguistics.In Thomas A. Sebeok (ed.), *Current Trends in Linguistics, vol. 12: Linguistics and the Adjacent Arts and Sciences*, 265–95. The Hague: Mouton.

Dammers, U., Walter Hoffmann and Hans-Joachim Solms. (1987). Flexion der starken und schwachen Verben. In Hugo Moser, Hugo Stopp, Werner Besch (eds.), *Grammatik des Frühneuhochdeutschen. Beiträge zur Laut- und und Formenlehre*. Heidelberg: Carl Winter.

de Mauro, Tullio. (1975). The Link with Linguistics. In Thomas A. Sebeok (ed.), 37–46.

Derrida, Jacques. (1976). *Of Grammatology*. Trans. G. C. Spivak. Baltimore: Johns Hopkins University Press.

— (1978). *Writing and Difference*. Trans. A. Bass. Chicago: University of Chicago Press.

de Saussure, Ferdinand. (1959). *Course in General Linguistics*. C. Bally *et al.* (eds.). Trans. W. Baskin. New York: Philosophical Library.

Devos, George. (1985). Dimensions of the Self in Japanese Culture. In A. Marsella, G. Devos, and F. L. K. Hsu (eds.), 141–84.

Dingwall, W. O. (1980). Human Communicative Behavior: A Biological Model. In I. Rauch and G. F. Carr (eds.), 51–86.

Doležel, Lubomír. (1976). Narrative Modalities. *Journal of Literary Semantics* 5: 5–14.

Donegan, P. J. and D. Stampe. (1979). The Study of Natural Phonology. In D.A. Dinnsen (ed.), *Current Approaches to Phonological Theory*, 126–73. Bloomington: Indiana University Press.

Dressler, Wolfgang U. (1973²). *Einführung in die Textlinguistik*. Tübingen: Niemeyer.

Dressler, Wolfgang U., Willi Mayerthaler, Oswald Panagl, and Wolfgang U. Wurzel (eds.). (1987). *Leitmotifs in Natural Morphology*. Amsterdam: John Benjamins.

Dressler, Wolfgang U. and Willi Mayerthaler. (1987). Introduction. In W. Dressler *et al.* (eds.), 3–9.

Eco, Umberto. (1975). Looking for a Logic of Culture. In Thomas A. Sebeok (ed.), 9–17.

— (1976). *A Theory of Semiotics*. Bloomington: Indiana University Press.

— (1978). Semiotics: A Discipline or an Interdisciplinary Method? In Thomas A. Sebeok (ed.), *Sight, Sound, and Sense*, 73–83. Bloomington: Indiana University Press.

— (1979). Preface. In Seymour Chatman, Umberto Eco, and J-M. Klinkenberg (eds.), v–viii.

— (1981). Der Einfluss Roman Jakobsons auf die Entwicklung der Semiotik. In Martin Krampen *et al.* (eds.), 173–204.

— (1990). *The Limits of Interpretation*. Bloomington: Indiana University Press.

— (1995). *The Search for the Perfect Language*. Trans. Fentress. Oxford: Blarkwell.

Eggers, Hans. (1985). Soziokulturelle Voraussetzungen und Sprachraum des Frühneuhochdeutschen. In Werner Besch, Oskar Reichmann, and Stefan Sonderegger (eds.), *Sprachgeschichte. Ein Handbuch zur Geschichte der deutschen Sprache und ihrer Erforschung*, 1295–1305. Berlin: Walter de Gruyter.

Engel, George L. (1985). Commentary on Schwartz and Wiggins' Science, Humanism, and the Nature of Medical Practice. *Perspectives in Biology and Medicine* 28: 362–6.

Enninger, Werner. (1983). Kodewandel in der Kleidung. Sechsundzwanzig. Hypothesenpaare. *Zeitschrift für Semiotik* 5: 23–48.

Eschbach, Achim. (1983). Prolegomena of a Possible Historiography of Semiotics: The Development of a Semiotical Fact. In Achim Eschbach and Jürgen Trabant (eds.), *History of Semiotics*, 25–38. Amsterdam: John Benjamins.

Eschbach, Achim and Viktoria Eschbach-Szabró. (1986). *Bibliography of Semiotics. 1975–1985*. I, II. Amsterdam: John Benjamins.

Fann, K. T. (1970). *Peirce's Theory of Abduction*. The Hague: Martinus Nijhoff.

Fauconnier, Gilles. (1994). *Mental Spaces: Aspects of Meaning Construction in Natural Language*. Cambridge: Cambridge University Press.

Feibleman, James K. (1969). *An Introduction to the Philosophy of Charles S. Peirce, Interpreted as a System*. Cambridge, Mass.: The M. I. T. Press.

Feldman, Richard S. (1978). Communicability Deficit in Schizophrenics Resulting from a More General Deficit. In Steven Schwartz (ed.), *Language and Cognition*, 35–53. Hillsdale, NJ: Lawrence Erlbaum Associates.

Feyerabend, Paul. (1978). *Against Method*. London: Verso.

Fick, August. (1883). *Göttinger gelehrte Anzeigen*. Göttingen.

Fillmore, Charles J. (1977). Preface. In L. Friedman (ed.), *On the Other Hand: New Perspectives on American Sign Language*. New York: Academic Press.

Fischer-Jørgensen, Eli. (1965). Louis Hjelmslev. *Acta Linguistica Hafniensia* 9 (1): iii–xxii.

Foucault, Michel. (1972). *The Archaeology of Knowledge*. Trans. A. M. Smith. New York: Pantheon Books.

Frederiksen, Carl H. (1977). Semantic Processing Units in Understanding Text. In R. O. Freedle (ed.), *Discourse Production and Comprehension*, 57–87. Norwood, NJ: Ablex.

Freud, Sigmund. (1905). Fragments of an Analysis of a Case of Hysteria. In E. Jones (ed.), *Collected Papers 3*, 13–146. New York.

— (1926 [1959]). *Inhibitions, Symptoms and Anxiety*. Standard Edition. Trans. J. Strachey. London: Hogarth Press.

Fromkin, Victoria. (1975). A Linguist Looks at "A Linguist Looks at Schizophrenic" Language. *Brain and Language* 2: 498–503.

Fuchs, H. P. and Schank, G. (1975). *Texte gesprochener deutscher Standardsprache III*. (Heutiges Deutsch, Series II: Texte, col. 3). Munich: Max Hueber.

Gallée, Johan Hendrik. (1910²). *Altsächsische Grammatik*. Halle: Niemeyer.

Garvin, Paul L. (1974). Specialty Trends in the Language Science. In Thomas A. Sebeok (ed.), *Current Trends in Linguistics 12*, 2889–2909. The Hague: Mouton.

Genette, Gérard. (1972). *Figures III*. Paris: Seuil.

Genzmer, Felix. (1956). *Heliand und die Bruchstücke der Genesis*. Stuttgart: Reclam.

Gerber, W. (1967). Philosophical Dictionaries and Encyclopedias. In P. Edwards (ed.), *The Encylopedia of Philosophy*, 170–99. New York: Macmillan.

Geschke, Susan Elsner. (1979). *A Linguistic-Semiotic Study of the Proliferation in the New High German Noun Plural Morphology*. Unpubl. dissertation, University of Illinois.

Giegerich, Heinz. (1985). *Metrical Phonology and Phonological Structure: German and English*. Cambridge: Cambridge University Press.

Giessmann, Ulrike. (1981). *Die Flexion von* gehen *und* stehen *im Frühneuhochdeutschen*. (Germanische Bibliothek. Series 3, Untersuchungen). Heidelberg: Carl Winter.

Goffman, Erving. (1979). Footing. *Semiotica* 25: 1–29.

Gopnik, M. (1977). Scientific Theories as Meta-Semiotic Systems. *Semiotica* 21: 211–25.

Greenberg, Joseph H. (1973). Linguistics as a Pilot Science. In Eric P. Hamp (ed.), *Themes in Linguistics: The 1970's* (Janua Linguarum, Series Minor 172), 45–60. The Hague: Mouton.

Greenfield, Meg. (1997). Brutus Denies All. *Newsweek* August 11: 76.

Greimas, Algirdas J. (1971). Narrative Grammar: Units and levels. *Modern Language Notes* 86: 793–806.

— (1977). Elements of a Narrative Grammar. *Diacritics* March: 23–39.

Greimas, Algirdas J. and Courtés, Joseph. (1976). The Cognitive Dimension of Narrative Discourse. *New Literary History* 7: 433–47.

— (1982). *Semiotics and Language. An Analytic Dictionary*. Bloomington: Indiana University Press.

— (1986). *Sémiotique — Dictionnaire Raisonné de la Théorie du Langage*. Paris: Hachette.

Greven, Jochen (ed.). (1971). *Das Gesamtwerk*. Geneva: Kossodo.

Grice, Paul H. (1975). Logic and Conversation. In Peter Cole and Jerry Morgan (eds.) *Syntax and Semantics. 3: Speech Acts,* 41–58. New York: Seminar Press.

Grienberger, Theodor. (1920). Althochdeutsche Texterklärungen II. *Beiträge zur Geschichte der deutschen Sprache und Literatur* 45: 404–29.

Grimm, Jakob, and Wilhelm Grimm. (1854). *Deutsches Wörterbuch I*. Leipzig: Hirzel.

Grimm, Jakob. (1831). *Deutsche Grammatik 3*. Göttingen: Dieterich.

Gülich, Elisabeth. (1970). *Gliederungssignale in der Makrosyntax des gesprochenen Französisch*. Munich: Wilhelm Fink.

Gülich, Elisabeth and Wolfgang Raible. (1977). *Linguistische Textmodelle: Grundlagen und Möglichkeiten*. Munich: Wilhelm Fink.

Gürtler, Hans. (1912, 1913). Zur Geschichte der deutschen -*er*-Plurale, besonders im Frühneuhochdeutschen. *Beiträge zur Geschichte der deutschen Sprache und Literatur* I, 37: 492–543; II, III, 38: 67–224.

Haiman, John B. (1980). The Iconicity of Grammar: Isomorphism and Motivation. *Language* 56: 515–40.

— (1983). Iconic and Economic Motivation. *Language* 59: 781–819.

Hall, Edward T. (1972). A System for the Notation of Proxemic Behavior. In John Laver and Sandy Hutcherson (eds.), *Communication in Face to Face Interaction*, 247–73. (*American Anthropologist* 65, 1963: 1003–26.) Harmondsworth, Middlesex, England: Penguin Books.

Halle, Morris. (1962). Phonology in Generative Grammar. *Word* 8: 54–72.

Halliday, Michael A.K. (1978). *Language as a Social Semiotic: The Social Interpretation of Language and Meaning*. Baltimore: University Park Press.

Halliday, Michael A. K., Angus McIntosh, and Peter Strevens. (1964). *The Linguistic Sciences and Language Teaching*. London: Longman.

Hankiss, A. (1980). Games Con Men Play: The Semiosis of Deceptive Interacton. *Journal of Communication* 30: 104–12.

Harris, Zelig S. (1952). Discourse Analysis. *Language* 28: 1–30.

Hartmann, Peter. (1971). Texte als linguistisches Objekt. In W.-D. Stempel (ed.) *Beiträge zur Textlinguistik*, 9–29. Munich: Wilhelm Fink.

Hartmann, R. R. K. (1921). *Contrastive Textology.* Heidelberg: Groos.

Hayano, D. (1980). Communicative Competency Among Poker Players. *Journal of Communication* 30: 113–20.

Heffner, R.-M.S. (1952). *General Phonetics.* Madison: University of Wisconsin Press.

Heidegger, Martin. (1981). *Poetry, Language, Thought.* Trans. A. Hofstadter. New York: Harper and Row.

Herzfeld, Michael and Lucio Melazzo. (eds.). (1988). *Semiotic Theory and Practice: Proceedings of the Third International Congress of the IASS, Palermo, 1984.* Berlin: Mouton de Gruyter.

Hill, A. A. (1958). *Introduction to Linguistic Structures.* New York: Harcourt, Brace and World.

Hjelmslev, Louis. (1963). *Prolegomena to a Theory of Language.* Trans. F. J. Whitfield,. Madison: University of Wisconsin Press.

Hobbes, T. (1839). *The English Works I.* W. Molesworth (ed.). Aalen: Scientia.

Hockett, Charles F. (1958). *A Course in Modern Linguistics.* New York: Macmillan.

— (1963). The Problem of Universals in Language. In Joseph H. Greenberg (ed.), *Universals of Language*, 1–22. Cambridge, MA: MIT Press.

— (1965). Sound Change. *Language* 41: 185–215.

Holthausen, Ferdinand. (1921[2]). *Altsächsisches Elementarbuch.* Heidelberg: Carl Winter.

Hooper, Joan B. (1976). *An Introduction to Natural Generative Phonology.* New York: Academic Press.

Horaček, Blanka. (1958). *Kleine historische Lautlehre des Deutschen.* Wien: Wilhelm Braumüller.

Humboldt, Wilhelm von. (1836[1988]). *On Language: The Diversity of Human Language—Structure and Its Influence on the Mental Development of Mankind.* Trans. P. Heath. Cambridge: Cambridge University Press.

Hurtig, Richard. (1977). Toward a Functional Theory of Discourse. In R.O. Freedle (ed.), *Discourse Production and Comprehension,* 89–106. Norwood, NJ: Ablex.

Innis, Robert E. (1982). *Karl Bühler: Semiotic Foundations of Language Theory.* New York: Plenum Press.

Isenberg, Horst. (1970). Der Begriff "Text" in der Sprachtheorie. *Arbeitsstelle Strukturelle Grammatik.* Berlin: Deutsche Akademie der Wissenschaften zu Berlin, Bericht 8.

Jackendoff, Ray S. and F. Lehrdahl. (1980). *Toward a Formal Theory of Tonal Music.* Cambridge: MIT Press.

Jakobson, Roman. (1958). Typological Studies and Their Contribution to Historical Comparative Linguistics. In *Proceedings of the Eighth International Congress of Linguistics,* 17–25. Oslo: Oslo University Press.

— (1962a). Observations sur le classement phonologique des consonnes. *Roman Jakobson Selected Writings I: Phonological Studies,* 272–79. The Hague: Mouton.

— (1962b). Remarques sur l'évolution phonologique du russe comparée à celle des autres langues slaves *Roman Jakobson Selected Writings I: Phonological Studies,* 7–116. The Hague: Mouton.

— (1965). Quest for the Essence of Language. *Diogenes: An International Review of Philosophy and Humanistic Studies* 51: 21–37.

— (1970). *Main Trends in the Science of Language,* 26. New York: Harper & Row.

— (1971a). The Phonemic and Grammatical Aspects of Language in Their Interrelations. *Selected Writings II: Word and Languages,* 103–14. The Hague: Mouton.

— (1971b). Linguistics in Relation to Other Sciences. *Roman Jakobson: Selected Writings II: Word and Languages,* 655–96. The Hague: Mouton.

— (1971c). Language in Relation to Other Communication Systems. *Selected Writings II: Word and Languages,* 679–708. The Hague: Mouton.

— (1979). Coup d'oeil sur le développement de la sémiotique. In Seymour Chatman, Umberto Eco, and J.-M. Klinkenberg (eds.), 3–18.

Jaworski, Adam. (1993). *The Power of Silence: Social and Pragmatic Perspectives.* Newbury Park, CA: Sage Publications.

Johnson, Frank A. (1985). The Western Concept of Self. In A. Marsella, G. Devos, and F. L. K. Hsu (eds.), 91–138.
— (1989). Psychotherapeutic Change: The Possible Application of a Semiotic Analysis. In I. Rauch, and G. F. Carr (eds.), 261–278.
Katz, Jerrold J. and Jerry A. Fodor. (1963). The Structure of a Semantic Theory. *Language* 39: 170–210.
Kelly, John and John Local. (1989). *Doing Phonology. Observing, Recording, Interpreting.* Manchester: Manchester University Press.
Kenner, Hugh. (1984). The Making of the Modernist Canon. In R. von Halberg (ed.), *Canons*, 363–75. Chicago: University of Chicago Press.
Kess, Joseph F. (1976). *Psycholinguistics: Introductory Perspectives.* New York: Academic Press.
King, Robert D. (1969). *Historical Linguistics and Generative Grammar.* Englewood Cliffs, N. J.: Prentice Hall.
Kiparsky, Paul (1965). *Phonological Change.* Unpubl. dissertation, MIT.
— (1968). Linguistic Universals and Linguistic Change. In Emmon Bach and Robert T. Harms (eds.), *Universals in Linguistic Theory*, 170–202. New York: Holt, Rinehart, Winston.
Klima, Edward (1965). *Studies in Diachronic Transformational Syntax.* Unpubl. dissertation, Harvard University.
Koutsoudas, A., G. Sanders, and C. Noll. (1974). The Application of Phonological Rules. *Language* 50: 1–28.
Krampen, Martin. (1979). Semiotische Klassiker des 20. Jahrhunderts. *Zeitschrift für Semiotik* 1 (1): 7.
Krampen, Martin, Klaus Oehler, Roland Posner and Thure von Uexküll (eds.). (1981). *Die Welt als Zeichen: Klassiker der modernen Semiotik.* Berlin: Severin and Siedler.
Kristeva, Julia. (1975). The System and the Speaking Subject. In Thomas A. Sebeok (ed.), 45–55.
Kuryłowicz, Jerzy. (1945–49). La nature de procès dits "analogiques." *Acta Linguistica* 5: 15–37.
— (1964). *The Inflectional Categories of Indo-European.* Heidelberg: Carl Winter.
Labov, William and Joshua Waletzky. (1967). Narrative Analysis: Oral Versions of Personal Experience. In *Essays on the Verbal and Visual Arts: Proceedings of the 1966 Annual Spring Meet-*

ing of the American Ethnological Society, 12–44. Seattle: University of Washington Press.

Ladefoged, Peter. (1982²). *A Course in Phonetics.* New York: Harcourt Brace Jovanovich.

Lakoff, George and Mark Johnson. (1980). *Metaphors We Live By.* Chicago: University of Chicago Press.

— (1987). *Women, Fire, and Dangerous Things: What Catergories Reveal about the Mind.* Chicago: University of Chicago Press.

Langacker, Ronald. (1987). *Foundations of Cognitive Grammar I: Theoretical Perspectives.* Stanford: Stanford University Press.

Lange-Seidl, Annemarie. (1977). *Approaches to Theories for Nonverbal Signs.* (Studies in Semiotics 17). Lisse: The Peter de Ridder Press.

— (1981). Konstitutionsbegriff und Zeichenkonstitution. In Annemarie Lange-Seidl (ed.), *Zeichenkonstitution: Akten des 2. Semiotischen Kolloquiums, Regenburg 1978,* 2–11. Berlin: Walter de Gruyter.

Leach, Edmund. (1976). Social Geography and Linguistic Performance. *Semiotica* 16: 87–97.

Leech, G. N. (1980). *Explorations in Semantics and Pragmatics* Amsterdam: John Benjamins.

Lees, R. B. (1980). Language and the Genetic Code. In I. Rauch and G. F. Carr (eds.), 218–26.

Lenneberg, Eric H. (1967). *Biological Foundations of Language.* New York: John Wiley.

Leskien, August. (1876). *Die Deklination in Slavish-Litauischen und Germanischen.* Leipzig: Hirzel.

Lévi-Strauss, Claude. (1963). *Structural Anthropology.* N.Y.: Basic Books.

— (1980). Die strukturalistische Tätigkeit. Ein Gespräch mit Marco d'Eramo. In A. Reif (ed.), *Mythos und Bedeutung.* Frankfurt: Suhrkamp.

Liles, Bruce. (1975). *An Introduction to Linguistics.* Englewood Cliffs, New Jersey: Prentice-Hall.

Lingren, Kaj B. (1953). *Die Apokope des MHD. -e in seinen verschiedenen Funktionen.* (Annales Academiae Scientiarum Fennicae B, 78,2) Helsinki: Suomalainen Tiedeakatemia.

Lorenz, Maria. (1961). Problems Posed by Schizophrenic Language. *Archives of General Psychiatry* 5: 406–10.

Lotman, J. M. *et al.* (1975). Theses on the Semiotic Study of Cultures (as Applied to Slavic Texts). In Thomas A. Sebeok (ed.), 57–84.

Lotman, J. M. (1977). The Dynamic Model of a Semiotic System. *Semiotica* 21: 93–210.

Lyons, John. (1977). *Semantics I, II.* Cambridge: Cambridge University Press.

— (1981). *Language and Linguistics.* Cambridge: Cambridge University Press.

— (1995). *Linguistic Semantics: An Introduction.* Cambridge: Cambridge University Press.

Machler, Robert (ed.). (1971). *Gedichte und Dramolette XI.* In Jochen Greven (ed.).

Maldonado, T. (1961). *Beitrag zur Terminologie der Semiotik.* Ulm:

Malkiel, Yakov. (1981). Drift, Slope, and Slant: Background of, and Variations upon, a Sapirian Theme. *Language* 57: 535–70.

Malmberg, Bertil. (1963). *Structural Linguistics and Human Communication.* New York: Academic Press.

Manczak, Witold. (1958). Tendences générales des changements analogiques. *Lingua* 7: 298–325, 387–420.

Marcella, Anthony, George Devos, and Francis L. K. Hsu (eds.). (1985). *Culture and Self: Asian and Western Perspectives.* New York: Tavistock.

Marshall, J. C. (1970). The Biology of Communication in Man and Animals. In John Lyons (ed.), *New Horizons in Linguistics,* 229–41. Harmondsworth, Middlesex, England: Penguin Books.

Marcus, Solomon. (1974). Linguistics as a Pilot Science. In T. A. Sebeok (ed.) *Current Trends in Linguistics 12,* 2871–87. The Hague: Mouton.

Martinet, André (1955). *Economie des changements phonétiques.* Bern: Francke.

Mathiot, Madeleine. (1978). Toward a Frame of Reference for the Analysis of Face to Face Interaction. *Semiotica* 24: 199–220.

— (1979). The Theoretical Status of Discourse. Paper Presented at the Fourth Annual Meeting of the Semiotic Society of America. Bloomington, Indiana.

Mayerthaler, Willi. (1987). System-Independent Morphological Naturalness. In W. U. Dressler *et al.* (eds.), 59–96.

Meid, Wolfgang. (1971). *Das germanische Präteritum*. (Innsbrucker Beiträge zur Sprachwissenschaft 3). Innsbruck: Institut für Vergleichende Sprachwissenschaft der Universität, Wien.

Merrell, Floyd. (1984). Deconstruction Meets a Mathematician: Meta-semiotic Inquiry. *American Journal of Semiotics* 2: 125–52.

— (1995). *Semiosis in the Postmodern Age*. West Lafayette: Purdue University Press.

— (1997). *Peirce, Signs, and Meaning*. Toronto: University of Toronto Press.

Mill, John Stuart. (1851³). *A System of Logic I*. London: J. W. Parker.

Miller, George A., and Philip Johnson-Laird. (1976). *Language and Perception*. Cambridge, MA: Belknap Press of Harvard University Press.

Mitzka, Walther. (1948/50). Die Sprache des Heliand und die altsächsische Stammesverfassung. *Niederdeutsches Jahrbuch* 71/73: 32–91.

Molz, Hermann. (1906). Die Substantivflexion seit Mittelhochdeutscher Zeit. II, *Beiträge zur Geschichte der deutschen Sprache und Literatur* 31: 277–392.

Moravcsik, J.M.E. (1975). *Understanding Language: A Study of Theories of Language in Linguistics and Philosophy*. (Janua Linguarum, Series Minor 169). The Hague: Mouton.

Morris, Charles. (1955²). *Signs, Language, and Behavior*. New York: Braziller.

Moulton, W. G. (1961). Zur Geschichte des deutschen Vokalsystems. *Beiträge zur Geschichte der deutschen Sprache und Literatur* (Veröffentlichungen des Instituts für Deutsche Sprache und Literatur 8), 40–79. Berlin: Akademie-Verlag. [Reprinted in Jürgen Eichhoff and Irmengard Rauch (eds.), *Der Heliand*, 200–46. Darmstadt: Wissenschaftliche Buchgesellschaft, 1973].

Nattiez, J.-J. (1972). The Place of Notation in Musical Semiology. Paper presented at the International Symposium on the Problematic of Today's Musical Notation. Rome, Italy.

Naville, Adrien. (1901). *Nouvelle classification des sciences*. Paris: Félix Alcan.

Nef, Frederic. (1977). Introduction to the Reading of Greimas: Toward a Discursive linguistics. *Diacritics* March: 18–22.

Nietzsche, Friedrich. (1874 [1922]). The Relation of the Rhetorical to Language. *Nietzsches Gesammelte Werke 5*: 297–300. Munich: Musarion.

Nöth, Winfred. (1990). *Handbook of Semiotics*. Bloomington: Indiana University Press.

O'Grady, W., M. Dobrovolsky and M. Aronoff. (1993^2). *Contemporary Linguistics: An Introduction*. N.Y.: St. Martins Press.

Oehler, Klaus. (1981). The Significance of Peirce's Ethics of Terminology for Contemporary Lexicography in Semiotics. *Transactions of the Charles S. Peirce Society* 17: 348–57.

Oehler, Klaus (ed.). (1984). *Zeichen und Realität*. Tübingen: Stauffenburg Verlag.

Oksaar, Els. (1984). Probleme der Artzt-Patient-Interaktion. In Oehler (ed.), 1101–10.

Orwell, George. (1949). *1984*. New York: Harcourt, Brace.

Osgood, Charles E. (1980). What is a language? In I. Rauch and G. F. Carr, 9–50.

Osthoff, Hermann. (1879). *Das physiologische und psychologische Moment in der sprachlichen Formenbildung*. Berlin: Carl Habel.

Ostwald, Peter. (1989). The Healing Power of Music: Some Observations on the Semiotic Function of Transitional Objects in Musical Communication. In I. Rauch and G. F. Carr (eds.), 279–96.

Owens, J. (1961). St. Thomas and Elucidation. *The New Scholasticism XXXV:* 421–44.

Parret, Herman. (1974). *Discussing Language*. The Hague: Mouton.

Paul, Hermann. (1880^4). *Prinzipien der Sprachgeschichte*. Halle: Niemeyer.

Paul, Hermann. (1966^7). *Prinzipien der Sprachgeschichte*. Tübingen: Niemeyer.

Pedersen, Holger. (1931). *Linguistic Science in the Nineteenth Century*. Trans. J. W. Spargo. Cambridge, Mass.: Harvard University Press. [Reprinted as *The Discovery of Language*. Bloomington: Indiana University Press, 1962.]

Peirce, Charles Sanders. (1902). Chapter II, Philological Notions. Section I, Classification of the Sciences (Logic II). Manuscript on microfilm at the University of Illinois Rare Book Room. Urbana, Illinois.

Peirce, Charles Sanders. (1913–1958). *Collected Papers of Charles Sanders Peirce I –VI.* C. Hartshorne and P. Weiss (eds.); *VII,* A. Burks (ed.). Cambridge, Mass.: Harvard University Press.

Pelc, Jerzy. (1970). A Functional Approach to the Logical Semiotics of Natural Language. In A.J. Greimas *et al.* (eds.), *Sign, Language, Culture.* 89–112. (Janua Linguarum, Series Major 1). The Hague: Mouton.

— (1989). Presidential address. *IASS-AIS Bulletin* (March-April), Special Issue. J. Bernard, A. Buttitta, and G. Withalm (eds.), 2–3.

Penn, Julia. (1972). *Linguistic Relativity versus Innate Ideas.* The Hague: Mouton.

Penzl, Herbert. (1984a). Das Frühneuhochdeutsche und die Periodisierung der Geschichte der deutschen Sprache. In Martin Bircher, Jörg-Ulrich Fechner and Gerd Hillen (eds.), *Barocker Lust-Spiegel,* 15–25. (Chloe 3). Amsterdam.

— (1984b). *Frühneuhochdeutsch.* Berlin: Peter Lang.

Petöfi, János S. (1973). Towards an Empirically Motivated Grammatical Theory of Verbal Texts. In Petöfi, Janos and H. Rieser (eds.), *Studies in Text Grammar,* 207–75. Dordrecht: D. Reidel.

Pettit, Philip. (1975). *The Concept of Structuralism: A Critical Analysis.* Berkeley: University of California Press.

Piaget, Jean. (1968). *Le Structuralisme.* Paris: Presses of Universitaires de France.

Piirainen, Ilpo Tapani. (1985). Die Diagliederung des Frühneuhochdeutschen. In Besch, Werner, Oskar Reichmann and Stefan Sonderegger (eds.), *Sprachgeschichte. Ein Handbuch zur Geschichte der deutschen Sprache und ihrer Erforschung,* 1368–79. Berlin: Mouton de Gruyter.

Pike, Kenneth L. (1954). *Language in Relation to a Unified Theory of the Structure of Human Behavior.* Preliminary edition, part 1. Glendale, California: Summer Institute of Linguistics.

Postal, Paul. (1966). Review article of *Elements of General Linguistics* by André Martinet. *Foundations of Language* 41: 183–9.

— (1968). *Aspects of Phonological Theory.* New York: Harper and Row.

Poyatos, Fernando. (1993). *Paralanguage: A Linguistic and Interdisciplinary Approach to Interactive Speech and Sound.* Amsterdam: John Benjamins.

Quirk, Randolph. (1970). Aspect and Variant Inflection in English Verbs. *Language* 46: 300–11.

Ramat, Paolo. (1975). Semiotics and Linguistics. *Versus* 10: 1–16.

Rauch, Irmengard. (1972). The Germanic Dental Preterite: Language Origin, and Linguistic Attitude. *Indogermanische Forschungen* 77: 215–33.

— (1975). Die phonologische Basis des Deutschen: unter- und überphonemische Faktoren. *Jahrbuch für internationale Germanistik* 6: 61–71.

— (1977). Review of *The Tell-Tale Sign: A Survey of Semiotics*, Thomas A. Sebeok (ed.). *Lingua* 41: 183–9.

— (1978). Distinguishing Semiotics from Linguistics and the Position of Language in Both. In R.W. Bailey, L. Matejka and P. Steiner (eds.),*The Sign: Semiotics Around the World*, 328–34. Ann Arbor: Michigan Slavic Publications.

— (1979a). Linguistic Method: A Matter of Principle. In I. Rauch and G. F. Carr (eds.), 1979: 19–23 .

— (1979b). The Language-inlay in Semiotic Modalities. *Semiotica* 25: 67–76.

— (1979c). First-language Syntax in the New High German of Swiss Authors. *Amsterdamer Beiträge zur neueren Germanistik* 9: 23–32.

— (1980). Between Linguistics and Semiotics: Paralanguage. In I. Rauch and G. F. Carr (eds.), 1980: 284–9.

— (1981a). Inversion, Adjectival Participle, and Narrative Effect in Old Saxon. *Jahrbuch des Vereins für niederdeutsche Sprachforschung 104: 22–30*.

— (1981b). Semiotics in Search of Method: Narrativity. *Semiotica* 34: 167–76.

— (1981c). What is cause? *The Journal of Indo-European Studies* 9: 319–28.

— (1982). Historical Analogy and the Peircean Categories. In Peter Maher *et al.* (eds.), *Proceedings of the Third International Conference on Historical Linguistics*, 359–67. (Current Issues in Linguistic Theory). Amsterdam: John Benjamins.

— (1983). The Semiotic Paradigm and Language Change.In John N. Deely and Margot D. Lenhart (eds.), *Semiotics 1981*, 193–200. New York: Plenum Press.

— (1984). 'Symbols Grow': Creation, Compulsion, Change. *American Journal of Semiotics* 3: 1–23.

— (1985). Semiotists on semiotists: The Hearbeat of the Sign. *Semiotica* 55: 227–50.

— (1987a). How Do Germanic Linguistic Data React to Newer Literary Methods? In Daniel Calder and T. Craig Christie (eds.), *Germania: Comparative Studies in the Old Germanic Languages and Literatures,* 97–111. UCLA Center for Medieval and Renaissance Studies. New Hampshire: D. S. Brewer.

— (1987b). Old Saxon *hell,* Drawl and Silence. In R. Bergmann, H. Kolb, K. Matzel, K. Stackmann, H. Tiefenbach, L. Voetz (eds.), *Althochdeutsch,* 1145–51. Heidelberg: Carl Winter.

— (1987c). Peirce, Saussure, Uexküll. In Hans Arsleff, Louis G. Kelly, Hans-Josef Niederehe (eds.), *Papers in the History of Linguistics,* 575–83. (Studies in the History of the Language Scienes 38). Amsterdam: John Benjamins.

— (1987d). Peirce: "With No Pretentsion to Being a Linguist," *Semiotica* 65: 29–43.

— (1988). The Saussurean Axes Subverted. *Dispositio* 12: 35–44.

— (1990a). Evidence of Language Change. In Polomé (ed.), *Research Guide for Language Change,* 37–70. (Trends in Linguistics 48). Berlin: Mouton de Gruyter.

— (1990b). Review of *Praguiana: Some Basic and Less Known Aspects of the Prague Linguistic School.* Josef Vachek and Libuse Disková (eds.), *Zeitschrift für Dialektologie und Linguistik* 8: 336–8.

— (1991) Semiotics: (No) Canon, (No) Theses. *Semiotica* 86: 85–92.

— (1992a). Deconstruction, Prototype Theory, and Semiotics. *The American Journal of Semiotics* 9: 129–38.

— (1992b). Icon Destruction and Icon Construction. In Gérard Déledalle, Michel Balat, Janice Déledalle-Rhodes (eds.), *Signs of Humanity/ L'homme et ses signes,* 401–5. Berlin: Mouton de Gruyter.

— (1992c). *The Old Saxon Language: Grammar, Epic Narrative, Linguistic Interference.* (Berkeley Models of Grammars 1). New York: Peter Lang.

— (1995). Formal and Less Formal Rules. In I. Rauch and G. F. Carr (eds.), 1995: 265–73.

— (1996 a).'My Language is the Sum total of Myself:' Humboldt and Peirce. *Ensaios em Homenagem A Thomas A. Sebeok (Cruzeiro Semiotico 22/25),* 109–17.

— (1996 b). 'Symbols Grow' II. In I. Rauch and G. F. Carr (eds.), *Semiotics Around the World: Synthesis in Diversity I*, 87–93. Berlin: Mouton de Gruyter.

— (Forthcoming). Semiotic Pronominal Configurations: A Question of Pathological Language. *Semiosis.*

Rauch, Irmengard and Gerald F. Carr (eds.). (1979). *Linguistic Method. Essays in Honor of Herbert Penzl.* The Hague: Mouton.

— (1980). *The Signifying Animal: The Grammar of Language and Experience.* Bloomington: Indiana University Press.

— (1989). *The Semiotic Bridge: Trends from California.* (Approaches to Semiotics 86). Berlin: Mouton de Gruyter.

— (1995). *Insights in Germanic Linguistics I: Methodology and Transition.* Berlin: Mouton de Gruyter.

— (1996). *Semiotics Around the World: Synthesis in Diversity I, II.* (Approaches to Semiotics 126). Berlin: Mouton Gruyter.

Rauch, Irmengard *et al.* (1995). "BAG IV: Phonological Interference," In I. Rauch and G. F. Carr (eds.), 1995: 275–92.

Reichenbach, H. (1947). *Elements of Symbolic Logic.* New York: Masmillan.

Reichmann, Oskar. (1985). Zur Abgrenzung des Mittelhochdeutschen vom Frühneuhochdeutschen. In Wolfgang Bachofer (ed.), *Mittelhochdeutsches Wörterbuch in der Diskussion. Symposion zur mhg. Lexikographie. Hamburg, Oktober 1985,* 119–147. (Reihe Germanistische Linguistik 84). Tübingen: Niemeyer.

Rewar, Walter. (1976). Notes for a Typology of Culture. *Semiotica* 18: 361–78.

— (1979). Cybernetics and Poetics: The Semiotic Information of Poetry. *Semiotica* 25: 273–305.

Ricoeur, Paul. (1979). The Ideality of Language and Contemporary Linguistics. *Semiotica* 25: 167–74.

Ries, John. (1880). *Die Stellung von Subject und Prädicatsverbum in Heliand. Nebst einem Anhang metrischer Excurse (Quellen und Forschung* 41). Strassburg: Trübner.

Robertson, John S. (1983). From Symbol to Icon: The Evolution of the Pronominal System from Common Mayan to Modern Yucatecan. *Language* 59: 781–819.

Robin, Richard S. (ed.). (1967). *Annotated Catalogue of the Papers of Charles Sanders Peirce.* Worcester, MA: University of Massachusetts Press.

Rooth, E. (1973). Über die Heliandsprache. In J. Eichhoff and I. Rauch (eds.), *Der Heliand*, 200–46. Darmstadt: Wissenschaftliche Buchgesellschaft.

Rosch, Eleanor and Carolyn Mervis. (1975). Family Resemblance. *Cognitive Psychology* 7: 573–605.

Rosenblatt, Roger. (1984). Journalism and the Larger Truth. *Time,* July 2: 88.

Rubenstein, Edward. (1980). Disease Caused by Impaired Communication among Cells. *Scientific American* 242: 102–21.

Ruwet, Nicolas. (1967). Musicology and Linguistics. *International Sound Science Journal* 19: 79–87.

— (1972). *Language, Musique, Poesie.* Paris: Editions du Seuil.

Ryan, Marie-Laure. (1979). Toward a Competence Theory of Genre. *Poetics* 8: 307–37.

Salzinger, Kurt, Stephanie Portnoy, and Thomas A. Sebeok (eds.). (1976). *Contributions to the Doctrine of Signs.* Bloomington: Indiana University Press and Lisse: The Peter de Ridder Press.

Sapir, Edward. (1921). *Language.* New York: Harcourt Brace.

— (1931). Conceptual Categories in Primitive Language. *Science* 74: 578.

Sauerbeck, Karl Otto, Hugo Stopp, Helmut Graser *et al.* (1973). *Grammatik des Frühneuhochdeutschen. Beiträge zur Laut- und Formenlehre.* Hugo Moser and Hugo Stopp (eds.) 1.2: *Vokalismus der Nebensilben II.* Heidelberg: Carl Winter.

Savan, David. (1980). Abduction and Semiotics. In I. Rauch and G. F. Carr (eds.), 252–62.

Schaff, Adam. (1970). Specific Features of the Verbal Sign. In Algirdas Greimas *et al.* (eds.), *Sign, Language, Culture.* (Janua Linguarum, Series Major 1). The Hague: Mouton.

Scherer, Wilhelm. (1878[2]). *Zur Geschichte der deutschen Sprache.* Berlin: Weidman.

Schmitter, Peter. (1979). New Horizons in Semantics? *Semiotica* 25: 139–60.

Scholes, Robert. (1974). *Structuralism in Literature: An Introduction.* New Haven, Conn.: Yale University Press.

Schottel, Justus Georg. (1663). *Ausführliche Arbeit von der teutschen Haubt Sprache.* Braunschweig: Christoff Friedrich Zillingern Buchhandlern.

Schwartz, Michael Alan and Osborne Wiggins. (1985). Humanism, and the Nature of Medical Practice: A Phenomenological View. *Perspectives in Biology and Medicine* 28: 331–61.

Schwartz, Steven (ed.). (1978a). *Language and Cognition*. Hillsdale, NJ: Lawrence Erlbaum Associates.

— (1978b). Language and Cognition in Schizophrenia: A Review and Synthesis. In Steven Schwartz (ed.). (1978a) 237–76.

Scott, Mariana. (1966). *The Heliand*. (University of North Carolina Studies in the Germanic Languages and Literatures 52). Chapel Hill: University of North Carolina Press.

Searle, John. (1969). *Speech Acts. An Essay in the Philosophy of Language*. London: Cambridge University Press.

Sebeok, Thomas A. (1972). *Perspectives in Zoosemiotics* (Janua Linguarum Series Minor 122). The Hague: Mouton.

— (1974). Semiotics: A Survey of the State of the Art. In *Current Trends in Linguistics 12*. The Hague: Mouton, 211–64.

— (1976). *Contributions to the Doctrine of Signs*. Bloomington: Indiana University Press and Peter de Ridder Press.

— (1977a). Zoosemiotic Components of Human Communication. In Thomas A. Sebeok (ed.). *How Animals Communicate*, 1055–77. Bloomington: Indiana University Press.

— (1977b). Ecumenicalism in Semiotics. In Thomas A. Sebeok, (ed.), *A Perfusion of Signs*, 180–206. Bloomington: Indiana University Press.

— (1979). *The Sign & Its Masters*. Austin: University of Texas Press.

— (1984). Signs of life. *International Semiotic Spectrum* 2: 1–2.

— (1986a). On the Goals of Semiotics. *Semiotica* 61: 369–88.

— (1994). *Signs: An Introduction to Semiotics*. Toronto: University of Toronto Press.

Sebeok, Thomas A. (ed.). (1975). *The Tell-Tale Sign: A survey of Semiotics*. Lisse: The Peter de Ridder Press.

— (1986b). *Encyclopedic Dictionary of Semiotics 1, 2, 3*. (Approaches to Semiotics 73). Berlin: Mouton de Gruyter.

Sebeok, Thomas A., Alfred S. Hayes, and Mary Catherine Bateson (eds.). (1964). *Approaches to Semiotics*. The Hague: Mouton.

Segre, Cesare. (1974). Greimas's Dictionary: Form Terminology to Ideology. *Semiotica* 50: 269–78.

Sehrt, Edward H. (1966²). *Vollständiges Wörterbuch zum Heliand und zur altsächsischen Genesis.* Göttingen: Vandenhoeck and Ruprecht.

Selinker, Larry. (1969). Interlanguage. *International Review of Applied Linguistics* 10: 209–31. [Reprinted in D.Nehls (ed.), *Studies in Contrastive Linguistics and Error Analysis I*, 55–77. Heidelberg: Groos, 1979].

Shands, Harley C. (1970). *Semiotic Approaches to Psychiatry.* The Hague: Mouton.

Shands, Harley C. and James D. Meltzer. (1977). Unexpected Semiotic Implications of Medical Inquiry. In Sebeok, Thomas A. (ed.) *A Perfusion of Signs,* 77–89. Bloomington.

Shapiro, Michael. (1969). *Aspects of Russian Morphology: A Semiotic Investigation.* Cambridge, Mass.: Slavica Publishers, Inc.

— (1980). Russian Conjugation: Theory and Hermeneutic. *Language* 56: 67–93.

— (1991). The Sense of Change: Language as History. Bloomington: Indiana University Press.

Shaumyan, Sebastian K. (1970). Semiotics and the Theory of Generative. In Algirdas Greimas *et al.* (eds.), *Sign, Language, Culture,* 244–255. (Janua Linguarum, Series Major 1). The Hague: Mouton.

— (1976). Linguistics as a Part of Semiotics. *Forum Linguisticum* 1: 60–6.

— (1984). Semiotic Laws in Linguistics and Natural Science. In James E. Copeland (ed.), *New Directions in Linguistics and Semiotics,* 231–57. Houston: Rice University Press,.

Shukman, Ann. (1976). *Literature and Semiotics: A Study of the Writings of Yuri Lotman.* Amsterdam: North Holland.

Sievers, Eduard. (1878). *Heliand.* Halle: Verlag der Buchhandlung des Waisenhauses.

— (1924). Ziele und Wege der Schallanalyse. *Stand und Aufgaben der Sprachwissenschaft* (Wilhelm Streitberg Festschrift) 65–111. Heidelberg: Carl Winter.

Silverman, Kaja. (1979). The Site of Reading. *Semiotica* 25: 257–71.

Singer, Milton. (1978). For a Semiotic Anthropology. In Thomas A. Sebeok (ed.). *Sight, Sound, and Sense,* 202–31. Bloomington: Indiana University Press.

Staiano, Kathryn Vance. (1979). A Semiotic Definition of Illness. *Semiotica* 28: 107–25.

— (1981). Alternative Therapeutic Systems in Belize: A Semiotic Framework. *Social Science and Medicine* 15: 317–32.

Stefani, G. (1972). "Semiotics Prospects in Musicology." Paper Presented at the International Symposium on the Problematic of Today's Musical Notation, Rome, Italy.

Steiner, George. (1978). A Note on the Distribution of Discourse. *Semiotica* 22: 185–209.

Sternberger, D. (1974). Nachbemerkung. In H. Weinrich (ed.) *Linguistik der Lüge,* 79–80. Heidelberg: Carl Winter.

Stevick, R. D. (1963). The Biological Model and Historical Linguistics. *Language* 39: 159–69.

Stokoe, W. (1974). Classification and Description of Sign Languages. In Thomas A. Sebeok (ed.), *Current Trends in Linguistics 12,* 345–71. The Hague: Mouton.

Stolt, Birgit. (1974). Rhetorik and Gefühl im Ackermann aus Böhmen. *Wortkampf: Frühneuhochdeutsche Beispiele zur rhetorischen Praxis,* 11–30. Frankfurt: Athenäum.

Sturtevant, Edgar H. (1947). *An Introduction to Linguistic Science.* New Haven: Yale University Press.

Szulc, Aleksander. (1987). *Historische Phonologie des Deutschen.* Tübingen: Niemeyer.

Talbott, Strobe. (1992). The Birth of the Global Nation. *Time* , July 20: 70–1.

Tarnas, Richard. (1990). "The Western Mind at the Threshold," Paper Presented at the Center for Psychological Studies in the Nuclear Age. Cambridge, MA: Affiliate of Harvard Medical School at the Cambridge Hospital.

Tarone, Elaine. (1984). On the Variability of Interlanguage Systems. In F. R. Eckman, H. Bell, and D. Nelson (eds.), *Universals of Second Language Acquisition,* 3–23. Rowley, MA.: Newbury House.

Tarski, A. (1949). The Semantic Conception of Truth and the Foundations of Semantics. In H. Feigl and W. Sellers (eds.), *Readings in Philosophical Analysis,* 52–84, New York: Appleton-Century-Crofts.

Taylor, John R. (1989). *Linguistic Categorization: Prototypes in Linguistic Theory.* Oxford: Oxford University Press.

Taylor, John R. and Robert E. MacLaury (eds.). (1995). *Language and the Cognitive Construal of the World.* Berlin: Mouton de Gruyter.

Thibault, Paul J. (1997). *Re-reading Saussure: The Dynamics of Signs in Social Life.* London: Routledge.

Thom, René. (1975). *Structural Stability and Morphogenesis.* Trans. D. H. Fowel. Reading: W. A. Benjamin.

Thompson, D'Arcy. (1917). *On Growth and Form.* Cambridge: Cambridge University Press.

Thorpe, W. H. (1972). The Comparison of Vocal Communication in Animals and Man. In R. A. Hinde (ed.), *Non-Verbal Communication,* 27–47. London: Cambridge University Press.

Tobin, Ishai. (1997). *Phonology as Human Behavior: Theoretical Implications and Clinical Applications.* Durham: Duke University Press.

Todorov, Tzvetan. (1966). Les catégories du récit littéraire. *Communications* 8: 125–51.

— (1970). Language and Literature. In Richard Macksey and Eugenio Donato (eds.), *Languages of Criticism and the Sciences of Man: The Structuralist Controversy,* Baltimore: Johns Hopkins Press.

— (1975). Literature and Semiotics. In Thomas A. Sebeok (ed.), 97–102.

Toynbee, Arnold. (1966). *Change and Habit.* New York: Oxford University Press.

Trabant, Jurgen. (1981). Louis Hjelmslev: Glossematik als allgemeine Semiotik. In Martin Krampen *et al.* (eds.), 143–71.

Trager, George. (1958). Paralanguage: A First Aproximation. *Studies in Linguistics* 13: 1–12.

Trask, R. L. (1996). *Historical Linguistics.* London: Arnold.

Trovillo, P. V. (1939). A History of Lie Detection. *Journal of Criminal Law and Criminology* 29: 848–81.

Uexküll, Jakob von. (1940). *Bedeutungslehre* (BIOS 10). Leipzig: Johann Ambrosius Barth.

Uexküll, Thure von. (1981). Die Zeichenlehre Jakob von Uexkülls. In Martin Krampen *et al.* (eds.), 233–79.

— (1984). Symptome als Zeichen für Zustände in lebenden Systemen. *Zeitschrift für Semiotik* 6: 27–36.

Uspensky, Boris. (1976). *Semiotics of the Russian Icon.* Lisse: The Peter de Ridder Press.

Vachek, Josef and Libuse Dusková. (1983). *Praguiana: Some Basic and Less Known Aspects of the Prague Linguistic School.* (Linguistic and Literary Studies in Eastern Europe 12). Amsterdam: John Benjamins.

Valesio, Paolo. (1969). Icons and Patterns in the Structure of Language. *Actes du Xme Congrès des Linguistes.* The Hague: Mouton.

van Coetsem, Frans. (1975). Generality in Language Change. The Case of the Old High German Vowel Shift. *Lingua* 35: 1–34.

van Dam, Jan. (1961⁵). *Handbuch der deutschen Sprache I. Einleitung und Lautlehre.* Groningen: J. B. Wolters.

— (1963⁴). *Handbuch der deutschen Sprache II. Wortlehre.* Groningen: J. B. Wolters.

van Dijk, Teun A. (1972a). Foundations for Typologies of Texts. *Semiotica* 6: 297–323

— (1972b). *Some Aspects of Text Grammars.* The Hague: Mouton.

— (1977). *Text and Context: Explorations in the Semantics and Pragmatics of Discourse.* London: Longman.

van Ginneken, J. (1956). Roman Jakobson, Pioneer of Diachronic Phonology. In Morris Halle *et al.* (eds.), *For Roman Jakobson: Essays on the Occasion of his Sixtieth Birthday,* 574–81. The Hague: Mouton.

Vennemann, Theo. (1972). Phonetic Analogy and Conceptual Analogy. In Theo Vennemann and Terence Wilbur (eds.), *Schuchardt, the Neogrammarians, and the Transformational Theory of Phonological Change,* Frankfurt a. M.: Athenäum.

— (1975). An Explanation of Drift. In C. N. Li (ed.), *Word Order and Word Order Change,* 269–305. Austin: University of Texas Press.

— (1986). *Neuere Entwicklungen in der Phonologie.* Berlin: Mouton de Gruyter.

von Wright, Georg Henrik and Walter Methlagl (eds.). (1969). *Briefe an Ludwig von Ficker I.* Salzburg: Otto Müller.

Voyles, Joseph. (1971). The Phonology of Old Saxon (2). *Glossa* 5: 3–30.

Walser, Robert. (1978). *Belege: Gedichte aus der deutschsprachigen Schweiz seit 1900.* Zurich: Artemis Verlag.

Wardhaugh, Ronald. (1977). *Introduction to Linguistics.* New York: McGraw-Hill.

Warfield, Gerald. (1976). *Layer Analysis: A Primer of Elementary Tonal Structures.* New York: David McKay.

Watt, W. C. (1990). Forgotten Figures in Semiotics XXXIII: John Ruskin. Paper Presented at the Fifth Meeting of the Semiotic Circle of California, Berkeley, CA.

Webster's New International Dictionary of the English Language Unbridged. (1964). Springfield, MA.

Wegera, Klaus-Peter. (1987). *Grammatik des Frühneuhochdeutschen.* In Hugo Moser, Hugo Stopp, and Werner Besch (eds.), *Beiträge zur Laut- und Formenlehre, 3: Flexion der Substantive.* Heidelberg: Carl Winter.

Weinreich, Uriel. (1963). On the Semantic Structure of Language. In Joseph H. Greenberg (ed.), *Universals of Language,* 114–71. Cambridge, Mass.: The M.I.T. Press.

Weinreich, Uriel, William Labov, and Marvin I. Herzog. (1968). Empirical Foundations for a Theory of Language Change. In Winfrid Lehmann and Yakov Malkiel (eds.), *Directions for Historical Linguistics.* 97–195. Austin: University of Texas Press.

Wellek, Albert. (1968). Karl Bühler. *International Encyclopedia of the Social Sciences* 2: 199–202.

Wells, Rulon S. (1947). De Saussure's System of Linguistics. *Word* 3: 1–31.

— (1964). The True Nature of Peirce's Evolutionism. In E. C. Moore and R. S. Robin (eds.), *Studies in the Philosophy of Charles Sanders Peirce,* 304–22. Amherst, MA: University of Massachusetts Press.

— (1971). Distinctively Human Semiotic. In Julia Kristeva, J. Rey-Debove, and D. J. Umiker (eds.), *Essays in Semiotics,* 95–119. (Approches to Semiotics 4). The Hague: Mouton.

Werner, Otmar. (1969). Das deutsche Pluralsystem. Strukturelle Diachronie. In *Sprache, Gegenwart und Geschichte. Probleme der Synchronie und Diachronie. Jahrbuch des Inst. f. Dt. Sprache.* 1968: 92–128. (Sprache der Gegenwart 5). Düsseldorf: Schwann.

Wescott, R. W. (1971). Linguistic Iconism. *Language* 47: 416–28.

White, Alan R. (1975). *Modal Thinking.* Ithaca, New York: Cornell University Press.

Whitney, William Dwight. (1869). *Language and the Study of Language.* New York: C. Scribner & Company.

Whorf, Benjamin Lee. (1964). A Linguistic Consideration of Thinking in Primitive Communities. In Dell Hymes (ed.), *Language in Culture and Society,* 129–141. New York: Harper and Row.

Wiese, Richard. (1986). Zur Theorie der Silbe. *Studium Linguistik* 20: 1–15.

Will, George. (1997). Torricelli's Larger Point. *Newsweek* September 1: 78.

Wise, David. (1997). Big Lies and Little Green Men. *New York Times* August 8: A 21.

Wolff, L. (1934). Die Stellung des Altsächsischen. *Zeitschrift für Deutsches Altertum* 71: 129–54.

Woods, J. D. (1975). *A Synchronic Phonology of the Old Saxon of Heliand – M.* Unpubl. dissertation, University of Massachusetts.

Worth, Sol. (1969). The Development of a Semiotic of Film. *Semiotica* 1: 282–321.

Wright, Joseph. (1958^2). *Grammar of the Gothic Language.* Oxford: Clarendon Press.

Wurzel, Wolfgang U. (1987a). Morphologische Regeln in historischer Sicht. In Ferenc Kiefer (ed.), *Morphologie und generative Grammatik.* 259–87. (Linguistische Forschungen 24). Frankfurt a. M.: Athenäum.

— (1987b). System-Dependent Morphological Naturalness in Inflection. In W. U. Dressler *et al.* (eds.), 25–58.

Yates, F. E. (1986). Semiotics as Bridge Between Information (Biology) and Dynamics (Physis). *Recherches Sémiotique/Semiotic Inquiry* 5: 347–60.

Young, Robert. (1981). *Untying the Text: A Post-Structuralist Reader.* Boston: Routledge and Kegan Paul.

Zuckerman, M., B. M. DePaulo, and R. Rosenthal. (1981). Verbal and Nonverbal Communication of Deception. In L. Berkowitz (ed.). *Advances in Experimental Social Psychology,* 1–59. New York.

Name Index

Subject Index

abduction 5, 7, 12, 28, 42–3, 58–9, 63, 86, 88, 164, 177, 181, 231, 233
ablaut (sets) 212–3. *See also* vowel alternation.
abstract relevance 140
adaptive rule 177
action (theory) 57–8, 91–2, 97, 99, 101, 109
allophonic swarming 152
Analogists/Anomalists 2
analogy 9, 42–3, 59, 173, 178–81, 187, 190, 229, 231; and cause 45, 185; and competence/performance 180; iconic 12, 44, 181, 183–5; indexical 44, 181, 183, 185, 187, 190; morphological 182–3; orthographic 184; phonological 182–4; proportional 43; semantic 182–3
anthropology 112, 124
anthroposemiotic 146, 148
apocope 13, 169, 197, 200, 205–6; drift 198; law 199
apperception 116, 142, 144
arbitrariness 59, 77–79, 154
architecture 5, 83, 85–7

Armenian 41
articulatory basis 205
assimilation 159
autoambience 26, 72, 113, 116, 154. *See also Umwelt.*

Basel Recipe 15–6, 219–21
Behaghel Rule I/Rule II 215
behavior: animal 147; linguistic 105; piece of conversational 106; verbal 102, 109
behavioreme 75
biology 6, 8, 29, 34, 37, 45, 47, 55, 112, 116–7, 126, 142, 144, 146
biosemiotics 37, 47, 150
biuniqueness: *See* isomorphism

cademe 75
catastrophe 5, 8, 14, 26, 45–7, 51, 72, 113, 147–8
categorization 23–4
cause/causation 45, 171, 175–9, 185; and philosophy 171; and psychological/biological factors 175; and rule ordering 174; necessity/compulsion within 177–8, 187, 190, 193,